359   Q

Chant, Christopher
Warships of the 20th century
                                16.98
                                2/97

Southbury Public Library
561 Main Street South
Southbury, Conn. 06488

GAYLORD MG

WARSHIPS

of the 20TH CENTURY

Christopher Chant

Illustrated by John Batchelor

TIGER BOOKS INTERNATIONAL
LONDON

This edition published in 1996 by
Tiger Books International PLC, Twickenham
© Graham Beehag Books, Christchurch, Dorset
All rights reserved
Printed and bound in Singapore

ISBN 1-85501-803-9

Contents

The Battleship and Battle-Cruiser

As its name suggests, the battleship was the modern successor of the type of capital ship known in the navies of the sailing era as the line of battle ship which, with its armament of 60 or more guns on two or more decks, was regarded as the arbiter of naval warfare fought between fleets of ships operating in lines of battle. As sail power was replaced by steam power and as wooden construction was superseded by iron (later steel) construction in the second and third quarters of the nineteenth century, the term battleship was introduced to reflect the new type of modern warship, whose creation was also facilitated if not actually made inevitable in the 1840s and 1850s by the development of the rifled gun supplementing and then replacing the short-ranged and less accurate smooth-bore gun, and of the explosive shell replacing the less damaging solid shot. In short, the development in little more than 25 years of iron (for additional protection and then as the primary structural medium), steam propulsion, the rifled gun and the explosive shell rendered obsolete the line of battle ship that had reigned supreme on the world's seas for more than three centuries.

The first such ship of this type was perhaps the French *Gloire* which was launched in 1859, but this was built primarily of wood with her sides provided with additional protection by a plating of iron. It is generally accepted, therefore, that the first true battleship was the British *Warrior*, which was launched in 1860, with a hull of iron construction. Both of these ships were officially rated as frigates and were completely ship-rigged, but this should not be allowed to disguise the fact that they were the harbingers of a new type of naval warfare, for with their auxiliary steam propulsion arrangements they could steam at 13 knots, which made it possible for them to overhaul, outmanoeuvre and thereby gain a decisive tactical advantage over any line of battle ship with its greater multitude of guns on several decks.

This should not be construed as suggesting that there was an immediate shift to the new concept of warship as a fully fledged type, however, for in the absence of any major European war that might otherwise have provided both the stimulus and the operational validation of the concept, the process was gradual. The transition from ship of the line to battleship was thus characterised by the conversion of many line of battle ships toward the newer standard by the addition of iron protection plating on the outside of the hulls and the lengthening of their hulls to allow the incorporation of a primitive steam propulsion arrangement that supplemented but certainly did not replace their original sailing ship rig, and also by the creation of new iron-hulled and steam-powered battleships which nonetheless retained the sailing ship rig and massive gun batteries of the earlier generation's ships.

Thus it was only with the development of improved and more reliable steam propulsion arrangements, offering greater power as well as radically

The capital ship of World War II is seen in classic form in this painting of the German battle-cruiser *Scharnhorst* in action with heavy ships of the British Home Fleet in northern waters.

improved economy of operation, that the battleship began to emerge in the third quarter of the nineteenth century as a type radically different from the line of battle ship. The new breed of battleship was made possible not only by its new steam propulsion arrangement but also by the adoption of more advanced guns with breech rather than muzzle loading, rifled rather than smooth-bore barrels, and efficient smokeless nitrocellulose propellant in place of the inefficient smoke-producing black powder. Steady improvements in metallurgy allowed the construction of larger ships whose armoured sides provided better protection against incoming fire, and the evolution of more advanced propulsion arrangements and hull designs facilitated higher speeds. (Although hull designs were generally improved in terms of a better underwater line and a higher length-beam ratio, an anachronism that lasted well into the twentieth century, at least in vestigial form, was the ram bow: this had apparently proved itself by deliberate and successful use in the second Battle of Lissa in July 1866, when the Austro-Hungarian flagship rammed and sank the Italian *Re d'Italia*, and by accidental but also successful use in 1893 when the *Victoria*, flagship of the Mediterranean Fleet, was rammed and sunk by another British battleship.)

The first battleships relying on steam rather than sail as their prime mover were generally known as mastless ships, and the first of these was the British *Devastation* launched in 1869 as what was really a sea-going monitor as it was very low in the water and lacked any forecastle or poop. The masted and mastless ships were still produced in parallel however, and the last masted iron battleships survived until the late 1880s.

Even so, technical progress made in the period between 1870 and 1890 in the development of steam power, gun technology and armour protection ensured that the battleship began to appear as a distinct type with the main guns mounted in trainable turrets. It was at this stage that the battleship

Designed in the UK by Mackrow as an improved 'Majestic' class battleship of the pre-dreadnought type, the *Hatsuse* is seen here on trials shortly after being launched on the River Tyne in 1899. The *Hatsuse* and her near-sister *Shikishima* differed only in their hull forms, and the details of the Imperial Japanese navy's *Hatsuse* included a full-load displacement of 15,255 tons, length of 439ft 0in (133.8m), armament of four 12in (305mm) guns in two twin turrets, fourteen 6in (152mm) guns in single mountings, twenty 3in (76mm) guns in single mountings, twelve 47mm guns in single mountings and four 18in (457mm) torpedo tubes, protection in the form of a 9.05in (230mm) belt, 14in (355mm) barbettes and 4in (102mm) deck, propulsion in the form of triple-expansion steam engines delivering 14,500hp (10,810kW) to two shafts for a speed of 18 knots, and complement of 740.

emerged from experimental status to be built in classes by the world's major powers. Each of these classes introduced improvements in capability that were reflected in greater size and displacement, the latter increasing typically from the 9,200 tons of the *Warrior* to the 15,000 tons of the *Majestic*, a British battleship launched in 1895. Whereas the *Warrior* was a single-ship type 420ft (128m) long, fully ship-rigged with an auxiliary steam powerplant delivering 5,267hp (3,927kW) to one propeller for a speed of 14.1 knots, protected by 4.5in (114mm) of iron over 18in (457mm) of wood, and armed with ten 110lb (49.9kg) and four 70lb (31.75kg) breech-loading guns as well as twenty-eight 68lb (30.8kg) muzzle-loading guns, the *Majestic* was the lead vessel of a 10-ship class to a design that included a length of 421ft (128.32m), triple-expansion steam engines delivering 12,000hp (8,947kW) to two propellers for a speed of 16.1 knots, protection based on steel up to 14in (357mm) thick, and an armament of four 12in (305mm) breech-loading guns in two centreline turrets supported by twelve 6in (152mm) breech-loading rifled guns in casemated mountings, sixteen 12pdr quick-firing guns and twelve 3pdr quick-firing guns.

The 'Majestic' class marked the start of a battleship type that became standard, with local changes, in most of the world's major navies and was built in large numbers in the period up to 1905 with changes limited mainly to greater size, thicker protection, more power for slightly increased speed, and secondary and tertiary gun batteries increased in calibre: this last factor is reflected in the two 'Swiftsure' class ships of 1904 with a secondary battery of fourteen 7.5in (191mm) guns, the eight 'King Edward' class ships of 1905 with a secondary battery of four 9.2in (234mm) guns and ten 6in (152mm) guns, and the two ships of the 'Lord Nelson' class of 1907 with a secondary battery of ten 9.2in guns. The largest-calibre guns were seen as the primary weapons for the engagement of opposing battleships, with the secondary battery adding to the weight of fire and also providing a capability against secondary targets such as armoured cruisers, which could also be hit by the tertiary battery that was provided mainly for the protection of the battleship against the attentions of torpedo boats. These boats were regarded as a major threat to the battle fleet, as they operated in flotillas designed to exploit their speed and manoeuvrability to get in close and decimate the battle fleet with waves of potent torpedoes.

Seen in the period leading up to World War I, the *Indefatigable* was lead ship of a class of three battle-cruisers designed to an improved 'Invincible' class standard for the Royal Navy, with a full-load displacement of 22,080 tons, length of 590ft 0in (179.8m), armament of eight 12in (305mm) guns in four twin turrets, sixteen 4in (102mm) guns in single mountings, four 3pdr guns in single mountings and two 18in (457mm) torpedo tubes, protection in the form of a 6in (152mm) belt, 7in (178mm) barbettes and turrets, 2.5in (64mm) decks and 10in (254mm) conning tower, propulsion in the form of steam turbines delivering 44,000hp (32,805kW) to four shafts for a speed of 25 knots, and complement of 800. Although fast and moderately well armed, the ships were woefully deficient in protection.

The performance of these guns was considerable: the 12in (305mm) weapon, for example, could fire an 850lb (386kg) projectile to a range of more than 20,000yds (18,290m). Yet it was still standard at the beginning of the twentieth century to think of fleet engagements at ranges of only a few thousand yards. This meant that virtually every gun on a battleship would be capable of striking its opponent, and this raised the enormous difficulty of spotting the fall of shot, for with guns of three or more calibres hitting the target ship it became crucially important to differentiate the explosions of the shells fired by the various guns: there was little point in an enemy capital ship being blanketed in the fire of the 6in (152mm) or smaller guns of the tertiary battery, which could inflict relatively little decisive damage, if this obscured the fact that the fire of the secondary and primary batteries was not hitting the target.

That this might well be the case was illustrated by Captain Percy Scott, a decided advocate of accurate gunnery at a time in which the Royal Navy, followed by most other navies, believed that protracted gunnery practice was expensive and unnecessary for the type of short-range engagements that were envisaged, with rate of fire and general accuracy more important than truly aimed fire, and that gunnery practice also damaged the ship's paintwork and brightwork. Even so, it came as a shock in 1899 when Scott's command, the cruiser *Scylla*, achieved 80 per cent of hits with her 4.7in (120mm) guns in the Mediterranean Fleet gunnery competition, easily winning over ships whose average score was a paltry 30 per cent.

Scott's technique was based on the use of a telescopic sight on each gun and the following of the target through his own ship's roll rather than firing only when the guns of his own ship were brought to bear by the ship's roll. Scott also devised an effective training system for his gunners, who trained with the 'otter', 'loader' and 'deflection teacher' aids for practice in roll, loading and allowance for the target ship's horizontal movement. Such was Scott's success that the inertia of other commanders and the Admiralty was overcome and by 1902 most British warships were using the same methods. Scott became Inspector of Target Practice in 1905, and in 1907 the average number of hits being secured by British ships had risen to 81 per cent. Scott returned to sea in 1908 as commander of a cruiser squadron in the Channel Fleet, but his involvement in an extraordinary vitriolic quarrel between Admiral Sir Charles Beresford and Admiral Sir John Fisher, respectively the commander of the Channel Fleet and the First Sea Lord, ended his active career. Fisher

Seen in her original form in 1913, the *Kirishima* was a 'Kongo' class battle-cruiser of the Imperial Japanese Navy, but in 1933 and 1934 was reconstructed as a fast battleship. The four ships were designed in the UK, and the lead ship was also built in that country as the last Japanese capital ship constructed outside Japan. The specification for the four ships, as completed to an improved 'Lion' class design offering superiority to all current capital ships in the arrangement of the main armament, weight of the secondary armament and extent of the protection, included a full-load displacement of 32,200 tons, length of 704ft 0in (214.6m), armament of eight 14in (356mm) guns in four twin turrets, sixteen 6in (152mm) guns in single mountings, sixteen 3.1in (78mm) guns in single mountings and eight 21in (533mm) torpedo tubes, protection in the form of an 8in (203mm) belt, 10in (254mm) barbettes, 9.1in (230mm) turrets and 10in (254mm) conning tower, propulsion in the form of steam turbines delivering 64,000hp (47,720kW) to four shafts for a speed of 27.5 knots, and complement of 1,220.

was well aware of the importance of Scott's thinking, however, and Scott was encouraged to continue with his most important work: this was the creation of the director sight.

This concept took overall control of each ship's gunnery into a gunnery control position mounted in the battleship's foretop, now located at the junction of a sturdy tripod mast to ensure rigidity, from which a good view of the engagement could be obtained and the laying and firing of all guns could be controlled in replacement for the individual aiming that was otherwise standard despite the fact that each gunner was located relatively low in the ship and could have his sight of the target obscured by spray, smoke, cordite haze, and mist or fog, especially as ranges began to increase as a result of the Scott-inspired improvement of gunnery accuracy. Director firing involved the use of a single telescopic sight in the director position. The target was held in this sight, which was located above most obstructions to its field of view, and the individual gunners then had to align their gunsights with a pointer controlled from the director position: once each gunsight had been aligned with the pointer it was accurately laid in azimuth and elevation, and then all the guns were fired electrically and in unison from the director position, which ensured a higher level of accuracy and also simplified the spotting of the fall of shot and thus the generation of error corrections.

Scott perfected the system in 1910, but met with considerable opposition from officers who claimed that reliance on a single director position and electrical controls opened the way to a disastrous failure in the event of a single shell hit, for reliance on this system would have

The 'Bellerophon' class battleships of the Royal Navy were the first class-built dreadnoughts to enter British service, and the three ships were completed to an improved 'Dreadnought' class standard with two tripod masts, a full-load displacement of 22,100 tons, length of 526ft 0in (160.3m), armament of ten 12in (305mm) guns in five twin turrets, sixteen 4in (102mm) guns in single mountings, four 3pdr guns in single mountings and three 18in (457mm) torpedo tubes, protection in the form of a 10in (254mm) belt, 9in (229mm) barbettes, 11in (280mm) turrets and conning tower, and 4in (102mm) decks, propulsion in the form of steam turbines delivering 23,000hp (17,140kW) to four shafts for a speed of 20.75 knots, and complement of 735.

ensured that little training was given to individual gunners. The matter was settled in 1912 during trials between two battleships, one using the Scott system of director firing and the other relying on individual aiming: the director-equipped ship scored six times as many hits at a range of 9,000yds (8,230m), and director firing was adopted by the British in 1913, only later being utilised by the Germans and Americans. It is worth noting that the accuracy of director firing was considerably enhanced from 1913 by the simultaneous adoption for the director position of Captain Frederic Charles Dreyer's 'fire-control table', which was in essence a mechanical computer for the solution of fire-control problems on the basis of inputted data for target bearing, bearing rate change, range, range rate change, and speed.

The director firing concept would have been useful for the type of battleship described above with its three or even four calibres of guns, but in fact came into its own with a new type of conceptually simpler but tactically superior battleship that first appeared in October 1906 with the completion of the British ship *Dreadnought*.

The impetus for the creation of this new type of battleship can be traced to 1896 and the passing of the First Naval Law designed to pave the way for the creation of a German navy that would eventually rival that of the UK. This led to a numerical and strategic destabilisation of the naval *status quo* in Europe at a time when the UK was already becoming concerned about the threat to its pre-eminent world position posed by Germany's growing industries and mercantile marine, and coincided with the simultaneous introductions of several new technologies that were all to exert considerable influence upon naval warfare. These technologies included the 'locomotive torpedo' in a perfected form, the submarine, radio communication, the internal-combustion engine including its safe and very economical diesel engine form, oil- rather than coal-fired boilers, steam turbines in place of triple-expansion engines for smoother running as well as higher power in less volume, and, from 1903, the aeroplane.

These and other factors combined to make inevitable the introduction of what might reasonably be called the 'all big gun' battleship with its primary and secondary batteries (typically four 12in/305mm primary guns in two centreline turrets fore and aft of the central superstructure, and ten 7.5in/190mm secondary guns in casemated mountings round and below the superstructure) replaced by a larger number of turreted main guns located on or as close to the centreline as possible and complemented by large numbers of small guns. The task of the main guns was to deal with major adversaries, and the function of the small guns was to provide protection against the attentions of torpedo boats, which were thought to offer a significant threat but were lightly built in order to secure high speed, and were thereby vulnerable to the fire of quick-firing weapons such as 12pdr guns.

A primary armament of single-calibre guns had been tested in the 1870s in a few British and Italian battleships, but the failure of these vessels had led to the general retention of at least three main calibres for battleship armament. Then in 1904-05 the Russo-Japanese War revealed the limitations of such a mixed armament: the primary guns were used accurately at the unprecedented range of 20,000yds (18,290m), and spotting of the fall of shot of the secondary and tertiary batteries proved almost impossible even at considerably shorter ranges.

The lesson was clear to all who considered the implications of the Japanese victory in the Russo-Japanese War: the day of the secondary and tertiary batteries as offensive weapons was over, and it was therefore sensible to concentrate all the offensive firepower in a larger number of main guns, which could concentrate an overwhelming weight of fire at very long range and sink or disable an enemy before it could close to a range at which its medium-calibre guns might become effective. The Japanese were in the position to reach this conclusion before anyone else, and laid down the first 'all big gun' battleships as the *Aki* and *Satsuma* with a planned armament of twelve 12in (305mm) guns in two centreline twin turrets and, on each beam, one twin and two single turrets. Completion of the ships was delayed not only by Japan's limited industrial capacity, however, but also by the realisation that it was not cost-effective to have two four-gun beam batteries that would never be used simultaneously: these were therefore replaced by an intermediate-calibre battery of twelve 10in (254mm) guns in three twin turrets on each beam. It was therefore the British, now thoroughly concerned about the pace and extent of Germany's growing naval strength, who produced the first 'all big gun' battleship as the *Dreadnought*, with the Americans close behind them with the 'South Carolina' class and the Germans also in the running with the 'Nassau' class.

The ship that marked the emergence of a new era in battleship concepts was the *Dreadnought*, which was commissioned in 1906. The details of this historically important warship, which introduced a main armament of 10 large-calibre guns in turrets located as three on the centreline and two in 'wing' positions, included a full-load displacement of 21,845 tons, length of 527ft 0in (160.6m), armament of ten 12in (305mm) guns in five twin turrets, twenty-seven 12pdr guns in single mountings and five 18in (457mm) torpedo tubes, protection in the form of 11in (280mm) belt, barbettes, turrets and conning tower, and 4in (102mm) deck, propulsion in the form of steam turbines delivering 23,000hp (17,140kW) to four shafts for a speed of 21 knots, and complement of 695. The ship was completed in a remarkably short time by the use of materials and components already on order for other ships, but was too slow for first-line service by 1916 and was broken up in 1921.

This was the eighth ship of this name in the Royal Navy, and certainly the most important as she ushered in a new type of warship. The *Dreadnought* gave her name to the new type of 'all big gun' battleship, the ships of the previous generation with mixed batteries becoming known as 'pre-dreadnought' battleships. The ship was laid down at Portsmouth Dockyard in October 1905 and launched in February 1906 for completion later in the year, and this was a truly remarkable construction effort made possible only by using matériel already ordered and built for other ships. The ship was described by Fisher, her conceptual father, as "the hard-boiled egg — because she cannot be beat". The ship was the first capital ship in the world to be fitted with steam turbines as her primary propulsion arrangement, in this instance four sets of turbines delivering 23,000hp (17,150kW) to four shafts for a maximum speed of 22 knots, which was considerably faster than any 'pre-dreadnought' battleship despite her longer length of 526ft (160.3m) and greater displacement of 20,700 tons at full load. Fisher had a penchant for major warships that secured their advantage through an offensive combination of firepower and speed rather than ta defensive strength of thick armour, and the *Dreadnought* was therefore only modestly well protected with a maximum thickness of 11in (280mm) on the waterline belt. It was in her armament that the *Dreadnought* excelled, however, for the primary battery comprised ten 12in (305mm) guns installed in five twin turrets as one forward and two aft on the centreline, and the other two in 'wing' positions abreast the superstructure for a broadside of eight 12in guns. Intended only for the task of repelling torpedo boats, the secondary armament comprised twenty-four 12pdr guns in single mountings.

The completion of the ship was a matter of enormous pride for the British people, but also a subject of much anxiety as the ship had, at a stroke, revolutionised naval warfare by making all 'pre-dreadnought' battleships obsolete. This meant that the Royal Navy currently enjoyed a numerical advantage of only one in terms of its best battleship strength, and naval superiority would therefore go to the country which could build 'dreadnought' battleships more quickly in what came to be called the 'naval race'.

The primary threat was Germany, but by striking first the UK had secured a significant advantage, and by the time Germany had completed its first class of four 'dreadnoughts', the UK had seven as well as three examples of the battle-cruiser, a still more revolutionary and controversial type of capital ship. The origins of the battle-cruiser can be traced back to 1896 and the suggestion of Emile Bertin, the great French ship designer, for a large warship combining the speed and protection of the armoured cruiser with the main-calibre guns of the battleship to create a type notable for its great offensive power (speed and firepower) but only limited defensive capability. The concept appealed strongly to Fisher, who considered offensive capability to be all-important and saw in the proposal a means of producing a cost-effective type

The Austro-Hungarian *Viribus Unitis* was the last unit of the four-strong 'Tegetthof' class of dreadnought battleships completed from 1913 as comparatively small but nonetheless useful ships with their main armament in two pairs of superfiring triple turrets. The details of the class included a full-load displacement of 21,595 tons, length of 499ft 4in (152.2m), armament of twelve 12in (305mm) guns in four triple turrets, twelve 5.9in (150mm) guns in single mountings, eighteen 2.6in (66mm) guns in single mountings, two 47mm guns in single mountings and four 21in (533mm) torpedo tubes, protection in the form of an 11in (280mm) belt, barbettes, turrets and conning tower and 1.4 in (36mm) deck, propulsion in the form of steam turbines delivering 25,000hp (18,640kW) to four shafts for a speed of 20 knots, and complement of 1,045.

Based on misleading information put out by the British about its 'Invincible' class battle-cruisers, the *Blücher* was a neat but badly undergunned and underprotected ship that lay in the bracket between armoured cruiser and battle-cruiser. The ship's specification included a full-load displacement of 17,500 tons, length of 530ft 10in (161.8m), armament of twelve 8.3in (210mm) guns in six twin turrets, eight 5.9in (150mm) guns in single mountings, sixteen 3.4in (88mm) guns in single mountings and four 17.7in (450mm) torpedo tubes, protection in the form of a 7.1in (180mm) belt and turrets, 9.8in (250mm) conning tower and 2.75in (70mm) deck, propulsion in the form of triple-expansion steam engines delivering 34,000hp (25,350kW) to three shafts for a speed of 24.8 knots, and complement of 890.

that would be able to function in typical cruiser roles (scouting for the main fleet and protection of British maritime trade routes all over the world) and have the capability for active participation in fleet engagements as a result of its powerful and long-ranged main battery.

The result was the battle-cruiser, of which the first three were laid down in 1906 as 'armoured cruisers'. Completed at three-monthly intervals in 1908, the ships of the 'Invincible' class were then revealed as vessels altogether different from anything that had gone before. Although their protection was along armoured cruiser lines, with a maximum armour thickness of 7in (178mm), the main armament of these ships, each displacing 19,940 tons at full load, was eight 12in (305mm) guns in four twin turrets of which two were located on the centreline fore and aft of the superstructure and the other two in echeloned 'wing' positions on each beam. A secondary armament more capable than that of the *Dreadnought* was installed, in the form of sixteen 4in (102mm) guns, and the other primary distinguishing features of these handsome ships were their fine lines on a length of 567ft 0in (172.82m) and the high speed of 26.6 knots provided by the delivery of 41,000hp (30,570kW) to four shafts by four sets of steam turbines.

In overall terms, the battle-cruiser was basically a development of the 'dreadnought' battleship with one less main turret, a considerably reduced area and thickness of armour, and a combination of a longer hull and a more powerful propulsion arrangement for notably higher speed. The result was a highly impressive type of warship designed to outfight any ship it could not outrun, and outrun any ship it could not outfight, but as operations in World War I (1914-18) were to prove, the lack of effective protection was a fatal flaw in the concept of these fine vessels.

The 'dreadnought' ships that followed in the period up to 1910 were the British 'Bellerophon' class of three ships based on the *Dreadnought* but with two tripod masts and a secondary armament of sixteen 4in (102mm) guns, the 'St Vincent' class of three ships with slightly thinner bow and stern armour as well as 50- rather than 45-calibre main guns for higher muzzle velocity and greater penetrative capability, the Japanese Satsuma interim type with its hybrid armament, and the German 'Nassau' class of four ships with a main armament of twelve 11in (280mm) guns in six twin turrets located as two centreline units fore and aft of the two superstructure blocks and four 'wing' turrets, a secondary armament of sixteen 3.4in (88mm) gun, protection up to a maximum of 12in (305mm), and a propulsion arrangement based on triple-expansion reciprocating steam engines delivering 26,244hp (19,568kW) to three shafts for a speed of 20 knots.

It is interesting to note that the Germans had considered that the protection of the British ships was too light, and therefore opted for better protection using the weight saved by the adoption of a slightly smaller-calibre main gun that nevertheless possessed a high muzzle velocity as well as the flatter trajectory that simplified the creation of a valid fire-control solution and also permitted the use of a lower and therefore lighter turret design.

The *Seydlitz* was an enlarged 'Moltke' class battle-cruiser of the Imperial German army, and its most important details included a full-load displacement of 28,550 tons, armament of ten 11in (280mm) guns in five twin turrets, twelve 5.9in (150mm) guns in single mountings and twelve 3.4in (88mm) guns in single mountings, and a speed of 26.5 knots.

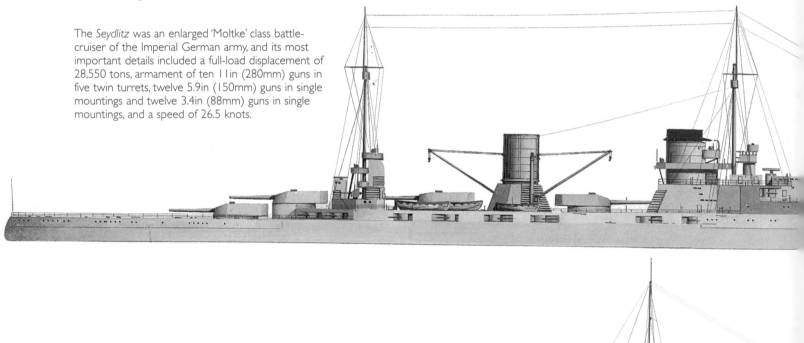

Lead ship of its four-strong class, the *Iron Duke* was a development of the 'King George V' class design with 6in (152mm) secondary guns and improved underwater protection. The ship's most important details included a full-load displacement of 30,280 tons, armament of ten 13.5in (343mm) guns in five twin turrets, twelve 6in (152mm) guns in single mountings and four 3pdr guns in single mountings, and a speed of 21 knots.

The *Rheinland* was one of the four 'Nassau' class ships that were Germany's first dreadnought battleships with a full-load displacement of 20,535 tons, armament of twelve 11in (280mm) guns in six twin turrets, twelve 5.9in (150mm) guns in single mountings and sixteen 3.4in (88mm) guns in single mountings, and a speed of 19.5 knots.

Another unit of the 'Nassau' class, the *Westfalen* was typified by armour protection in the form of an 11.4in (290mm) belt, 11in (280mm) turrets, 12in (305mm) conning tower and 3.15in (80mm) deck. The ships were shorter and beamier than the *Dreadnought*, possessed a more old-fashioned propulsion arrangement, were less well armed, and had a poor main armament disposition with only two centreline and four 'wing' turrets that limited the broadside to eight guns.

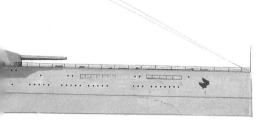

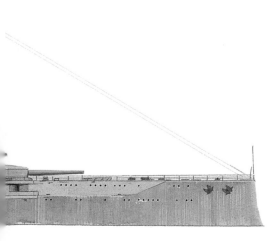

The completion of the *Dreadnought* gave the UK an early lead in the 'dreadnought race' within the 'naval race'. From the end of the first decade of the twentieth century, the pace of naval rearmament increased in direct proportion to the decrease in international relations as the UK's rapid start was now matched by developments in other countries. The first evidence of this world-wide response to the British lead was the commissioning of the 'Nassau' class ships in 1909 and 1910, and then of the two 'South Carolina' class battleships for the US Navy with a main armament of eight 12in (305 mm) guns in four centreline turrets. Further 'dreadnoughts' were: the two 'Minas Gerais' class ships built in the UK for Brazil; the two 'Delaware' class ships for the USA with ten 12in guns in five centreline turrets; the four ships of the 'Helgoland' class for Germany with twelve 12in (305mm) main guns in six twin turrets disposed as in the 'Nassau' class, the single ship of the 'Neptune' class for the UK with an armament of ten 12in main guns in five two-guns turrets installed as three (including a superfiring after pair) on the centreline and echeloned 'wing' turrets for the possibility of a 10-gun broadside, the two 'Colossus' class ships for the UK similar to the 'Hercules' class but with only one tripod mast; the two ships of the 'Florida' class for the USA as an improved version of the 'Delaware' class with rearranged cage masts and turbine propulsion on four shafts rather than triple-expansion engines on three shafts; the two ships of the 'Kawachi' class for Japan with an armament of twelve 12in main guns disposed as in the 'Helgoland' class, the two ships of the 'Wyoming' class for the USA with a main armament of twelve 12in guns of a longer design in six twin-gun centreline turrets installed as a superfiring pair forward and two superfiring pairs aft; the four ships of the 'Viribus Unitis' class for Austria-Hungary with an armament of twelve 12in main guns in four triple turrets located in fore and after superfiring pairs; the six ships of the 'Kaiser' class for Germany with an armament of ten 12in guns in five twin turrets located as three on the centreline (with the two after units in a superfiring arrangement) and two echeloned 'wing' turrets; the single ship of the 'Dante Alighieri' class for Italy with an armament of twelve 12in main guns in four triple turrets on the centreline; the three smallest-ever 'dreadnoughts' of the 'España' class for Spain with an armament of eight 12in main guns in four twin turrets located as two on the centreline and two in echeloned 'wing' positions; the four ships

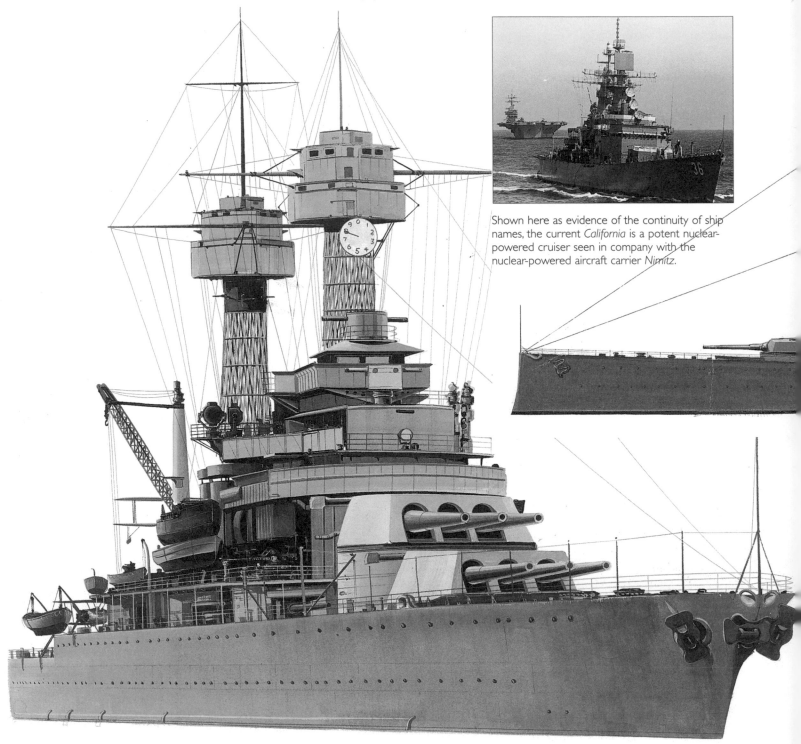

Shown here as evidence of the continuity of ship names, the current *California* is a potent nuclear-powered cruiser seen in company with the nuclear-powered aircraft carrier *Nimitz*.

Completed shortly after World War I and seen here in 1920, the *Hood* was reckoned to be the greatest and most beautiful capital ship of its time. The type was a battle-cruiser based on an enlarged version of the 'Queen Elizabeth' class battleship design to counter the Germans' planned 'Mackensen' class battle-cruisers, and with a full-load displacement of 42,500 tons and speed of 32 knots, it carried an armament of eight 15in (381mm) guns in four twin turrets backed by twelve 5.5in (140mm) guns in single mountings.

of the 'Courbet' class for France with an armament of twelve 12in main guns in four triple turrets installed on the centreline in forward and aft superfiring pairs; the four ships of the 'König' class for Germany with an armament of ten 12in (305mm) main guns in five twin turrets located on the centreline; the single 'Rio de Janeiro' class ship built for Argentina but taken over by the UK with an armament of no fewer than fourteen 12in main guns in seven twin turrets located as five on the centreline (a superfiring pair forward and three aft including one superfiring pair) and two echeloned 'wing' turrets; the two ships of the 'Rivadavia' class for Argentina built in the USA with a main armament of twelve 12in main guns in six twin turrets located on the

The *Invincible* was the first of three ships comprising the world's first battle-cruiser class, and was an impressive ship modelled conceptually on the Dreadnought with a longer and narrower hull, less protection, and a main armament of eight 12in (305mm) guns in four twin turrets. The result was the high speed of 25 knots but wholly inadequate protection based on a 6in (152mm) belt.

One of the definitive American 'super-dreadnought' classes, the two-ship 'Tennessee' class (here epitomised by the *California*) was an improved version of the 'New Mexico' class with two thinner funnels and a hull line clear of gun ports. The ship has the type of cage masts typical of American capital ships of the period, and its details included a full-load displacement of 33,190 tons, length of 624ft 6in (190.3m), armament of twelve 14in (356mm) guns in two pairs of superfiring triple turrets, fourteen 5in (127mm) guns in single mountings, four 3in (76mm) guns in single mountings and two 21in (533mm) torpedo tubes, protection in the form of a 13.5in (353mm) belt, 13in (330mm) barbettes, 18in (457mm) turrets, 16in (406mm) conning tower and 3.5in (89mm) deck, propulsion in the form of turbo-electric drive delivering 26,800hp (19,880kW) to four shafts for a speed of 21 knots, and complement of 1,085.

centreline and including superfiring forward and after pairs, the four ships of the Russian 'Gangut' class with an armament of twelve 12in main guns in four triple turrets located on the centreline; the two ships of the 'Caio Duilio' class for Italy with a main armament of thirteen 12in main guns in three triple and two twin turrets on the centreline with the twin turrets firing over the forward and after triple turrets; the two ships of the 'Conte di Cavour' class for Italy with basically the same armament as the 'Caio Duilio' class ships; and the three ships of the 'Imperatritsa Maria' class for Russia with a similar main armament to the 'Gangut' class ships but in a revised layout, thicker protection, a heavier secondary armament of eighteen 5.1in (130mm) guns in place of sixteen 4.7in (120mm) guns, and reduced speed and range as the ships were designed for service exclusively within the confines of the Black Sea.

The same period saw the spread, although not to so large an extent, of the battle-cruiser concept. In the UK the three ships of the 'Invincible' class were followed by the single ship of the 'Von der Tann' class for Germany with an armament of eight 11in (280mm) main guns in four twin turrets located as two on the centreline and the other two in echeloned 'wing'

Laid down for Brazil, bought by Turkey and taken over by the British in 1914, the *Agincourt* was extremely long and carried more main-calibre guns in more centreline turrets than any other capital ship before or since: this armament comprised fourteen 12in (305mm) guns in seven twin turrets.

positions. By comparison with the British battle-cruisers, the German ship had a lower combination of freeboard and superstructure (which made it difficult to secure a good range figure), better armour protection and, for the first time in German practice, a propulsion arrangement based on two sets of steam turbines driving four shafts for high speed and great reliability. The British followed the 'Invincible' class with the 'Indefatigable' class of three ships that differed from their predecessors mainly in the greater echeloning of their 'wing' turrets, making possible an eight- rather than six-gun broadside. The Germans countered with the two ships of the 'Moltke' class to an enlarged 'Von der Tann' design and with a fifth 11in (280mm) twin turret in a superfiring after position for a total of ten such weapons. The single ship of the 'Seydlitz' class that followed was basically an improved 'Moltke' class unit with the same armament on a longer and narrower hull for improved speed and better sea-keeping qualities. The final vessels of the pure 'dreadnought' type of battle-cruiser were the three ships of the 'Derrflinger' class for Germany, which differed quite significantly from the 'Moltke' and 'Seydlitz' class ships in being flush-decked and in having their eight 12in (305mm) main guns in twin turrets located in superfiring pairs

A fine example of a late-generation armoured cruiser that verged on the pre-dreadnought battleship, the Japanese *Ibuki* of 1904 was a member of a two-ship 'Kurama' class and was the first Japanese ship completed with turbine propulsion. The full-load displacement was 17,200 tons, the armament was four 12in (305mm) guns in two twin turrets complemented by eight 8in (203mm) guns in single mountings, the protection was based on a 7in (178mm) belt, and a speed of 21.5 knots was achieved on the 24,000hp (17,895kW) delivered to two shafts.

forward and aft of the superstructure, which contained the considerably enhanced secondary battery of twelve 5.9in (150mm) guns.

In the last stages of the 'dreadnought' era's first stage, the building race between the UK and Germany was complemented by a technological race in which each side sought to create successive classes of capital ship in which each succeeding class offered advantages over its predecessor. Thus the Germans, who had initially been content to rival the British 12in (305mm) gun with their 11in (280mm) weapon firing a lighter shell at a higher muzzle velocity for a flatter and therefore more aimable trajectory for roughly comparable armour-penetration capability, soon planned the switch to a 12in weapon firing an 893lb (405kg) shell to a maximum range in the order of 21,000yds (19,200m) for increased penetrative effect at longer range.

Anticipating such a move by the Germans, the British had planned a development of the 'dreadnought' into the 'super-dreadnought' type of battleship with a primary armament of 13.5in (343mm) guns. This weapon fired a larger shell than the 12in (305mm) weapon and at a lower muzzle velocity, resulting in more than adequate hitting power at long range in combination with greater accuracy and lower barrel erosion, the last factor providing a significant increase in barrel life. The first result of this process was the 'Orion' class of four ships, which introduced the new gun in five twin turrets located on the centreline (superfiring pairs of turrets fore and aft with a singleton turret amidships), increased the height as well as the thickness of the armour belt, and despite a significant increase in displacement was able to attain a higher speed than the *Dreadnought* as the result of its improved propulsion arrangement, in which four steam turbines delivered 27,000hp (20,130kW) to four shafts for a speed of 21 knots.

The British capitalised on the availability of the new 13.5in gun by adopting it for a series of battleship and battle-cruiser classes. Among the battleships were the four ships of the 'King George V' class with the same basic armament but an improved pattern of main gun; the four ships of the 'Iron Duke' class with the same main armament as the 'King George V' class but with the improved secondary armament of twelve 6in (152mm) guns in place of sixteen 4in (102mm) guns supplemented – for the first time in a

Below left: Lead unit of a three-ship class of *Panzerschiffe* known in the English-speaking world as pocket battleships, the *Deutschland* was completed in 1933 as a long-range commerce-raiding ship that could outrun anything that it could not outfight, and outfight anything that it could not outrun. With a full-load displacement of 15,900 tons and length of 610ft 3in (186.0m), the ship carried an armament of six 11in (280mm) guns in two triple turrets, eight 5.9in (150mm) guns, three 3.4in (88mm) anti-aircraft guns and eight 21in (533mm) torpedo tubes.

Built in reply to the British 'Queen Elizabeth' class, the *Baden* was lead ship of a four-strong class of which only two were completed in the later part of World War I to a specification that included a full-load displacement of 32,200 tons, length of 590ft 6in (180.0m), armament of eight 15in (381mm) guns in four twin turrets, sixteen 5.9in (150mm) guns in single mountings, eight 3.4in (88mm) guns in single mountings and five 23.6in (600mm) torpedo tubes, protection in the form of a 13.8in (350mm) belt and turrets, 15.75in (400mm) conning tower and 3.9in (100mm) deck, propulsion arrangement of geared steam turbines delivering 35,000hp (26,095kW) to three shafts for a speed of 22 knots, and complement of 1,170.

British battleship class – with anti-aircraft armament in the form of two 3in (76mm) high-angle guns; the single ship of the 'Reshadieh' class built for Turkey but taken over by the UK as the *Erin* with the same basic armament as the 'Iron Duke' class; and the single ship of the 'Admiral Latorre' class built for Chile but taken over by the UK as the *Canada* with a primary armament of ten 14in (356mm) guns in the same dispositions as the British ships with 13.5in (343mm) guns.

The first battle-cruisers with 13.5in guns were the three ships of the 'Lion' class, which were known as the 'splendid cats' and were the largest warships yet planned when they were laid down in 1912 and 1913 with a full-load displacement of 29,680 tons and a length of 700ft 0in (213.36m). The main armament comprised eight 13.5in weapons in four centreline turrets, of which the forward two were installed as a superfiring pair, and this was complemented by a secondary armament of sixteen 4 in (102mm) guns. Protection was provided by armour up to 10in (254mm) thick, and the

Completed in the late 1920s and seen here in 1930, the *Norfolk* was designed as the lead ship of a four-strong class of heavy cruisers of which only two were completed to a standard that included a displacement of 9,925 tons, length of 630ft 0in (192.0m), armament of eight 8in (203mm) guns in four twin turrets, eight 4in (102mm) anti-aircraft guns in four twin turrets, sixteen 2pdr anti-aircraft guns in two octuple mountings, eight 0.5in (12.7mm) machine guns in two quadruple mountings and eight 21in (533mm) torpedo tubes in two quadruple mountings.

Designed in the later 1930s as replacement for the 'Royal Sovereign' class, the 'King George V' class of five battleships is exemplified here by the *King George V*, photographed in January 1941. To avoid the loss of time that would have resulted from redesign with larger-calibre main guns, the type retained the 14in (356mm) weapons that had already been planned within Treaty constraints, but was nonetheless a capable type whose specification included a full-load displacement of 44,460 tons, length of 745ft 0in (227.1m), armament of ten 14in (356mm) guns in two quadruple and one twin turret, sixteen 5.25in (133mm) dual-purpose guns in eight twin turrets, forty-eight 2pdr anti-aircraft guns in six octuple mountings and eight 40mm anti-aircraft guns in four twin mountings, protection in the form of 14.7in (374mm) belt, 12in (305mm) barbettes, 12.8in (325mm) turrets, 4.5in (114mm) conning tower and 6in (152mm) deck, propulsion in the form of geared steam turbines delivering 125,000hp (93,200kW) to four shafts for a speed of 27.5 knots, and complement of 1,640.

propulsion arrangement comprised four sets of steam turbines delivering 73,800hp (55,025kW) to four shafts for a speed of 27 knots. The *Tiger*, planned as the fourth unit of the class, was completed slightly later to a design that resulted from a measure of revision in light of British knowledge of the Japanese 'Kongo' class, of which four were being built in the UK. The *Tiger* therefore appeared with the improved secondary armament of twelve 6in (152mm) guns and slightly greater beam and displacement to allow an enlargement and reorganisation of the machinery spaces to allow the delivery of 108,000hp (80,525kW) to four shafts for a speed of 20 knots. Detractors of the battle-cruiser's protective arrangements felt that too much offensive power and performance had been built into the 'splendid cats', but

it is worth emphasising that at the Battle of Jutland in May 1916, the *Tiger* took hits from 21 shells (including 17 large-calibre) without suffering major damage, and was repaired in less than one month.

The major increase in operational capability represented by the 'Orion' class, together with her battleship and battle-cruiser successors, meant that other navies had to respond to the 'super-dreadnought' concept by adopting larger-calibre main guns, improved defensive measures (secondary armament and armour) and, where they had not already done so, a centreline disposition for the main armament.

First off the mark was Japan with the four battle-cruisers of the 'Kongo' class, of which the lead ship was built in the UK largely so that Japan could become accustomed to the latest design and construction techniques used by the British. The design was derived from that for the Turkish 'Reshadieh' class battleship and resulted in the most powerful battle-cruiser of its time, considerably improving on the standards set by the 'splendid cats' in terms of protection (with a longer, deeper and thicker belt closed off at the ends by armour bulkheads as well as considerable internal compartmentalisation) and gun power, which was based on a primary armament of

From front to back, this quartet of Japanese battleships photographed in the period leading up to World War II comprises the *Nagato*, *Kirishima*, *Ise* and *Hiuga*. Most noticeable are the enormous 'pagoda' foremast arrangements.

An 'armoured ship' or pocket battleship of the 'Deutschland' class, the *Admiral Scheer* was launched in April 1933 and completed in November 1934. During World War II the ship was used initially for anti-commerce raids into the Atlantic and Indian Oceans before being transferred to the Arctic coast of Norway in 1942 and then into the Baltic late in 1944. The ship was bombed at Kiel during April 1945 and then capsized.

eight 14in (356mm) guns in four twin turrets on the centreline with the forward pair in a superfiring installation, a secondary armament of sixteen 6in (152mm) guns and a tertiary armament of sixteen 3in (76mm) guns. With 64,000hp (47,720kW) delivered by four sets of steam turbines to four shafts, the ships had a speed of 27.5 knots.

The battle-cruisers were matched by four battleships, namely the vessels of the two-ship 'Fuso' and 'Ise' classes that were originally to have been four units of the 'Fuso' class. Entirely designed and built in Japan with Japanese weapons and equipment, the ships confirmed the full arrival of the Japanese navy to world class status, for the 'Fuso' class battleships outgunned the contemporary 'Texas' and 'Oklahoma' class battleships of the US Navy and were basically equal to the 'Pennsylvania' class battleships. The Japanese ships were less well protected than these American counterparts and carried their main armament in twin rather than triple turrets: the main battery of 12 guns required six turrets rather than the American ships' four turrets, which required additional length. The resulting finer hull line, however, which translated into higher speed: 23 knots was attained on the 40,000hp (29,825kW) delivered by the steam turbines to four shafts. Other details of the 'Fuso' class battleships included a secondary armament of sixteen 6in (152mm) guns and a maximum armour thickness of 13.75in (349mm).

Although planned as standard 'Fuso' class ships, the last two units were completed to a standard that differed from that of the 'Fuso' class sufficiently for them to be recategorised in their own 'Ise' class. The main changes were the relocation of the two amidships twin gun turrets as a superfiring pair, and the replacement of the 6in guns of the secondary battery by more modern 5.5in (140mm) weapons.

The USA also opted for the 14in (356mm) main gun, but avoided the concept of the battle-cruiser, which ran contrary to American notions. The Americans therefore opted for maximum firepower and maximum protection even if this meant a sacrifice in speed to typical battleship levels. The first of the US Navy's ships built to the 'super-dreadnought' standard were the two vessels of the 'Texas' class, with the typical US flushdecked design derived from that of the beamy 'Wyoming' class and originally designed for a primary armament of fifteen 12in (305mm) guns in five centreline triple turrets. Then the advent of the 'Orion' class forced a rethink

The *Bismarck* was the lead ship of the two-strong class whose other unit was the Tirpitz, and these were the only German battleships completed in the lifetime of the Third Reich. The ships were visually impressive and exercised a horrid fascination on the minds of the British Admiralty despite the fact that they had an unfortunate propulsion arrangement, possessed a considerable weight of armour that was not particularly well disposed, and had a cluttered deck arrangement in its combination of secondary and tertiary gun batteries (due to the German navy's lack of dual-purpose guns and fire-control systems). The specification for the Bismarck included a full-load displacement 50,900 tons, length of 813ft 8in (248.0m), armament of eight 15in (380mm) guns in four twin turrets, twelve 5.9in (150mm) guns in six twin turrets, eight 4.1in (105mm) anti-aircraft guns in four twin mountings and sixteen 37mm anti-aircraft guns in single mountings, protection in the form of a 12.6in (320mm) belt, 14.2in (360mm) turrets, 13.8in (350mm) conning tower and 4.7in (120mm) deck, propulsion in the form of geared steam turbines delivering 138,000hp (102,895kW) to three shafts for a speed of 29 knots, and complement of 2,400.

on the US Navy, which then opted for a primary armament of ten 14in guns in five centreline twin turrets (superfiring pairs forward and aft with a singleton unit amidships), and a secondary armament of twenty-one 5in (127mm) guns. Protection was provided by well-arranged armour up to 14in (356mm) thick, but a retrograde step – forced on the Americans by the inability of US turbine manufacturers to meet the exacting official requirement – was the use of reciprocating machinery delivering 28,100hp (20,950kW) to two shafts for a speed of 21 knots.

Further development along the same lines resulted in the two ships of the 'Nevada' class, which carried basically the same armament as the 'Texas' class battleships but were considerably better protected (firing trials against an old battleship revealed that light and medium armour were no protection against large-calibre shells). The Americans therefore adopted the 'all or nothing' principle for armour protection, demanding that all armour protecting the ship's vital spaces and other essential areas should be proof against penetration by large-calibre shells fired at typical ranges, and that other areas should receive no protection at all. This meant that the Americans now began to produce battleships with excellent firepower and protection although this inevitably meant a slight sacrifice in theoretical performance to typical battleship levels, and effectively ended any possibility of American battle-cruisers. The two ships of the 'Nevada' class

The *Bismarck* rides through the North Atlantic swell in May 1941, somewhat low in the bows after suffering damage and taking on water, in the aftermath of the Battle of the Denmark Strait in which its accurate long-range gunfire sank the Hood, still the pride of the Royal Navy despite its age and lack of adequate horizontal protection against plunging fire.

had armour up to 18in (457mm) thick. The propulsion arrangement was now based on steam turbines, in this instance delivering 26,500hp (19,760kW) to two shafts for a speed of 20.5 knots.

The final expression of the American 'super-dreadnought' concept was to be found in the five ships of the two-ship 'Pennsylvania' and three-ship 'New Mexico' classes completed in the early part of World War I and while the USA was still a neutral nation. The 'Pennsylvania' class design was basically an improved version of the 'Nevada' class with the earlier type's combination of two triple and two twin superfiring turrets replaced by four triple turrets in superfiring pairs. The same armament of 12 main-calibre guns was carried in the contemporary 'Fuso' class for the Japanese navy, although in

Above: The most famous of the three 'Deutschland' class 'pocket battleships', the *Admiral Graf Spee* was launched in June 1934 and completed in January 1936, and was scuttled off Montevideo in December 1939 after suffering only modest damage in the Battle of the River Plate, against a force of three British cruisers, at the end of a commerce-raiding cruise in which the German ship had sunk or captured nine British merchant ships.

Only two of the four 'Richelieu' class battleships, planned in the late 1930s as the major surface fighting element of the French navy were completed. This is the *Richelieu*, seen in partially completed state off Dakar in French West Africa during 1941 after the ship's hasty departure from France in June 1940. The ship's details included a full-load displacement of 47,500 tons, length of 813ft 0in (247.8m), armament of eight 15in (380mm) guns in two quadruple turrets, nine 6in (152mm) guns in three triple turrets, twelve 3.9in (100mm) anti-aircraft guns in six twin turrets and sixteen 37mm anti-aircraft guns in eight twin mountings, protection in the form of a 12.9in (327mm) belt, 15.9in (404mm) barbettes, 16.9in (430mm) turrets, 13.3in (340mm) conning tower and 6.7in (170mm) deck, propulsion in the form of geared steam turbines delivering 155,000hp (115,570kW) to four shafts for a speed of 30 knots, and complement of 1,550. The design was a development of that evolved for the smaller 'Dunkerque' battleships, with better protection and heavier armament based on a primary battery of eight guns in two superfiring quadruple turrets forward of the superstructure and a secondary battery of nine guns in three triple turrets abaft the superstructure.

Below: The *Gneisenau* was the second of the two 'Scharnhorst' class battle-cruisers completed in Germany in the late 1930s as highly impressive ships with a full-load displacement of 34,900 tons, length of 754ft 0in (229.8m), armament of nine 11in (280mm) guns in three triple turrets, twelve 5.6in (150mm) guns in six twin turrets, fourteen 4.1in (105mm) anti-aircraft guns in seven twin mountings and sixteen 37mm anti-aircraft guns in eight twin mountings.

this instance the guns were carried in six twin turrets that demanded an additional 65ft (19.8m) of length and additional 15,000hp (11,185kW) of power for a speed 2 knots higher on the same displacement.

The 'New Mexico' class design was a much improved version of the 'Pennsylvania' class design with basically the same armament, although the main guns were mounted in separate sleeves to allow individual rather than collective elevation and the secondary guns were installed one deck higher. The main improvements in the class were a more refined hull, which introduced an elegant clipper bow and a bulbous forefoot, increased internal compartmentalisation for greater survivability and, in the New Mexico, the first installation in a capital ship of a turbo-electric propulsion arrangement in which two steam turbines powered electrical generators supplying current to the four electric motors that delivered 27,500hp (20,505kW) to four shafts for a speed of 21 knots. Although bulky and heavy, the turbo-electric drive was highly economical and a decided asset to manoeuvrability.

The French had lagged somewhat behind in the 'dreadnought race', and it was only in May 1912 that the first of three 'Provence' class 'super-dreadnought' battleships was laid down. This was based on the hull design of the 'Courbet' class 'dreadnought' battleship to save in design time, but

Second of a two-strong battle-cruiser class whose other unit was the lead ship *Scharnhorst*, the *Gneisenau* was launched in December 1936 and completed in May 1938. In the early months of World War II the two ships undertook a raid into the North Atlantic before being damaged by the fire of the British battle-cruiser *Renown* off Norway in April 1940; the *Gneisenau* later sank the British aircraft carrier *Glorious* and was damaged when the destroyer *Glowworm* rammed it. Further damage resulted from a torpedo hit from the submarine Clyde in June 1940, and after this more serious damage had been repaired, the two German battle-cruisers made a further sortie into the North Atlantic during the first three months of 1941 before returning to Brest. The two battle-cruisers, together with the heavy cruiser Prinz Eugen, made a classic run up the English Channel to Germany in February 1942, suffering mine damage near the end of the trip and then bomb damage while in dock at Kiel. The ship was decommissioned in July 1942, and expended as a blockship at Gdynia in March 1945.

made a new departure for the French as it was armed with ten 13.4in (340mm) main guns in five centreline twin turrets (superfiring pairs forward and aft with a singleton unit amidships).

Meanwhile, the British had been pushing ahead with their next development in response to the latest German ships. These were now armed with 12in (305mm) main guns, which the British deemed to be comparable in operational terms to their 13.5in (343mm) weapons as the German guns had a higher muzzle velocity for greater range and penetrative power in combination with a flatter trajectory that made for greater accuracy. The British response was the 15in (381mm) gun designed to provide a significant measure of advantage over the German 12in weapon and also the 14in (356mm) gun that was entering service with other navies. The 15in gun proved itself an excellent weapon, with a 1,920lb (871kg) shell fired at a muzzle velocity of 2,655ft (809m) per second to attain a range of 35,000yds (32,005m); moreover, the gun soon revealed the additional advantage of suffering little barrel wear even in protracted firing, and this offered excellent economics. The additional weight of this larger gun, its mounting and the turret required to carry them in a twin installation

Operation 'Cerberus'

OPERATION 'Cerberus' was the German designation for the dash up the English Channel between 11 and 13 February 1942 by three major German warships, namely the battle-cruisers Scharnhorst and Gneisenau with the heavy cruiser Prinz Eugen, all of which had arrived in the Breton port of Brest after commerce-raiding cruises into the Atlantic, resulting in the sinking of 22 British ships. Brest had since suffered a protracted series of British bombing raids, including one on April 10 during which the Gneisenau had been hit by four bombs and another on July 22 in the course of which the Scharnhorst had been hit by five bombs. Although Grossadmiral Erich Raeder, commander-in-chief of the German navy, was convinced that the ships should be left at Brest for further raids into the Atlantic, Adolf Hitler demanded that they be brought home to Germany as insurance against the expected British invasion of Norway, and it was decided that a high-speed dash under massive fighter protection offered the best chance of breaking through the inevitable British attacks. The squadron sailed at 22.45 on 11 February, and caught the British so completely by suprise that it was not until 11.30 on 12 February that the German squadron was positively identified and marked for attack. By this time the German units were off Boulogne, and managed to fight through determined but unco-ordinated British air and surface attacks to reach Wilhelmshaven (Scharnhorst) and Brunsbuttel (Gneisenau and Prinz Eugen) on the morning of 13 February. The Gneisenau was slightly damaged after hitting one mine, but the Scharnhorst was more seriously affected by striking two mines. British aircraft losses were heavy as a result of the ships' massive anti-aircraft armaments and the superb fighter escort provided by the Luftwaffe. The Scharnhorst was repaired and re-entered combat in September 1943, when the ship bombarded Spitsbergen, but in December of the same year, the British battleship Duke of York and an accompanying cruiser and destroyer force caught up with the German battle-cruiser off the North Cape. The resulting battle ended with the sinking of the Scharnhorst and the loss of 1,803 German officers and men.

demanded a ship somewhat larger than had become the norm. The result was the 'Queen Elizabeth' class of five ships based on a hull design adapted from that of the 'Iron Duke' class, with an additional 2,500 tons of displacement provided by a lengthening of 20ft (6.1m) and a widening of 6in (0.15m). Another development was the introduction, for the first time anywhere in the world, of boilers that were exclusively fired by oil. The elimination of the bunkerage previously required for coal saved a considerable amount of weight, and this was used to improve the protection, which was based on a deeper belt up to 13in (330mm) thick, five armoured decks that yielded a greater overall thickness than the individually thicker decks of the 'Iron Duke' class ships, and two longitudinal bulkheads to provide improved underwater protection. On this massive hull, with a full-load displacement of 33,020 tons and capable of 23 knots on the 75,000hp (55,920kW) delivered to four shafts, the 'Queen Elizabeth' class battleships carried a main armament of eight 15in main guns in four centreline turrets (superfiring pairs forward and aft) and a secondary armament of sixteen 6in (152mm) guns.

The 'Queen Elizabeth' class ships opened the definitive period in the development of the 'all big gun' battleship, for further progress was now based not so much on any conceptual developments but rather on increased

Below: The *Tirpitz* was the sister-ship of the *Bismarck*, from which it differed only in details such as a full-load displacement of 52,600 tons, length of 823ft 6in (251.0m) and the addition of eight 21in (533mm) torpedo tubes. The ship was launched in April 1939 and completed in February 1941, and its sole success in World War II (apart from tying down large numbers of British capital ships) was a bombardment of Spitsbergen in September 1943. The ship was damaged by British midget submarine attack later in that month, damaged by aircraft attack in April 1944 (with the loss of 122 men after being hit by 14 bombs), rendered unseaworthy by further aircraft bombs in September 1944, and finally sunk in November 1944 when the ship capsized with the loss of 902 men after being hit by 'Tallboy' bombs.

The last British battleship to be completed, and virtually the last ship of its type to enter service anywhere in the world, the *Vanguard* was an improved and enlarged version of the 'King George V' class battleship with a revised main armament comprising the eight guns originally manufactured in World War I for the light battle-cruisers *Courageous* and *Glorious* and installed in four new twin turrets. The specification for the *Vanguard* included a full-load displacement of 51,420 tons, length of 814ft 4in (248.2m), armament of eight 15in (381mm) guns in four twin turrets, sixteen 5.25in (133mm) dual-purpose guns in eight twin turrets and seventy-one 40mm anti-aircraft guns, protection in the form of 12.8in (325mm) belt, barbettes and turrets, 2.9in (74mm) conning tower and 6in (152mm) deck, propulsion in the form of geared steam turbines delivering 130,000hp (96,930kW) to four shafts for a speed of 30 knots, and complement of 1,600.

size for the greater power and thicker (as well as better disposed) armour that provided a higher speed and improved protection, in combination with a centreline main armament arrangement often involving larger-calibre guns, a better secondary armament arrangement in which casemated single-purpose guns were generally replaced by turreted weapons that were often of the dual-purpose type, and a tertiary armament arrangement designed to supplement the secondary armament with a dedicated anti-aircraft fit to provide protection against the warplane, which became the primary threat to the capital ship after the end of World War I.

This was still in the future, however, as countries started to respond to the British lead exemplified by the battleships of the 'Queen Elizabeth' class and then exploited by the five ships of the 'Royal Sovereign' class, which was a further development based on the hull design of the 'Iron Duke' class with a primary armament of eight 15in (381mm) guns in four twin superfiring turrets (forward and aft) and a secondary armament of fourteen 6in (152mm) guns. Revisions were incorporated to improve the design's steadiness, to improve protection by an increase in the depth of the belt, the enhancement of the internal underwater protection and, in the last ship of the class, the introduction of the external 'bulges' that became standard in the 1920s and 1930s. With a speed of 22 knots on the 42,650hp (31,800kW)

Eventually numbering four out of a planned six ships, the
'Iowa' class battleships were without doubt the most capable
battleships ever designed, even though the two completed units
of the Japanese 'Yamato' class were larger and more heavily armed.
Exemplified here by the *Iowa*, the class carried basically the same
armament as its predecessors but was better protected on a longer hull
whose high length/beam ratio allowed the attainment of speeds never exceeded
by other battleships. The specification of the ships as completed included a full-load
displacement of 55,250 tons, length of 887ft 3in (270.4m), armament of nine 16in
(406mm) guns in three triple turrets, twenty 5in (127mm) dual-purpose guns in ten twin
turrets and eighty 40mm anti-aircraft guns, protection in the form of a 12.2in (310mm) belt, 17.3in
(440mm) barbettes, 17in (432mm) turrets, 17.5in (445mm) conning tower and 5.5in (140mm) decks,
propulsion in the form of geared steam turbines delivering 212,000hp (158,065kW) to four shafts for a
speed of 33 knots, and complement of 2,750. The ships were retained after World War II for further
operational service in the Korean and Vietnam Wars, and were finally decommissioned only in the early 1990s after
having been updated to a considerably more potent form with provision for Tomahawk cruise and Harpoon anti-ship
missiles. The two photographs, taken in the late 1980s, show the *Iowa*'s forward main turrets – that on the left
in action and that on the right after suffering a turret explosion and fire.

delivered to four shafts, the 'Royal Sovereign' class battleships were for a time considered inferior to the 'Queen Elizabeth' class ships, but were in fact superior as a result of their improved protection and siting of secondary armament.

The battleships armed with 15in main guns were complemented by battle-cruiser equivalents, starting with the two ships of the 'Renown' class with a main armament of six 15in guns in three centreline twin turrets (a superfiring pair forward and a singleton unit aft), armour up to a maximum of 11in (280mm) but only 6in (152mm) on the belt, and a speed of 32.7 knots on the 126,300hp (94,170kW) delivered to four shafts. The last three British battle-cruisers of World War I were distinctly eccentric ships, reflecting Fisher's obsession with speed and firepower to the detriment of protection and, in this instance, his desire to undertake a landing, in collaboration with Russian forces, on the north German coast in the Baltic with the support of shallow-draught battle-cruisers. This resulted in the three ships of the 'Glorious' class. The first two of these were completed with a main armament of four 15in guns in two twin turrets and a secondary armament of eighteen 6in guns in six triple turrets, an armoured belt whose maximum

The *Ferre* is a British 'Daring' class destroyer of the Peruvian navy, which received two such ships in 1969. Manned and operated almost as light cruisers, the class numbered eight ships completed in the early 1950s with a full-load displacement of 3,580 tons, length of 390ft 0in (118.8m), armament of six 4.5in (114mm) dual-purpose guns in three twin turrets, up to six 40mm anti-aircraft guns in up to three twin mountings and one 'Squid' anti-submarine projector, propulsion in the form of geared steam turbines delivering 54,000hp (40,260kW) to two shafts for a speed of 34.75 knots, and complement of 330.

thickness was only 3in (76mm), and a speed of 32 knots on the 93,780hp (69,920kW) delivered to four shafts: they were a pair of magnificent but wholly impractical ships whose basic concept was taken to the limit, or indeed beyond it, by their half-sister *Furious* in which the main armament comprised two 18in (457mm) guns in single turrets and the secondary armament eleven 5.5in (140mm) guns. Before completion, the *Furious* was modified into a hybrid aircraft carrier with the forward main-gun turret replaced by a long flightdeck, and in 1918 the ship was revised as a true aircraft carrier, a standard to which the two half-sister ships were modified in the 1920s.

The German response to the British ships with 15in guns was the 'Baden' class projected at four units of which only two were completed. The design of this class reflected a change in German thinking from an original capital ship philosophy of gun power inferiority but protective superiority vis-à-vis British ships, to an equality of gun power and protection. This philosophy was posited on the new 15in gun developed by Krupp, which was in fact inferior to the British gun of the same calibre as it fired a lighter 1,653lb

Opposite top: One of three 'Tourville' or 'C67' class guided missile destroyers completed for the French navy in the mid-1970s, the *Tourville* is a multi-role destroyer optimised for the anti-submarine role with a full-load displacement of 5,745 tons, length of 501ft 0in (152.5m), armament of two 3.9in (100mm) dual-purpose guns in single turrets, six MM.38 Exocet anti-ship missiles, one Crotale octuple launcher for twenty-six surface-to-air missiles and one Malafon launcher for thirteen anti-submarine rockets, propulsion in the form of geared steam turbines delivering 54,400hp (40,560kW) to two shafts for a speed of 31 knots, and complement of 305.

Epitomised here by the *Zeeland*, the Dutch 'Holland' class of destroyers totalled four ships completed in the mid-1950s to a specification that included a full-load displacement of 2,765 tons, length of 371ft 0in (113.1m), armament of four 4.7in (120mm) guns in two twin turrets, one 40mm anti-aircraft gun and two 14.75in (375mm) anti-submarine mortars, propulsion in the form of geared steam turbines delivering 45,000hp (33,550kW) to two shafts for a speed of 32 knots, and complement of 250.

Below: Completed for the French navy in the late 1950s, the five destroyers of the 'Duperré' or 'T53' class were produced to a standard evolved from that of the 12 destroyers of the 'Surcouf' or 'T47' class and are epitomised here by the *Jaureguiberry*. The details of this important multi-role type included a full-load displacement of 3,740 tons, length of 422ft 0in (128.6m), armament of six 5in (127mm) dual-purpose guns in three twin turrets, six 57mm anti-aircraft guns in three twin mountings, two or four 20mm cannon in single mountings, one 14.75in (375mm) anti-submarine rocket launcher and six 21.7in (550mm) torpedo tubes in two triple mountings, propulsion in the form of geared steam turbines delivering 63,000hp (46,975kW) to two shafts for a speed of 34 knots, and complement of 345.

(750kg) shell at the lower muzzle velocity of 2,297ft (700m) per second to the shorter range of 22,200yds (20,300m) at an elevation of 16 degrees. Eight of these guns were located in four centreline twin turrets installed as superfiring pairs, and the secondary armament was sixteen 5.9in (150mm) guns in casemated mountings. The hull was basically an improved version of that developed for the 'König' class but with greater length and beam for a larger displacement and space for a more powerful propulsion arrangement, with three sets of steam turbines delivering 52,000shp (38,770kW) to three shafts for a speed of 22.25 knots.

German plans for the completion of the remaining two ships of the class, and also for the construction of other ships with 15in guns, were overtaken by the end of the war, but British assessment of these and other German ships after the war revealed that they were basically inferior to their British counterparts in structural integrity as well as in a number of operational features.

The end of World War I, brought about by the political, social, economic and military collapse of Germany and its Central Powers' allies, most

The two largest battleships to be completed were the Japanese super-battleships of the 'Yamato' class. The ships were designed and built in great secrecy with the intention of providing the Imperial Japanese navy with ships that could individually fight groups of enemy battleships through their superb protection and very long-range main armament based on the largest guns ever installed on a battleship. The details of these magnificent ships, which were almost immediately made obsolete by overwhelming American air power in the Pacific campaign of World War II, included a full-load displacement of 71,695 tons, length of 862ft 10in (263.0m), armament of nine 18.1in (460mm) guns in three triple turrets, twelve 6.1in (155mm) guns in four triple turrets, twelve 5in (127mm) anti-aircraft guns in six twin turrets, twenty-four 25mm anti-aircraft guns in eight triple mountings later increased to one hundred and fifty-two 25mm anti-aircraft guns, and six aircraft launched with the aid of two catapults, protection in the form of a 16.1in (410mm) belt, 22in (559mm) barbettes, 25.6in (650mm) turrets, 19.7in (500mm) conning tower and 9.1in (231mm) deck, propulsion in the form of geared steam turbines delivering 150,000hp (111,810kW) to four shafts for a speed of 27 knots, and complement of 2,500. The three illustrations of the *Yamato* on this spread include (top left) the ship manoeuvring at speed while under American air attack, the massive and gun-covered superstructure with the 'pagoda' foremast and single large funnel (centre), and the starboard side elevation (bottom).

notably Austria-Hungary and Turkey, was a relief for the almost equally exhausted Allied powers, especially France and the UK. For a variety of reasons, none of these countries could consider large-scale naval development or construction in the years following World War I, and this left the USA and Japan to move up in the 'naval race'. The USA now felt itself compelled to operate a navy 'second to none' as a protector of its world-wide mercantile interests and main bastion of democracy, while Japan had grown enormously in power across the eastern Pacific during the war and now felt that parity with the USA was a realisable and indeed worthy objective that was reflected in the so-called 8-8' programme to build eight new battleships and eight battle-cruisers by the end of the 1920s. Moreover, despite its exhaustion the UK felt in the early 1920s that it could not allow its naval superiority to be challenged without any British response, and thus it appeared that a new 'naval race' might be in the making.

Efforts to prevent such a race, with its financial burdens and destabilising influences, resulted in the Washington Naval Conference of 1921-22 that resulted in a treaty signed in February 1922. This was a far-ranging document that sought to impose artificial limits on the tonnage of warships

This illustration reveals the 'Kongo' class battle-cruiser *Kirishima* after its reconstruction in the early 1930s as a fast battleship to a specification that included a full-load displacement of 36,600 tons, length of 728ft 3in (222.0m), armament of eight 14in (356mm) guns in four twin turrets, fourteen 6in (152mm) guns in single mountings, eight 5in (127mm) anti-aircraft guns in four twin turrets, four 40mm anti-aircraft guns in single mountings, twenty 25mm anti-aircraft guns in 10 twin mountings and three aircraft, protection in the form of an 8in (203mm) belt, 10in (254mm) barbettes, 11in (280mm) turrets, 4.7in (120mm) deck and 10in (254mm) conning tower, propulsion in the form of steam turbines delivering 136,000hp (101,400kW) to four shafts for a speed of 30 knots, and complement of 1,435.

that could be built and on the calibre of the weapons that they might carry. In qualitative terms the treaty fixed 35,000 tons and 16in (406mm) as the maximum displacement and maximum gun calibre that might be used, and in quantitative terms it imposed limits so acute that an immediate result was the scrapping of many American, British and Japanese capital ships then under construction or being planned. These types, some of which were converted into aircraft carriers, included the American 43,200-ton 'South Dakota' class battleships with an armament of twelve 16in (406mm) guns and the 43,500-ton 'Lexington' class battle-cruisers with an armament of eight 16in guns; the British 48,400-ton 'G3' class battle-cruisers with an armament of nine 16in guns and the 48,500-ton 'N3' class battleships with an armament of nine 18in (457mm) guns; and the Japanese 40,640-ton 'Amagi' class battle-cruisers with an armament of ten 16in guns and the 40,570-ton 'Tosa' class battleships with an armament of ten 16in guns.

As well as the disruption caused by their politically inspired changes and limitations, capital ships' designers now had to come to terms with a number of changed technical factors. On the offensive side these were basically the revision of turrets and their guns to allow firing at higher elevation angles for the type of longer-range engagement that was now increasingly the norm, the replacement of casemated secondary-armament guns by turreted guns installed at a higher level for greater range and continued operability in a seaway, the adoption of director firing for the secondary armament, and the increased sophistication of the main armament's director firing system with a longer-base rangefinder for the maintenance of accuracy at longer ranges and a gyroscopic platform whose electric output was used to keep the guns in the same position relative to the horizon despite the ship's roll, thereby much enhancing the accuracy of fire to a given range.

On the defensive side, the designers had to come to grips with the changed protective requirements imposed by the potential arrival of projectiles at higher impact angles (shells fired at longer range and therefore descending at a more acute angle, and aircraft-dropped bombs arriving at a near-vertical angle). The latter threat demanded an increase in horizontal protection to resist the penetration of these high-angle weapons, although no loss of vertical protection could be entertained because of the continued threat of short-range fire, the torpedo and the mine. Early trials with bombs dropped by warplanes had been largely discounted because of their inaccuracy under all but artificial conditions, but the tendency to ignore the air-launched bomb and its effects was regretted in the early days of World War II (1939-45), when the bomb delivered with considerable accuracy by the dive-bomber became a decisive weapon that was matched later in the war by the bomb dropped by the level bomber. The fact that the threat of the warplane was not ignored, however, was shown by modest improvements in horizontal armour and the introduction of larger numbers

Spain's two 'Roger de Lauria' class destroyers, here epitomised by the lead ship, were completed in the late 1960s after having been laid down as the second and third units of the 'Oquendo' class that comprised only one ship, the other six units having been cancelled. The 'Roger de Lauria' class ships were completed with American weapons and electronics to a specification that included a full-load displacement of 3,785 tons, length of 391ft 6in (119.3m), armament of six 5in (127mm) dual-purpose guns in three twin turrets, six 12.75in (324mm) tubes in two triple mountings for lightweight anti-submarine torpedoes, two 21in (533mm) tubes for heavyweight anti-submarine torpedoes and one helicopter, propulsion in the form of geared steam turbines delivering 60,000hp (44,735kW) to two shafts for a speed of 31 knots, and complement of 320.

The triple turret and three 16in (406mm) Mk 7 Mod 0 guns carried by the 'Iowa' class battleships weighs 1,700 tons complete with its mounting, has a crew of 79, can fire at the rate of two rounds per minute per gun, and can fire its 2,700lb (1,225kg) armour-piercing projectile to a maximum range of 40,185yds (36,745m), or alternatively its 1,900lb (862kg) high-capacity projectile to a maximum range of 41,625yds (38,060m).

of dedicated anti-aircraft guns. The standard in the later part of World War I had generally been two 3in (76mm) or similar weapons, but during the 1920s the numbers of anti-aircraft guns were increased significantly in the forms of larger-calibre weapons for the engagement of high-flying attackers at longer ranges, and smaller-calibre weapons, often of the multiple type, for the creation of a barrage through which any low-level attacker would have to fly at shorter ranges. As the navies of the world and their designers were dealing with the limits imposed on them by the Washington Naval Treaty, the last of the World War I capital ships were being completed. The finest of these, and arguably the most beautiful, was the British battle-cruiser *Hood*, which resulted directly from the revelation in 1915 that the Germans were preparing a battle-cruiser design with 15in (381mm) main guns. The

Admiralty decided to respond not with larger-calibre weapons, but rather with a battle-cruiser that combined superior speed, greater firepower than was available in the 'Renown' class ships and greater protection than was afforded in the 'splendid cats'. The result was a design that was in effect a 'Queen Elizabeth' class battleship with a longer and less thickly armoured hull containing a more potent propulsion arrangement for significantly higher speed despite a full-load displacement of 44,600 tons. Four of the class were ordered in April 1916, but the only unit to be completed was the *Hood*, which had a main armament of eight higher-angle 15in guns in four superfiring twin turrets on the centreline as well as a secondary armament of twelve 5.5in (140mm) guns, a maximum armour thickness of 12in (305mm) including a measure of inclined armour to provide protection against plunging fire, and steam turbines powered by more efficient small-tube boilers for the delivery of 151,280hp (112,795kW) to four shafts for a speed of 32.1 knots.

Whereas it was generally the British who had led the way with capital ship design up to this period, the Japanese led the way to the adoption of the 16in (406mm) gun in the two ships of the 'Nagato' class that entered service in the early 1920s. These were excellent examples of the 'fast battleship' concept, for the adoption of eight 16in main guns in two pairs of superfiring twin turrets permitted a significant reduction in armament weight by comparison with the ships of the 'Hyuga' class with their primary armament of twelve 14in (356mm) weapons in six turrets. The broadside weight of the 'Hyuga' class ships was 17,857lb (8,100kg) in comparison to the 'Nagato' class ships' 17,513lb (7,944kg). The 'Nagato' class was based on the same hull as the 'Hyuga' class, but this was revised with significantly more and better disposed armour and a propulsion arrangement in which four steam turbines delivered 80,000hp (59,650kW) to four shafts for a speed of 26.75 knots. Other improvements over the 'Hyuga' class included a secondary armament of twenty 5.5in (140 mm) guns and a control top located on what came to be called a 'pagoda' foremast, after this highly distinctive feature of the Japanese capital ship.

American battleships completed in this period included the two ships of the 'Tennessee' class that were in essence improved versions of the 'New Mexico' class ships with turbo-electric drive and the secondary armament of fourteen 5in (127mm) guns located one deck higher: although one-third less than that of the 'New Mexico' class in purely numerical terms, the secondary battery of the 'Tennessee' class was operationally superior because of its higher siting. There followed the ships of the 'Maryland' class that was basically a repeat of the 'Tennessee' class with the twelve 14in (356mm) guns replaced by eight 16in (406mm) guns. The class was to have totalled four ships, but the completion of the fourth unit was overtaken by the Washington Naval Treaty. The incomplete ship was therefore used for tests into explosions and blast, and as such probably played as important a part in the development of the American battleship as she would have done if completed.

The two American battleships of the 'Tennessee' class, here epitomised by the lead ship later in its career during World War II, were planned in the early part of World War I as improved versions of the two 'New Mexico' class battleships and were completed to a specification that included a full-load displacement of 33,190 tons, length of 624ft 6in (190.3m), armament of twelve 14in (356mm) guns in four triple turrets, fourteen 5in (127mm) guns in single mountings, four 3in (76mm) anti-aircraft guns in single mountings and two 21in (533mm) torpedo tubes, protection in the form of a 13.5in (343mm) belt, 13in (330mm) barbettes, 18in (457mm) turrets, 16in (406mm) conning tower and 3.5in (89mm) deck, propulsion in the form of turbo-electric drive delivering 26,800hp (19,980kW) to two shafts for a speed of 21 knots, and complement of 1,085. Both ships were completely rebuilt in 1943 to emerge as potent escort and gunfire support vessels with a full-load displacement of 40,300 tons, beam increased from 97ft 4in (29.67m) to 114ft 0in (34.75m), and an armament of twelve 14in guns in four triple turrets, sixteen 5in dual-purpose guns in eight twin turrets, forty 40mm anti-aircraft guns in 10 quadruple mountings, fifty-two 20mm cannon in single mountings, and three aircraft.

In the years following World War II, the rapid development of the 'Cold War' between the superpower blocs of the USA and the USSR led to the US Navy's retention of its better World War II destroyers in a form optimised for the escort of major surface forces. Two of the fleet destroyer classes that were taken in hand for adaptation to ocean escort standard were the 'Fletcher' and 'Allen M. Sumner' classes. Seen (top) is the 'Fletcher' class destroyer *Halsey Powell* in 1962 after its conversion but before its 1968 transfer to South Korea as the *Seoul*. Seen (above) is the 'Allen M. Sumner' class destroyer *James C. Owens* in 1969 before its transfer to Brazil as the *Sergipe* in 1973.

The first country to design a battleship without the constraints of the Washington Naval Treaty was the UK with the two-strong 'Nelson' class, which was designed to provide parity with the Japanese 'Nagato' and American 'Maryland' class ships. The design was basically a cut-down version of the projected 'G3' class battle-cruiser with the same primary armament and level of protection, although displacement limitations meant that thick armour was applied to a reduced area and the propulsion arrangement was considerably down-rated. The principal expedient adopted to provide adequate protection over the vital spaces was the grouping of all three triple turrets, each carrying three 16in guns, ahead of the superstructure block, resulting in a very truncated stern. The propulsion arrangement comprised just two sets of steam turbines delivering 45,000hp (33,550kW) to two shafts for a speed of only 23.5 knots.

This was basically the extent of capital ship construction in the 1920s as limited by the Washington Naval Treaty, although considerable effort was expended by the major powers on improvements to the capabilities of their existing ships, especially in terms of their defensive capabilities – for which an additional 3,000 tons of displacement were permitted per ship – which included enhanced anti-aircraft capability in the form of additional armour and extra anti-aircraft weapons, and improved anti-torpedo capability in the form of bulges on and below the waterline. Other changes that were effected were a revitalisation of the propulsion arrangement, with oil-fired boilers replacing surviving coal-fired units, and the addition of one or more catapults for the launch of floatplanes that could extend the parent ship's search horizon and also serve in the gunnery spotting role in long-range engagements. Some countries also went to the trouble and expense of virtually gutting their older battleships and battle-cruisers so that they could be revised into altogether more modern and capable warships. The Japanese, for example, rebuilt their 'Kongo' class ships with a lengthened hull for the improved length-beam ratio that allowed considerably higher speed, while the Italians revised their 'Conte di Cavour' and 'Caio Duilio' class battleships virtually out of recognition with extended and reshaped bow lines, heavier main armament achieved by boring out the original weapons, a completely new secondary armament arrangement, and a totally rebuilt superstructure. This last revision was also a feature of Japanese battleships, which all began to sport a 'pagoda' type of superstructure. British battleships were also extensively revised with new superstructures and main batteries in which the guns' maximum elevation angle was increased to 30 degrees from the original 20 degrees as a means of extending their range.

Plans were also laid in the 1930s for more extensive rebuilds of older ships, but these were generally curtailed on the outbreak of World War II, when the ships were required for immediate service, and the combination of dockyard facilities and other resources were earmarked for more important programmes such as the construction of new vessels and the rapid repair of damaged ships.

A revitalisation of battleship-building programmes resulted from the 1929 decision by Germany, prohibited by the terms of the Treaty of Versailles from building warships with a displacement of more than 10,000 tons, to build a class of armoured ships (*Panzerschiffe*) that were really cruisers with a main armament of 11in (280mm) guns. This led to the First and Second London Naval Conferences of 1930 and 1935-36, together with the resulting treaties that sought to maintain the basic concept of the Washington Naval Treaty but added a number of provisos allowing individual countries to react in various ways in response to the actions of other countries. The First London Naval Conference involved Japan, the UK and the USA while the

The *Perkins* was another FRAM II conversion to the ocean escort role, in this instance from the 'Gearing' class fleet destroyer standard. The ship is seen here in 1969 before its 1973 transfer to Argentina, in whose navy it became the *Py*. In its modernised form, the ship had a full-load displacement of 3,945 tons, length of 390ft 2in (119.0m), armament of four 5in (127mm) dual-purpose guns in two twin turrets, one ASROC anti-submarine rocket system with 17 weapons, six 12.75in (324mm) tubes in two triple mountings for lightweight anti-submarine torpedoes and one DASH remotely piloted helicopter, propulsion in the form of geared steam turbines delivering 60,000hp (44,735kW) to two shafts for a speed of 32 knots, and complement of 310.

In some respects resembling a destroyer of the period after World War II, the Italian navy's *San Giorgio* was completed in 1943 as a light cruiser named *Pompeo Magno*, but was renamed when converted into a training ship in the mid-1960s. The ship was deleted in 1980, and in training ship configuration had a full-load displacement of 4,450 tons, length of 466ft 6in (142.2m), armament of four 5in (127mm) dual-purpose guns in two twin turrets, three 3in (76mm) dual-purpose guns in single turrets, six 12.75in (324mm) tubes in two triple mountings for lightweight anti-submarine torpedoes and one Menon three-barrel launcher for anti-submarine rockets, propulsion in the form of a CODAG arrangement with four diesels and two gas turbines delivering 18,000hp (13,420kW) and 15,000hp (11,185kW) respectively to two shafts for a speed of 27 knots, and complement of 315 excluding 130 midshipmen.

Second Conference involved France, the UK and the USA, and with hindsight both can be appreciated as attempts to re-establish a situation that was already disappearing even if it had not actually disappeared.

The first result of the Germans' decision to build a class of three 'Deutschland' class *Panzerschiffe* was the French order for two 'Dunkerque' class fast battleships with a main armament of eight 13in (330mm) guns in two quadruple turrets ahead of the superstructure, and a secondary armament of sixteen 5.1in (130mm) dual-purpose guns in three quadruple turrets aft and two twin turrets amidships. Protection was on the light side, with a maximum of 13.6in (345mm) on the barbettes and 9.5in (240mm) on the belt, but this allowed the ships to achieve 29.5 knots on the 112,500hp (83,880kW) delivered to four shafts by four sets of steam turbines.

This was a period of steadily deteriorating relations between France and Italy, and the former's decision to build two ships was soon followed by the latter's order for two more potent 'Vittorio Veneto' class battleships with a main armament of nine 15in (381mm) guns in three triple turrets and a secondary armament of twelve 6in (152mm) guns in four triple turrets located in beam pairs abreast the superfiring unit of the two forward main-gun turrets and the after main-gun turret. The Italians preferred to rely on speed and manoeuvrability for protection, and the armour of the two 'Vittorio Veneto' class ships was therefore on the thin and light side by contemporary standards, but this permitted a speed of 31.4 knots on the 134,616hp (100,370kW) delivered to four shafts by four sets of steam turbines.

The final nails were put into the 'battleship holiday', which had started

Lead ship of possibly the last type of 'battleship' to be built, the Soviet battle-cruiser *Kirov* is seen here during its trials in February 1981. This class was the USSR's first nuclear-powered surface combatant type, and with the exception of aircraft carriers and major amphibious warfare vessels is the largest type of surface warship built since the end of World War II.

with the Washington Naval Treaty, by the German decision to renounce the terms of the Treaty of Versailles and start a programme of rearmament that included two improved *Panzerschiffe*, namely the battle-cruisers of the 'Gneisenau' class, and by the revelation that Japan had no intention of abiding by the terms of the 1936 London Naval Treaty, which ordained that signatory countries could build as many battleships as they liked so long as none of these ships exceeded a displacement of 40,000 tons and a main gun calibre of 14in (356mm). The Treaty also contained a provision that in the event of a Japanese non-ratification, the signatories could switch to 16in (406mm) main guns, but American and British moves in this direction were hampered by their continued attempts to limit battleship displacement to 45,000 and 40,000 tons respectively. In the event, all these negotiations were overtaken by the outbreak of World War II in September 1939.

Another attempt to limit the growth of Europe's fleet of expensive capital ships was the Anglo-German Naval Treaty of 1935, in which the UK agreed to a measure of German rearmament in exchange for a German agreement to limit its capital ship programme to the two battleships of the 'Bismarck' class with an armament of eight 15in (381mm) guns in four twin turrets against which the British laid down the first of its 'King George V' class of modern battleships with a main armament of ten 14in guns in two quadruple turrets and one superfiring twin turret. This British effort was designed to persuade other countries to limit their main gun calibre to 14in, but the fact that the originating country did not have much confidence in the success of its effort was signalled by the preparation of plans for the 'Lion' class battleships with an armament of nine 16in guns in three triple turrets, but these were later cancelled because of the exigencies of the war.

The two 'Gneisenau' class battle-cruisers were planned as the fourth and fifth units of the 'Deutschland' class of 'pocket battleships' before it was decided to develop them into altogether larger and more powerful ships to give the Germans parity with the French 'Dunkerque' class of fast battleships. Further delay was occasioned by Adolf Hitler's initial insistence that the ships should have the same main armament as the 'Deutschland' class vessels, namely six 11in (280mm) guns in two triple turrets and the German navy's demand that the minimum feasible armament for ships of this type should be nine 11in weapons in three triple turrets. The navy had really wanted a larger calibre of gun, and was hard pressed to justify its resistance to Hitler's next demand, which was that the ships should be designed and built with provision for subsequent rearmament with 15in weapons when these became available. The basic design was modelled on that of two uncompleted battle-cruiser designs of World War I, which were the most advanced types of which Germany had direct experience, with a number of improvements to features such as the disposition of the armour, the introduction of considerably more modern fire-control systems, and provision for catapult-launched aircraft. Completed in the second half of the 1930s and later revised with a clipper bow for improved seakeeping capabilities, the two ships were small but nonetheless impressive vessels of their type, and their details included a primary armament of nine 11in guns in three triple turrets including a superfiring pair forward of the superstructure, a secondary armament of twelve 5.9in (150mm) guns, a tertiary armament of fourteen 4.1in (105mm) anti-aircraft guns, armour up to a maximum thickness of 13.8in (350mm), and a propulsion arrangement in which three sets of steam turbines delivered 160,000hp (119,360kW) to three shafts for a speed of 31 knots. A propulsion arrangement based on diesel engines had originally been considered for very long cruising range, the ships being designed for extended commerce raiding capability in the Atlantic, but this was rejected in favour of the higher speed provided by steam turbine propulsion.

Epitomised here by its lead ship, the 'Georges Leygues' or 'F70/ASW' class of seven ships is the French navy's most advanced type of anti-submarine destroyer, these ships having entered service between 1979 and 1990 with a full-load displacement of 4,380 tons, length of 455ft 11in (139.0m), armament of one 3.9in (100mm) dual-purpose gun in a single turret, two 20mm cannon in single mountings, four MM.38 Exocet anti-ship missiles, one Crotale octuple launcher for 26 surface-to-air missiles, two 21in (533mm) tubes for heavyweight anti-submarine torpedoes, and two helicopters, propulsion in the form of a CODOG arrangement with diesels and gas turbines delivering 10,400hp (7,755kW) and 42,600hp (31,765kW) respectively to two shafts for a speed of 21 or 30 knots respectively, and complement of 220. There are also two ships of the 'Cassard' or 'Type F70A/A' class of anti-aircraft half-sisters with basically the same hull but with a diesel powerplant and a different combination of sensors and primary weapons.

The two 'Gneisenau' class battle-cruisers were followed by the two 'Bismarck' class battleships. These were designed and built with commendable speed on the basis of theoretical work which German naval architects had completed during the period in which Germany was prohibited from the construction of warships displacing more than 10,000 tons, but reflected the fact that Germany was short of practical experience in the design, construction and use of modern battleships. The most important aspect of this limitation was that the basic hull concept of the World War I 'Baden' class was reused, albeit in a more refined form with a greater length-beam ratio to allow a higher speed. Considerable development of the basic hull allowed the incorporation of much-improved underwater protection and an enhanced armament fit, which now comprised a main battery of eight 15in (381mm) main guns in two pairs of superfiring twin turrets, a secondary battery of twelve 5.9in (150mm) guns in six twin turrets, and a tertiary battery of sixteen 4.1in (105mm) anti-aircraft guns in eight twin turrets complemented by large numbers of 37mm and 20mm cannon wherever deck space could be found; but the basic obsolescence of the hull was evident in the poor protection provided for the rudders and associated steering gear, the location of the main armoured deck toward the bottom edge of the armoured belt at a time when other countries, drawing on experience in the destruction of older battleships, had moved this to a position farther up the belt to provide better protection for communications and data-transmission systems. Both of these faults played a decisive part in the eventual loss of the *Bismarck*. Three other weak points were the provision of separate low-angle secondary and high-angle tertiary gun batteries, making extensive demands on deck area and displacement as a result of Germany's failure to keep abreast of the latest developments in dual-purpose ship's armament, the indifferent quality of the armour that was designed to be proof against penetration by 15in fire in its key areas but was in fact penetrated by 8in (203mm) fire, and the poor quality of the 15in shells, which often failed to detonate. All these factors notwithstanding, the two 'Bismarck' class battleships were magnificent vessels that exercised a horrible fascination on the British, who retained powerful forces in home waters to meet the threat of these two battleships.

The slightly later British contemporaries of the 'Bismarck' class were the five ships of the 'King George V' class, which were originally designed within the constraints of the Washington Naval Treaty with a primary armament of nine 15in (381mm) guns in three triple turrets, a secondary armament of 6in (152mm) guns, and only modest speed. Revision of the core design in 1934 resulted in the replacement of the 6in weapons with 4.7in (120mm) guns, but the final selection was the excellent 5.25in (133mm) dual-purpose gun mounting introduced on the 'Dido' class of light cruisers. Finally, the 15in main guns were replaced by 14in (356mm) weapons ordained as the maximum by the London Naval Treaty: the British felt that Japan might not ratify the treaty, thereby opening the probability that other countries would opt for the 16in (406mm) weapons then allowed by the treaty, but as British plans were based on the possibility of war with Germany by 1940, which was the earliest date in which guns and turrets ordered in 1936 could be delivered, the British opted for the smaller calibre of main gun in combination with armour designed to provide survivability against 16in fire.

The plan was now to install twelve 14in guns in two pairs of superfiring triple turrets, but the need to provide additional horizontal armour meant the sacrifice of two guns to produce a final disposition of ten 14in guns installed in two quadruple turrets and one twin superfiring turret. The 'all or nothing' protection was based on armour up to 15in (381mm) thick, and the propulsion arrangement allowed for the delivery of 110,000hp (82,015kW) to four shafts by four sets of steam turbines for a speed of 29.25 knots.

At much the same time, France was planning a class of four battleships offering greater capabilities than the two units of the 'Dunkerque' class and thus providing the French navy with a counter to the German 'Bismarck' and Italian 'Vittorio Veneto' class battleships. These were the 'Richelieu' class battleships, of which only one was completed in World War II and another in the period immediately after the end of the war. The type retained the basic configuration of the 'Dunkerque' class ships, with the primary armament grouped in the forward part of the ship, although in this instance the main armament was eight 15in (381mm) guns in two quadruple turrets. The secondary armament comprised nine 6in (152mm) guns in three triple turrets in the after part of the ship, and the tertiary armament was twelve 3.9in (100mm) anti-aircraft guns in six twin turrets clustered round the 'mack'.

The blast pattern on the surface of the water is telling evidence of the power generated by the 16in (406mm) main guns of the 'Iowa' class, seen here in the form of the *New Jersey* shelling Palestinian positions near Beirut in Lebanon during 1984. Such a capability in the shore bombardment role is no longer available to any navy in the world.

Protection was adequate, and a speed of 32 knots was possible on the 155,000hp (115,570kW) delivered to four shafts by four sets of steam turbines.

The only other countries to complete new classes of battleship in this period were Japan and the USA. The Japanese offering was the extraordinary 'Yamato' class, of which two were completed during World War II as the largest, most strongly defended and most powerfully armed battleships ever placed in service. The result of an evolutionary process that had seen the creation of 23 designs in the period between 1934 and 1937, the 'Yamato' class design resulted in ships of magnificent appearance with a full-load displacement of 71,660 tons, armour up to a maximum of 25.6in (650mm) thick on the turrets and 16.1in (410mm) thick on the belt, a propulsion arrangement in which steam turbines delivered 150,000hp (111,840kW) to four shafts for a speed of 27 knots, and a comprehensive armament fit that included a main battery of nine 18.1in (460mm) guns in three triple turrets (including a superfiring pair forward), a secondary battery of twelve 6.1in (155mm) guns in three triple turrets clustered round the superstructure, and a tertiary battery of twelve 5in dual-purpose guns in twin mountings. The two 6.1in turrets in the 'wing positions' were later replaced by an additional twelve 5in guns for increased anti-aircraft protection at a time when American land-based and carrierborne warplanes were rampant in the Pacific, and by the end of her life in 1945 the *Yamato* had a specialised anti-aircraft armament of no fewer than 150 25mm cannon. There can be no denial of the fact that the two completed ships were obsolete by the time of their service debuts, and saw little effective use in the face of overwhelming American air power superiority. Both ships were in fact lost to air attack, the strength of their construction being attested by the fact that the *Musashi* absorbed between 11 and 19 torpedo hits and at least 17 bomb strikes before succumbing, while the *Yamato* took between 11 and 15 torpedo hits and seven bomb strikes before sinking.

The last American battleships were the two ships of the 'North Carolina' class, the four ships of the 'South Dakota' class, and the four ships of the

The *Long Beach* was the first nuclear-powered surface combatant to enter service anywhere in the world, an event that took place in September 1961. The ship was also the first cruiser to be designed in the USA after World War II, and was also the world's first warship with a primary armament of guided missiles, in this instance surface-to-air missiles for the defence of American carrier battle groups. In its present form, the ship has a full-load displacement of 17,525 tons, length of 721ft 3in (219.9m), armament of two 5in (127mm) dual-purpose guns in a twin turret, two 20mm Vulcan six-barrel cannon in two Phalanx close-in weapon system mountings, two twin launchers for 120 Standard Missile SAMs, two quadruple launchers for eight Tomahawk cruise missiles, two quadruple launchers for eight Harpoon anti-ship missiles, one ASROC octuple launcher for anti-submarine rockets and six 12.75in (324mm) tubes in two triple mountings for lightweight anti-submarine torpedoes, propulsion in the form of nuclear-powered geared steam turbines delivering 80,000hp (59,650kW) to two shafts for a speed of 30 knots, and complement of 960.

'Iowa' class. The 'North Carolina' class was the first American battleship type built after the end of the Washington Naval Treaty limitations, but was originally planned round the London Naval Treaty armament of twelve 14in (356mm) guns in two pairs of superfiring turrets. When the Japanese refused to ratify the treaty, the Americans recast the 'North Carolina' class ships with a primary armament of nine 16in (406mm) guns in three triple turrets, and this arrangement, with a superfiring pair of turrets forward and a single turret aft, became standard in the two succeeding classes: this gun fired a 2,700lb (1,225kg) shell to a range of 36,900yds (33,740m) at an elevation of 45 degrees, and was a notably successful weapon. The secondary armament comprised twenty 5in (127mm) guns around the superstructure. 'All or nothing' protection was based on armour up to 16in (406mm) thick, and a speed of 28 knots was provided by four shafts receiving 121,000hp (90,220kW) from four sets of steam turbines.

The four ships of the 'South Dakota' class were built to what was a basically improved version of the 'South Carolina' class design with reduced habitability, an increased level of blast interference from the 5in guns, and a hull shortened by 50ft (15.2m) to allow the incorporation of much-improved horizontal and underwater protection.

The four ships of the 'Iowa' class were the last American battleships to be completed, and were designed as successors to the 'South Dakota' class with a longer and finer hull whose additional volume and displacement were used for increased protection and power rather than greater armament. This resulted in a type possessing basically the same primary and secondary armaments as carried by the two preceding classes, but armoured to a maximum of 19.7in (495mm) and capable of 33 knots on the 212,000hp (158,065kW) delivered to four shafts by four sets of steam turbines.

The 'Iowa' class battleships were in every respect superb fighting ships, but the obsolescence of the type as 'the' capital ship had been highlighted by World War II operations, including the Japanese air attack on the US Pacific Fleet in Pearl Harbor during December 1941. The American battleships of World War II were generally not used in the effort to bring Japanese battleships to decisive action; the older ships were used to provide gunfire support for amphibious operations, while the more modern ships typically operated as force flagships and/or escorts for aircraft carrier task forces. Most of the American battleships were retired shortly after the end of World War II, but the four 'Iowa' class ships were recalled to active service in the Korean War (1950-53) and during the Vietnam War (American involvement between 1961 and 1973), and were later upgraded with offensive and defensive missile capability for continued service into the early 1990s in the gunfire support and flagship roles.

It is also worth noting two other capital ship types. The British Vanguard, completed in 1946 and little used in any meaningful fashion as the day of the battleship was past, was a singleton type resulting from the survival of the four 15in (381mm) twin turrets removed from the Courageous and Glorious after World War I. These turrets were installed in superfiring pairs on a hull that was basically an improved version of that designed for the 'King George V' class. Finally, there are the four units of the 'Kirov' class completed by the USSR (and succeeding Commonwealth of Independent States) between 1980 and the early 1990s. These are attractive and highly capable major surface combatants often dubbed battle-cruisers. With a full-load displacement of 23,400 tons, the ships have a hybrid propulsion arrangement in which the steam from two pressurised water-cooled nuclear reactors is superheated by two oil-fired burners to power two sets of steam turbines delivering 150,000hp (111,840kW) to two shafts for a speed of 30 knots. The ships are armoured, although the basis of this armour

The Soviet 'Kynda' class of four anti-ship cruisers was designed in the late 1950s as the world's first surface combatant designed with a primary armament of large anti-ship missiles.

has not been revealed, and the primary armament is missiles rather than the guns that had been used in all previous capital ship designs: this armament comprises twenty SS-N-19 'Shipwreck' anti-ship missiles with a conventional or nuclear warhead, and is complemented by three types of surface-to-air missile, a hybrid surface-to-air missile/30mm cannon system for close-in defence against aircraft and missiles, a twin launcher for SS-N-14 'Silex' anti-submarine missiles, and a gun armament comprising two main guns (3.9in/100mm or 5.1in/130mm depending on ship) and eight 30mm 'Gatling' cannon for close-in defence.

The Cruiser

I N its original form as a sailing ship, the cruiser (often spelt cruizer at the time), was a fourth-rate ship or large frigate detached from the main fleet to sail independently in search of the enemy, whose position was then reported back to the fleet so that engagement could be brought about. The term was also employed for frigates and smaller vessels operated independently against the enemy's maritime lines of communication in the *guerre de course* role. In both these tasks, the essential requirement of any successful cruiser was a sailing ability superior to that of the enemy, especially in terms of speed and ability to point high into the wind.

All this changed with the advent of steam propulsion and iron (later steel) protection in the first half of the nineteenth century, when the cruiser ceased to be a generic name for any warship acting independently of the main fleet and became a type of warship in its own right. The cruiser was evolved in the middle and later years of the nineteenth century in four basic types, namely the armoured cruiser with a displacement of up to 14,600 tons and comprehensive protection matched by powerful guns, and the protected cruiser that was built in three subclasses with horizontal deck armour but no vertical belt armour and additional protection and survivability provided by the arrangement of the coal bunkers on the sides of the ship along the waterline and the compartmentalisation of the hull's interior spaces: in descending order of displacement, these three subclasses were the first-, second- and third-class protected cruisers with maximum displacements of 14,200, 6,000 and 3,000 tons.

The British built a total of 136 cruisers of these 'pre-dreadnought' types in the form of 35 armoured, 21 first-class protected, 51 second-class

The 8,800-ton *Deutschland*, launched in 1874 and completed in 1875, was the second unit of the two-strong 'Kaiser' class of central battery ironclads that paved the way for the armoured cruiser in German service. The two ships were built in the UK, and were in fact the last German major warships built outside Germany. As completed, the ships had a full sail rig, steel armour over a teak backing, and an armament of one 8.25in gun and eight 10.25in (260mm) guns. In 1882 the single 8.25in (210mm) weapon was replaced by seven 5.9in (150mm) guns complemented by four 3.15in (80mm) and six 37mm guns, and in the 1880s the two ships were rebuilt in Germany to cruiser standard, as illustrated in this 1898 photograph, with two military masts and the revised armament of eight 10.25in, eight 5.8in (150mm) and eight 3.4in (88mm) guns together with five 21in (533mm) torpedo tubes. Both ships became harbour vessels in the first decade of the twentieth century, the Deutschland being renamed Jupiter and then used as a target ship before being broken up in 1909.

protected and 29 third-class protected cruisers. The armoured cruisers were intended to provide a scouting capability within sight of the Royal Navy fleets to which they were attached, and also to serve as the flagships of overseas squadrons that did not need a battleship, while the task of the three subclasses of protected cruiser was the protection of British mercantile trade, the escort of troopship convoys to and from various parts of the British empire, and the provision of a 'naval outpost' capability in less advanced parts of the world. By the outbreak of World War I, 51 of these ships had already been deleted or reduced to non-combatant status, and another seven converted into minelayers. There were also 10 small cruisers with a displacement of up to 1,850 tons.

The evolution of the cruiser through the second half of the 19th century paralleled that of the battleship, starting as wooden vessels to which were added a layer of protective armour and steam machinery to supplement the three-masted ship rig with its full complement of sails, progressing through interim stages in which iron and then steel became the primary structural medium and the steam propulsion system gradually superseded the sailed arrangement, to reach the point at which the masts disappeared (except in vestigial form to provide the means of hoisting flags and carrying control tops) and the main armament was a mixed assortment of breech-loading weapons in which the largest-calibre guns were carried in trainable turrets and the intermediate-calibre guns were installed in casemates. The three main weapons carried by British cruisers were the 9.2in (234mm) gun firing a 380lb (172kg) shell, the 7.5in (190mm) gun firing a 200lb (91kg) shell, and the 6in (152mm) gun firing a 100lb (45kg) shell.

Typical of the British cruiser types before the advent of the 'dreadnought' era in 1906 were the first-class cruisers of the 'Warrior' armoured and 'Diadem' protected classes, the 'Challenger' second-class cruisers, and the 'Pelorus' third-class cruisers. The 'Warrior' class, of which four were launched in 1905, had a full-load displacement of 13,550 tons, an armament of six 9.2in guns, four 7.5in and twenty-three 3pdr quick-firing guns, armour protection up to a maximum thickness of 6in (152mm), and a speed of 23 knots on the 23,000hp (17,150kW) provided to two shafts by triple-expansion steam engines. The 'Diadem' class, of which eight were launched between 1896 and 1898, had a full-load displacement of 11,000 tons, an armament of sixteen 6in, fourteen 12pdr and three 3pdr quick-firing guns,

Completed in 1914, the two German light cruisers of the 'Regensburg' class, including the *Regensburg* illustrated, were basically improved versions of the 'Karlsruhe' class of three ships. As completed, the ships had a displacement of 5,500 tons, length of 468ft 0in (142.6m), armament of twelve 4.1in (105mm) guns in single mountings and four 19.7in (500mm) torpedo tubes, protection in the form of a 2.5in (65mm) belt and 0.75in (20mm) deck, propulsion in the form of steam turbines delivering 32,000hp (23,860kW) to two shafts for a speed of 27.25 knots, and complement of 420. During World War I, the armament was altered to seven 5.9in (150mm) guns in single mountings, two 3.4in (88mm) anti-aircraft guns in single mountings and up to 120 mines, and after the war the ships were handed over to France and Italy as war reparations, the *Regensburg* becoming the French *Strasbourg* and the *Graudenz* becoming the Italian *Ancona*.

armour protection up to a maximum thickness of 4.5in (114mm), and a speed of 20.25 knots on the 16,500hp (12,300kW) provided to two shafts by triple-expansion steam engines. The 'Challenger' class, of which five were launched in two subclasses between 1898 and 1902, had a full-load displacement of 5,880 tons, an armament of eleven 6in, nine 12pdr and six 3pdr quick-firing guns, armour protection up to a maximum thickness of 3in (76mm), and a speed of 21 knots on the 12,500hp (9,320kW) provided to two shafts by triple-expansion steam engines. The 'Pelorus' class, of which 11 were launched between 1896 and 1900, had a full-load displacement of 2,135 tons, an armament of eight 4in (102mm) and eight 3pdr quick-firing guns, armour protection up to a maximum thickness of 3in (76mm) on very limited areas, and a speed of twenty   knots on the 7,000hp (5,220kW) provided to two shafts by triple-expansion steam engines.

These ships were rendered obsolete by the development of the 'dreadnought' and the comparable development of improved warships in smaller classes, but were still in extensive service on the outbreak of World War I. The armoured cruisers were generally retained for service in home waters until their losses up to and including the Battle of Jutland in May 1916 revealed their fateful weakness against more powerfully armed opponents, but the protected cruisers served a useful function in overseas waters in the pursuit and destruction of Germany's merchant raiding force, and were also used for the convoy escort role in the North Atlantic.

A major turning point in the design of cruisers came in 1904-05 with the advent of the 'River' class of light warships, in which the torpedo boat and torpedo boat destroyer had come of age as a unified type offering genuine ocean-going rather than merely coastal or at best sea-going capability. The new ocean-going destroyer was a far greater threat to major surface forces than the earlier sea-going torpedo boat, and the commanders of major surface forces now had to take into consideration the possibility of massed attacks by torpedo-firing ships using their speed and agility to evade destruction. The threat of the destroyer in the early 1900s therefore called for the development of a new type of light cruiser

The *Novara* was one of the three-strong 'Improved Spaun' class of light cruisers delivered to the Austro-Hungarian navy in 1914 to a specification that included a displacement of 3,445 tons, length of 428ft 6in (130.6m), armament of eight 3.9in (100mm) guns in single mountings and six 17.7in (450mm) torpedo tubes in three twin mountings, protection in the form of a 2.5in (65mm) belt and 0.75in (20mm) deck, propulsion in the form of steam turbines delivering 25,000hp (18,640kW) to four shafts for a speed of 27 knots, and complement of 320.

Lead ship of a three-strong class of German light cruisers completed in 1908, the *Stettin* survived World War I and was assigned to the UK as part of Germany's war reparations and was later scrapped. The details of this ship, which fought at Jutland in 1916, included a displacement of 3,550 tons, length of 385ft 0in (117.3m), armament of ten 4.1in (105mm) guns in single mountings and two 17.7in (450mm) torpedo tubes, protection in the form of a 2in (51mm) deck, propulsion in the form of triple-expansion steam engines delivering 21,000hp (15,660kW) to two shafts for a speed of 25.5 knots, and complement of 350.

that was fast enough to work with destroyer flotillas, for which it provided a command capability, and also fast enough and sufficiently well armed with quick-firing guns to provide a defensive screen against attacks by the enemy's destroyer flotillas.

The first results of this new requirement were the 15 ships of the 'Scout' classes that were built between 1904 and 1912 with a displacement in the order of 2,700 to 3,500 tons, and the 21 ships of the 'Town' classes that were built between 1909 and 1915 with a displacement in the order of 4,800 to 5,500 tons with a much greater endurance and the ability to operate semi-independently from remote bases. There were six classes of 'Scout' type light cruisers, of which the last was the three-strong 'Active' class with a displacement of 3,440 tons, an armament of ten 4in (102mm) guns and two 21in (533mm) torpedo tubes, no protection, and a propulsion arrangement of steam turbines delivering 18,000hp (13,420kW) to two shafts for a speed of 26 knots. There were five classes of the 'Town' type light cruisers, of which the last was the two-strong 'Birkenhead' class with a displacement of 5,200 tons, an armament of ten 5.5in (140mm) guns and two 21in torpedo tubes, protection in the form of a 3in (76mm) belt, and a propulsion arrangement of steam turbines delivering 31,000hp (23,115kW) to four shafts for a speed of 26.5 knots.

Early experience with the 'Scout' and 'Town' types of light cruiser indicated that they were useful types of warship, but that a hybrid type would be best suited to the requirements of working with major surface forces in the North Sea, which was the area in which the Grand Fleet intended to secure a climactic victory over the German High Seas Fleet in the event of an outbreak of war. This hybrid type combined features of the 'Scout' and 'Town' types with a more potent propulsion arrangement for the higher speed required for effective use in collaboration with the Grand Fleet and its fast destroyer flotillas. The first of the new classes, which eventually totalled nine including the five ships of the 'Delhi' class completed after the end of the war, was the 'Arethusa' class of eight ships that started to enter service just before the outbreak of World War I. As built, the ships had a displacement of 3,512 tons, an armament of two 6in (152mm) and six 4in (102mm) guns as well as eight 21in (533mm) torpedo tubes, protection in the form of a 3in (76mm) belt and 1in (25mm) deck, and a speed of 30 knots on the 40,000hp (29,825kW) provided to four shafts by four sets of steam turbines. Wartime changes included a revision of the gun armament to three 6in and four 4in guns as well as one 4in or two 3in (76mm) anti-aircraft guns, and the original pole foremast was replaced by a tripod foremast. The ships were somewhat cramped but, soon proving themselves admirably well suited to their task, were used as the basis for steadily improved successor classes whose main changes were a larger number of 6in guns in replacement of 4in weapons. The details of the 'Delhi' class included a displacement of 4,650 tons, an armament of six 6in guns and two 3in anti-aircraft guns as well as twelve 21in torpedo tubes, protection in the form of a 3in (76mm) belt and 1in (25mm) deck, and a speed of 29 knots on the 40,000hp (29,825kW) provided to four shafts by four sets of steam turbines.

As the leading maritime power in the world during the last years of the nineteenth century, the UK was generally followed in terms of naval developments although rivals such as Germany sought to offset British numerical superiority with qualitative superiority in matters such as firepower and speed. At the beginning of World War I, the German navy had six armoured cruisers, of which the most advanced were the two ships of the 'Scharnhorst' class with a displacement of 11,600 tons, an armament of eight 8.2in (210mm), six 5.9in (150mm) and twenty 3.4in (88mm) guns as well as four 17.7in (450mm) torpedo tubes, protection in the form of a 6in (152mm) belt and 2in (51mm) deck, and a speed of 22.5 knots on the 26,000hp (19,385kW) provided to three shafts by triple-expansion steam engines.

It is also worth noting that Germany produced just one example of a heavy armoured cruiser, the *Blücher*, that was designed to provide a capability comparable to that of the 'Invincible' class, which were the Royal Navy's first battle-cruisers and originally described (for disinformation purposes) as being armed with 9.2in (234mm) guns. The Germans therefore responded with a design based on that of the 'Westfalen' class of 'dreadnought' battleships but scaled down and fitted with a primary armament of 8.2in guns. This resulted in a vessel characterised by a displacement of 15,500 tons, an armament of twelve 8.2in, eight 5.9in and sixteen 3.4in guns as well as four 17.7in torpedo tubes, protection in the form of a 6.75in (170mm) belt and turrets, and a speed of 26 knots on the 44,000hp (32,805kW) provided to three shafts by triple-expansion steam engines. Inevitably the *Blücher* was too lightly armed and armoured to be a real battle-cruiser, and paid the penalty at the Battle of the Dogger Bank in 1915, when she fought alongside the German battle-cruisers and was completely overwhelmed.

Germany also operated 17 protected cruisers, approximating in overall capabilities to the British second-class protected cruisers, and of these it was the 10 ships of the closely related 'Gazelle', 'Nymphe' and 'Frauenlob' classes

Second of the two-strong 'Karlsruhe' class of German light cruisers completed in 1913, the *Rostock* was sunk at Jutland in 1916. The details of the ship included a displacement of 5,500 tons, length of 468ft 0in (142.6m), armament of twelve 4.1in (105mm) guns in single mountings and four 17.7in (450mm) torpedo tubes, protection in the form of a 2.5in (65mm) belt and 0.75in (20mm) deck, propulsion in the form of steam turbines delivering 32,000hp (23,860kW) to two shafts for a speed of 27.25 knots, and complement of 420.

that were the most modern, all having been completed between 1899 and 1903 with a displacement of between 2,645 and 2,715 tons, a primary armament of ten 4.1in (105mm) guns and two 17.7in torpedo tubes, protection in the form of a 2in (50mm) deck, and a speed of 21.5 knots on the 8,500hp (6,340kW) delivered to two shafts by triple-expansion steam engines.

Like the UK, Germany came to appreciate in the first years of the twentieth century that the protected cruiser was obsolete in conceptual terms and that the immediate future lay with the light cruiser, of which the country built 14 classes in the period up to the end of World War I. The first of these, completed in 1904, was the 'Bremen' class of five ships with a displacement of 3,250 tons, an armament of ten 4.1in guns and two 17.7in torpedo tubes, protection in the form of a 2in (50mm) deck, and a speed of 23 knots on the 11,000hp (8,200kW) delivered to two shafts by triple-expansion steam engines. The last, completed in 1918, was the second 'Dresden' class of two ships with a displacement of 6,150 tons, an armament of eight 5.9in guns, two or three 3.4in anti-aircraft guns, and four 19.7in (500mm) torpedo tubes, protection in the form of a 2.5in (65mm) belt and a

The french World War II cruiser *Montcalm*, photographed in 1935.

0.75in (20mm) deck, and a speed of 28.5 knots on the 45,000hp (33,550kW) delivered to two shafts by steam turbines. The remarkable thing about these two classes, and this is a fact that was also evident in comparable British classes, was their conceptual similarity: the later class was larger, more heavily armed and armoured, and possessed a higher speed as a result of a more powerful propulsion arrangement based on steam turbines rather than triple-expansion engines, but in overall terms was merely a scaling-up of the earlier class with the incorporation of a number of operational improvements.

France, Italy and Russia followed basically the same course of development at slightly later dates and to smaller overall numbers of ships. The same was true of the US Navy, which entered the twentieth century with just two armoured cruisers, 15 protected cruisers and three unprotected cruisers, but then began a major programme of cruiser development and construction that saw the delivery of more advanced ships at an increasing rate. On the outbreak of World War I, when the USA remained neutral, the most modern type of armoured cruiser was the 'Tennessee' class of four ships launched between 1904 and 1906 with a

displacement of 14,500 tons, an armament of four 10in (254mm) guns in two twin turrets, sixteen 6in (152mm) guns in casemated mountings, twenty-two 3in (76mm) guns, twelve 3pdr guns and four 21in (533mm) torpedo tubes, protection in the form of a 5in (127mm) belt and 9in (229mm) turrets, and a speed of 22 knots on the 23,000hp (17,150kW) delivered to two shafts by triple-expansion steam engines. Dating from the same period was the 'St Louis' class of three protected cruisers with a displacement of 9,700 tons, an armament of fourteen 6in and eighteen 3in guns, protection in the form of a 4in (102mm) belt and 5in (127mm) conning tower, and a speed of 22 knots on the 21,000hp (15,660kW) delivered to two shafts by triple-expansion steam engines.

The only unprotected cruisers were three wholly obsolete ships of the 'Montgomery' class launched in 1891 and 1892, and the American cruiser force was completed by the three scout cruisers of the 'Chester' class launched in 1907 with a displacement of 3,750 tons, an armament of two 5in guns, six 3in guns and two 21in torpedo tubes, no protection, and a speed of 24 knots on the 16,000hp (11,930kW) delivered to two shafts by steam turbines.

Japanese developments reflected those of the Western powers, the last armoured cruisers being the two ships of the 'Kasuga' class ordered from an Italian yard by Argentina, which sold the two units to Japan in 1903. The ships had a displacement of some 7,650 tons, an armament of one 10in and two 8in or four 8in guns in one single and one twin or two twin turrets, fourteen 6in guns, ten 3in guns, six 3pdr guns and four 18in torpedo tubes, protection in the form of a 5.9in (150mm) belt, barbettes and conning tower, and a speed of twenty knots on the 13,500hp (10,065kW) delivered to two shafts by triple-expansion steam engines. The equivalent protected cruiser type was the 'Chikuma' class of three ships completed in 1912 with a displacement of 4,400 tons, an armament of six 6in guns, eight 12pdr guns and four 21in torpedo tubes, protection in the form of a 3in (76mm) deck and 4in (102mm) conning tower, and a speed of 26 knots on the 22,500hp (16,775kW) provided to two shafts by steam turbines. During World War I Japan kept a close watch on British warship developments, and in 1916 felt sufficiently confident in the utility of the new light cruiser concept to order an initial class of two 'Tenryu' class light cruisers modelled closely on the British 'C' type (the closely related 'Caroline', 'Cambrian', 'Centaur',

The Italian navy's heavy cruiser *Zara* was a classic ship of its type reflecting the Italians' realisation that French heavy cruisers offered superior all-round capabilities as a result of sacrificing a small measure of speed for significantly improved protection. The four ships of the 'Zara' class were launched in 1930 and 1931 for subsequent completion to a standard that included a full-load displacement of 14,600 tons, length of 599ft 5in (182.7m), armament of eight 8in (203mm) guns in four twin turrets, sixteen 3.9in (100mm) dual-purpose guns in eight twin turrets, eight 37mm anti-aircraft guns and two aircraft, protection in the form of 5.9in (150mm) belt and barbettes, 5.5in (140mm) turrets and 2.75in (70mm) deck, propulsion in the form of geared steam turbines delivering 108,000hp (80,535kW) to two shafts for a speed of 32 knots, and complement of 830. In March 1941 the *Zara, Fiume* and *Pola* were caught unawares at night off Cape Matapan by a powerful force of British ships including battleships that used radar direction to shatter and sink the Italian cruisers at very short range with 15in (381mm) shell fire.

A typical member of the 18-strong 'Baltimore' class of American heavy cruisers completed during the closing stages of and immediately after the end of World War II, the *St Paul* remained on the active list to 1971 and was scrapped in 1973. The details of the class included a full-load displacement of 17,070 tons, length of 675ft 0in (205.75m), armament of nine 8in (203mm) guns in three triple turrets, twelve 5in (127mm) dual-purpose guns in six twin turrets, forty-eight 40mm anti-aircraft guns in 11 quadruple and two twin mountings, twenty-two 20mm cannon in single mountings and four aircraft launched with the aid of two catapults, protection in the form of 6in (152mm) belt, barbettes and turrets, 8in (203mm) conning tower and 3in (76mm) deck, propulsion in the form of geared steam turbines delivering 120,000hp (89,470kW) to four shafts for a speed of 33 knots, and complement of 1,700.

'Caledon', 'Ceres' and 'Carlisle' classes). These two ships were completed only after the end of World War II, but paved the way for future Japanese light cruiser developments.

So far as the cruiser was concerned, the main lesson of World War I was that the naval reconnaissance role was better effected by aircraft than by the cruiser, which was thereafter operated mainly in alternative roles such as escort of major convoys, commerce protection and raiding, and gunfire support of amphibious operations.

This fact had become evident to the British in the later stages of World War I, when they had started to build cruisers somewhat larger than the otherwise standard cruisers that had proved so effective in the part of the war. Many of the latter were still comparatively new ships and were retained in service during the 1920s and 1930s, increasingly for second-line tasks such as the protection of trade routes. The oldest classes to survive into World War II were the 'Caledon', 'Carlisle' and 'Ceres' classes numbering three, five and five ships respectively. The 'Caledon' class ships were little altered in real terms from the standard in which they fought in World War I, but three of the 'Ceres' and all of the 'Carlisle' classes were considerably altered in overall capability by conversion to anti-aircraft cruisers. The *Coventry* and *Curlew* were prototype conversions with a primary armament of ten 4in (102mm) anti-aircraft guns in single mountings and sixteen 2pdr anti-aircraft guns in two octuple mountings, but the definitive standard adopted for the other six ships was eight 4in anti-aircraft guns in four twin turrets and four 2pdr anti-aircraft guns in a quadruple mounting.

Four of the five 'Improved Birmingham' class cruisers survived for limited service in World War II, and these larger and more capable ships were characterised by a displacement in the order of 9,700 tons, an armament of seven or five 7.5in (190mm) guns in single mountings and four or five 4in anti-aircraft guns in single mountings and, reflecting the increased threat posed by aircraft in World War II, eight 2pdr anti-aircraft guns in two quadruple mountings and ten 20mm anti-aircraft cannon, protection in the form of a 3in (76mm) belt and 1.5in (38mm) deck, and a speed of 30.5 knots on the 65,000hp (48,465kW) delivered to four shafts by steam turbines.

Another survivor from World War I and its immediate aftermath was the

'D' class of eight light cruisers originally built in the 'Danae' and 'Delhi' classes, and the two cruisers of the 'E' class completed in the early 1920s with a displacement of some 7,550 tons, an armament of seven 6in and three 4in anti-aircraft guns, protection in the form of a 2.5in (64mm) belt and 1in (25mm) deck, and a speed of 33 knots on the 80,000hp (59,650kW) delivered to four shafts by steam turbines.

These ships pre-dated the limitation treaties of the 1920s and 1930s, which did not in fact place any limit on the numbers of cruisers that could be built. Instead qualitative and later total tonnage restrictions were imposed, and replacement of over-age ships was also permitted. These conditions led to the general evolution of the cruiser into two species differentiated mainly by gun calibre: the light cruiser was generally a smaller type with guns of up to 6in calibre and indifferent armour protection, while the heavy cruiser was a larger type with guns of up to 8in calibre and relatively more effective armour protection.

The first of these modern cruiser classes in British service was the 'Kent' class of seven ships (including two for the Royal Australian Navy) with a displacement in the order of 9,800 tons, an armament of eight 8in guns in four twin turrets, eight 4in anti-aircraft guns in four twin turrets, eight 2pdr anti-aircraft guns in two quadruple mountings, and eight 21in (533mm) torpedo tubes, protection in the form of a 5in (127mm) belt and 4in (102mm) turrets, and a speed of 31.5 knots on the 80,000hp (59,650kW) supplied to four shafts by steam turbines. The same basic pattern of armament was followed in the 'London' class of three heavy cruisers and the 'Norfolk' class of two heavy cruisers, but the number of 8in main guns was reduced to six in three twin mountings in the two smaller heavy cruisers of the 'York' class that followed in the late 1920s.

Construction during the 1920s gave the Royal Navy a strong force of heavy cruisers, and in the 1930s attention switched to the replacement of the light cruiser types surviving from World War I with more advanced ships designed to complement the heavy cruisers. The first result of this effort was the 'Leander' class of light cruisers of which five were built for the UK and three for Australia. The British ships had a displacement in the order of 7,200 tons, an armament of eight 6in guns in four twin turrets, eight 4in anti-aircraft guns in four twin turrets, eight 2pdr anti-aircraft guns in two quadruple mountings, and eight 21in torpedo tubes, protection in the form of a 4in (102mm) belt and 2in (51mm) deck, and a speed of 32.5 knots on the

Built to too limited a design as a result of erroneous information about the first British battle-cruisers, the German navy's *Blücher* was a hybrid battle-cruiser/armoured cruiser that was completed in 1909 and lost in the Battle of the Dogger Bank during 1915. The details of the ship included a displacement of 15,500 tons, length of 530ft 6in (161.7m), armament of twelve 8.2in (208mm) guns in six twin turrets, eight 5.9in (150mm) guns in single mountings, sixteen 3.4in (88mm) guns in single mountings and four 17.7in (450mm) torpedo tubes, protection in the form of 6.75in (170mm) belt and turrets, propulsion in the form of triple-expansion steam engines delivering 44,000hp (32,805kW) to three shafts for a speed of 26 knots, and complement of 930. This artwork reveals the ship in its final configuration, which included a tripod rather than pole foremast as adopted in 1914.

72,000hp (53,685kW) delivered to four shafts by steam turbines. The three Australian ships differed in their displacement of some 6,900 tons and lack of 2pdr 'pom-pom' anti-aircraft guns. The following 'Arethusa' class of four ships was somewhat smaller with a displacement of some 5,250 tons, an armament of six 6in guns in three triple turrets, eight 4in anti-aircraft guns in four twin turrets, eight 2pdr anti-aircraft guns in two quadruple mountings and six 21in torpedo tubes, protection in the form of a 2in (51mm) belt and deck, and a speed of 32.25 knots on the 64,000hp (47,720kW) delivered to four shafts by steam turbines.

The next class of British ships was a hybrid type combining the size and most of the protection of the heavy cruiser with an augmented light cruiser armament. This was the 'Southampton' class built in three subclasses totalling five, three and two ships respectively. The first two subclasses had displacements of 9,100 and 9,400 tons respectively, an armament of twelve 6in guns in four triple turrets, eight 4in anti-aircraft guns in four twin turrets, eight 2pdr anti-aircraft guns in two quadruple mountings and six 21in torpedo tubes, protection in the form of a 4in (102mm) belt and 2in (51mm) deck and turrets, and a speed of 32 and 32.5 knots on the 75,000 or 82,500hp (55,920 or 61,510kW) respectively delivered to four shafts by steam turbines. The ships of the last subclass had a displacement of 10,000 tons, an armament of twelve 6in guns in four triple turrets, twelve 4in anti-aircraft guns in six twin turrets, sixteen 2pdr anti-aircraft guns in two octuple mountings and six 21in torpedo tubes, improved protection in the form of a 4.5in (114mm) belt and 2in (51mm) deck, and a speed of 32 knots on the 80,000hp (59,650kW) delivered to four shafts by steam turbines. The ships proved to be remarkably resilient, and saw very extensive service.

By the time the ships of the 'Southampton' class had been laid down in the mid-1930s, it had become clear that the warplane was rapidly becoming one of the most significant menaces faced by naval forces, and the British responded to this increasing threat with a classic class of dedicated anti-aircraft cruisers, the 'Dido' class of which 16 units were completed in 11- and five-ship subclasses with a displacement of 5,450 and 5,770 tons respectively and an armament in the first subclass of ten 5.25in (133mm) dual-purpose guns in five twin turrets, eight 2pdr anti-aircraft guns in two quadruple mountings and six 21in torpedo tubes, or in the second subclass of eight 5.25in dual-purpose guns in four twin turrets, twelve 2pdr anti-aircraft guns in three quadruple mountings and six 21in torpedo tubes. Features common to both subclasses were protection in the form of a 3in (76mm) belt and 2in (51mm) deck, and a speed of 33 knots on the 62,000hp (46,225kW) delivered to four shafts by steam turbines.

The next British cruiser type was the 'Fiji' class that reverted to the standard light cruiser concept, and these 11 ships were completed in eight- and three-ship subclasses whose common features included protection in the form of a 3.25in (83mm) belt and 2in (51mm) deck, and a speed of 33 knots on the 72,500hp (54,055kW) delivered to four shafts by steam

The light cruiser *Dresden* was the only major German ship to avoid destruction in the Battle of the Falkland Islands in 1914, but was severely damaged and was later scuttled off Juan Fernandez to avoid capture. The details of the ship, sister of the *Emden* that was a celebrated commerce raider brought to action and sunk off the Cocos Islands in 1914 by the Australian cruiser *Sydney*, included a displacement of 3,650 tons, length of 388ft 0in (118.25m), armament of ten 4.1in (105mm) guns and two 17.7in (450mm) torpedo tubes, protection in the form of a 2in (51mm) deck, propulsion in the form of steam turbines delivering 14,000hp (10,440kW) to four shafts for a speed of 24.5 knots, and complement of 360.

turbines: the first subclass had a displacement of 8,000 tons and an armament of twelve 6in guns in four triple turrets, eight 4in anti-aircraft guns in four twin turrets, nine 2pdr anti-aircraft guns in one single and two quadruple mountings and six 21in torpedo tubes, while the second subclass had a displacement of 8,800 tons, and an armament of nine 6in guns in three triple turrets, twenty 2pdr anti-aircraft guns in five quadruple mountings and twenty 20mm anti-aircraft cannon in ten twin mountings.

The final British cruiser class of the World War II period was the 'Minotaur' class, of which six were completed in three-ship subclasses during or immediately after the war to a design modelled on that of the second subclass of the 'Fiji' class. The principal common features were the hull and the protection, the latter in the form of a 3.5in (89mm) belt and 2in (51mm) deck and turrets. The first subclass had a displacement of 8,800 tons, an armament of nine 6in guns in three triple turrets, ten 4in anti-aircraft guns in five twin turrets, sixteen 2pdr anti-aircraft guns in four quadruple mountings, eight 40mm anti-aircraft guns in eight single mountings and six 21in torpedo tubes, and a speed of 32.5 knots on the 72,500hp (54,055kW) delivered to four shafts by steam turbines. The second subclass, which comprised the ships completed some time after the war, at whose termination construction had been suspended, had a displacement of 9,550 tons, an armament of four 6in dual-purpose guns in two twin turrets and six 3in anti-aircraft guns in three twin turrets, and a speed of 31.5 knots on the 80,000hp (59,650kW) delivered to four shafts by steam turbines. The

German Cruiser Identification

GERMAN light cruisers were generally similar in configuration, although size and the number of main guns increased in later ships, so one of the surest methods of identifying these useful vessels was by the combination of their funnel and bow configurations. The 'Bremen' class ships, for example, had three tall, raked funnels and an extended ram bow, while later types included the 'Leipzig' class with three tall funnels and an extended ram bow; the 'Stettin' class with three tall funnels (the forward two comparatively close together) and a ram bow; the 'Königsberg (1)' class had three tall funnels with steam pipes abaft the funnels, a ram bow and three 4.1in (105mm) guns on each beam; the 'Dresden' class had three tall funnels with steam pipes on their sides, a ram bow and three 4.1in guns on each beam; the 'Kolberg' class had three tall funnels, a ram bow and four 4.1in guns on each beam; the 'Breslau' class had four funnels with medium outer casings and a raked bow; the 'Karlsruhe' class had four funnels with low outer casing and a raked bow; the 'Elbing' class had three funnels including a taller forward unit and a straight bo;, and the 'Bremse' class had three tall, raked funnels and a clipper bow. The last four classes each had three funnels with low outer casings and a raked bow: the 'Regensburg' class had a circular first funnel and oval second and third funnels; the 'Frankfurt' class had a circular second funnel cased to its top and oval first and third funnels; the 'Königsberg (2)' class had a raised and circular first funnel and oval second and third funnels, and the 'Dresden (2)' class had a raised oval first, circular second and oval third funnel.

reduction in the number of guns in the second subclass was more than counterbalanced by the incorporation of the latest fire-control methods, which included extensive radar equipment.

During the course of the war, existing ships were extensively modified as they underwent refits or heavy repairs. The major part of this improvement effort was devoted to an upgrading of the ships' anti-aircraft capability by the addition of 20mm cannon in place of the original machine guns, the later replacement of these 20mm cannon by 40mm weapons, the supplementing of optical fire-control systems with radar fire-control systems, the removal of aircraft (between one and three depending on class) together with their associated hangar and catapult facilities (as long-range warning of ships and aircraft was increasingly and more reliably provided by radar), and in many ships the removal of one of the after main gun turrets to provide additional deck area for anti-aircraft weapons and radar equipment.

The US Navy disposed of most of its World War I cruisers during the 1920s and 1930s, but at the time of the USA's entry into World War II in December 1941 it had a total of 37 cruisers (18 heavy and 19 light). The size of this total was fortunate, for after the Japanese attack on Pearl Harbor and the loss, permanent or temporary, of many of its battleships, the US Navy was forced to rely on its cruiser force as its primary surface warfare capability as the surviving battleships were used for the escort of vital troop convoys. The intensity of this surface warfare in the period up to the middle of 1943 is attested by the fact that all of the pre-war cruisers involved in the protracted Solomons campaign were either sunk or damaged, and after the middle of 1943 the surviving cruisers were generally used for the gunfire support of amphibious landing and for the escort of carrier task forces. In common with their British counterparts, every protracted stay in port, either for refit or repair, was used to enhance the fighting capabilities of these very useful warships: radar was fitted and the anti-aircraft fit was considerably enhanced by the adoption of both specialised fire-control systems and additional weapons. The latter were of the lighter type designed to provide a high volume of fire for protection at shorter ranges against mass attacks, and may be typified by the enhancement of the 'Northampton' class ships, which each received sixteen 40mm guns in four quadruple mountings and nearly thirty 20mm cannon in single mountings.

Some of the ships suffered a fairly severe loss of stability as a result of the additional topweight, but even so the ships retained a remarkable tolerance to battle damage as a result of their construction, which was sturdy in the extreme although there were a number of structural failures as a result of poor welding: the *Pittsburgh*, for example, lost 90ft (27.4m) of her bows in a typhoon after a poor weld separated.

The two types of cruiser standardised in the US Navy during the 1920s were the heavy cruiser with an armament of 8in (203mm) guns and moderately thick armour, and the light cruiser with an armament of 6in (152mm) guns and comparatively thin armour.

The oldest heavy cruiser type in service during World War II was the 'Pensacola' class, of which the two units were launched in 1929. These were built in accordance with the dictates of the Washington Naval Treaty and were flushdecked ships with a low freeboard. The USA was the last of the treaty signatories to start on the construction of new heavy cruisers, and was therefore able to capitalise on the lessons that were discernible in the heavy cruisers that had already been built by other signatories: the French and Italians had opted for high speed at the expense of protection in the 'Duquesne' and 'Trento' class ships respectively, the Japanese had been influenced by initial reports of very heavy gun armament on the proposed American ships and had therefore adopted an additional main gun turret as well as good protection and a high turn of speed in the 'Myoko' class that in fact exceeded the treaty displacement limit by some 1,000 tons, and the British had opted in the 'Kent' class for a design that was altogether lighter than its contemporaries in firepower, protection and speed but which, as events were to prove, was robustly built and was an excellent seaboat. After assessing these other classes, the Americans opted for an approach similar to that of the Japanese with a main armament of ten 8in (203mm) guns located not in five twin turrets, as in the Japanese ships, but in superfiring pairs of triple and twin turrets. This primary armament was complemented by eight 5in (127mm) dual-purpose guns in single mountings, and other details of these ships included a full-load displacement of 12,050 tons, protection in the form of a 3in (76mm) belt and 2in (51mm) deck, and a speed of 32.5 knots on the 107,000hp (79,780kW) delivered to four shafts by steam turbines. A notable feature of the design was the considerable extent of weight saving that was effected in the design and construction of these fine ships, which emerged at a displacement some 900 tons below the Treaty standard displacement limit of 10,000 tons and were therefore considerably better value than the heavier Japanese ships.

The 'Pensacola' class set the pattern for the following heavy cruiser classes, which began with the six ships of the 'Northampton' class launched in 1929 and 1930. This was in effect a development of the 'Pensacola' class with a raised forecastle for improved seaworthiness and reduced wetness

Seen here behind its torpedo net defences in a Norwegian fjord during World War II, the *Lützow* was the pocket battleship *Deutschland*, which had been renamed in November 1939 in response to fears that the destruction of a ship named after the Fatherland would be a blow to morale. In 1940 the ship was reclassified as a heavy cruiser, but thereafter played only an undistinguished part in the war.

forward, and with further weight saving effected by the replacement of the ten 8in guns in a four-turret arrangement in the 'Pensacola' class with nine 8in guns in a three-turret arrangement. The ships were at first subject to a heavy rolling tendency, but this was cured by the installation of deeper bilge keels, and their primary details including a full-load displacement of some 12,250 tons, an armament of nine 8in guns and eight 5in dual-purpose guns, protection in the form of a 3in (76mm) belt and 2in (51mm) deck, and a speed of 32.5 knots on the 107,000hp (79,780kW) delivered to four shafts by steam turbines.

By the time the 'Northampton' class was under construction, the other signatories of the Washington Naval Treaty had produced their second generation of heavy cruiser, and the Americans were yet again able to profit from a survey of these vessels: the primary lesson learned was that the French and Italians had decided that their first-generation heavy cruisers had sacrificed too much protection in an effort to secure the highest possible speed, and the new 'Suffren' and 'Zara' classes, together with the 'Canarias' class designed for Spain in the UK, were notable for improved protection at a modest sacrifice in speed. The British and Japanese did not follow the same course as they had already opted for a better balance of protection and speed, and the Americans felt that this was the best option to be followed in the 'Indianapolis' class of two ships, which were very similar to the preceding 'Northampton' class except for a redistribution of the armour to provide additional protection amidships. The details of the ships, which were launched in 1931 and 1932, included a full-load displacement of 12,575 tons, an armament of nine 8in guns and eight 5in dual-purpose guns, protection in the form of a 4in (102mm) belt and 2in (51mm) deck, and a speed of 32.75 knots on the 107,000hp (79,780kW) delivered to four shafts by steam turbines.

The final American heavy cruisers built to Washington Naval Treaty limitations were the seven ships of the 'Astoria' class, which were in every way superlative ships matched in overall combat capability only by the single ship of the French 'Algérie' class and the three ships of the German 'Admiral Hipper' class. The principal changes from the 'Indianapolis' class were a lengthening of the forecastle to the rear for improved seaworthiness, pole rather than tripod masts, and improved protection in the form of a longer belt and thicker armour for the decks, turrets and conning tower. The details of the ships, which were launched between 1933 and 1936, therefore included a full-load displacement of 13,500 tons, an armament of nine 8in (203mm) guns, eight 5in (127mm) dual-purpose guns and sixteen 1.1in anti-aircraft guns, protection in the form of a 5in (127mm) belt and 3in (76mm) deck, and a speed of 32.75 knots on the 107,000hp (79,780kW) delivered to four shafts by steam turbines.

Launched in 1937, the single ship of the 'Wichita' class had been planned as the eighth ship of the 'Astoria' class but was completed to a standard resembling the 'Brooklyn' class of light cruiser except in its armament details. The ship had a full-load displacement of 13,700 tons, an armament of nine 8in (203mm) guns and eight 5in (127mm) dual-purpose guns, protection in the form of a 5in (127mm) belt and 3in (76mm) deck, and a speed of 32.5 knots on the 100,000hp (74,560kW) delivered to four shafts by steam turbines.

This similarity to the 'Brooklyn' class provides striking evidence of the gradual merging of American heavy and light cruiser design concepts, the heavy cruiser generally having slightly greater length and the light cruiser having five turrets each carrying three 6in (152mm) guns rather than the heavy cruiser's fit of three turrets each carrying three 8in guns. The Japanese also followed this concept, although not to so standardised a level, and were therefore able to upgrade the 'Mogami' class light cruisers to heavy cruiser standard by the replacement of the triple 6.1in (155m) turrets by twin 8in turrets.

The tendency towards the use of a conceptually similar design for light and heavy cruisers became fully evident with the 'Baltimore' class of 17 ships launched between 1942 and 1945 with an eighteenth following in 1951, although only 14 of these were completed in World War II. The design was based on that of the 'Cleveland' class of light cruisers with the hull lengthened

A notably potent heavy cruiser of the Imperial Japanese navy, the *Chokai* was a unit of the four-strong 'Takao' class and was completed in the early 1930s to a standard that included a full-load displacement of 13,160 tons, length of 661ft 6in (201.6m), armament of ten 8in (203mm) guns in five twin turrets (three forward and two aft), four 4.7in (120mm) anti-aircraft guns in single mountings, eight 24in (610mm) torpedo tubes in four twin mountings and two aircraft, protection in the form of a 4in (102mm) belt and 1.5in (38mm) turrets and decks, propulsion in the form of geared steam turbines delivering 135,000hp (100,655kW) to four shafts for a speed of 35.5 knots, and complement of 775. After suffering major damage from aircraft-launched torpedoes, the Chokai was scuttled off the Philippines in October 1944.

by 65ft (19.6m) and an increase in beam of 4ft (1.2m), and with the main armament revised to heavy cruiser standard. By the time of their completion, all other navies except that of Germany had effectively abandoned the heavy cruiser concept, but the US Navy still believed that with large oceans off its eastern and western seaboards there was not only scope but even demand for heavy cruisers offering a combination of firepower, protection, speed and range that was unrivalled by anything but a capital ship. The 'Baltimore' class heavy cruisers were superb examples of this concept, which certainly retained a full validity up to and indeed after the end of World War II. The main features of the 'Baltimore' class design were a large deck area allowing the siting of large numbers of short-range anti-aircraft weapons in addition to the turrets carrying the primary and secondary armaments, a shorter but thicker length of belt armour, and the absence of side scuttles so that all interior spaces had to be artificially ventilated and illuminated. The details of these fine fighting ships included a full-load displacement of 17,070 tons, an armament of nine 8in guns in three triple turrets, twelve 5in dual-purpose guns in six twin turrets, forty-eight 40mm anti-aircraft guns in 11 quadruple and two twin mountings, and up to twenty-eight 20mm anti-aircraft cannon in single mountings, protection in the form of a 6in (152mm) belt and 3in (76mm) deck, and a speed of 33 knots on the 120,000hp (89,470kW) delivered to four shafts by steam turbines.

To complete the story of American heavy cruisers with 8in guns, it is necessary to mention two classes that were designed during World War II but completed after the end of hostilities and then only in small numbers and in different forms. The 'Oregon City' class was planned as eight ships of which only four were completed to an improved 'Baltimore' class design with a single funnel rather than twin funnels to give the guns improved arcs of fire, and the 'Des Moines' class was planned as 12 ships of which only three were completed to an improved 'Oregon City' class design with automatic 8in guns, a tertiary battery of twenty-four 3in (76mm) anti-aircraft guns in 12 twin turrets to replace the 40mm guns of the preceding classes, and a longer and thicker belt of waterline armour.

Mention should also be made of the supremely elegant 'Alaska' class of large heavy cruisers, often but erroneously called battle-cruisers. The origins of the class are to be found in the pre-war report that Japan was emulating the German lead and building a class of 'pocket battleships', and to this report the US Navy responded with the 'Alaska' class projected as six large heavy cruisers of which only three were laid down and two actually completed to what was basically an enlarged version of the 'Baltimore' class design, with a primary armament of nine 12in (305mm) rather than 8in guns and the protection scaled up to approximately the same extent. With a full-load displacement of 34,250 tons and a length of 808ft 6in (246.43m), the 'Alaska' class large heavy cruiser carried a primary armament of nine 12in guns in three triple turrets including a superfiring pair forward, a secondary armament of twelve 5in dual-purpose guns in six twin turrets, and a tertiary armament of fifty-six 40mm guns in 14 quadruple mountings and thirty-four 20mm anti-aircraft cannon in single mountings. The ships were protected by extensive but only moderately thick armour that included an 8in (203mm) belt and 3.75in (95mm) deck, and the highly impressive sustained speed of 33 knots was attained on the 150,000hp (111,840kW) delivered to four shafts by steam turbines.

The oldest class of light cruisers still in service with the US Navy at the time of the American entry into World War II was the 'Omaha' class of 10 ships, planned in the aftermath of World War I as the first light cruisers designed in the USA for more than 10 years. The light cruiser had fully proved its worth in World War I, and as the starting point for its new type the US Navy took the British 'Danae' and 'Delhi' classes as well as the German 'Dresden' class. These classes had a speed of 29 and 28.5 knots respectively for the British and German types, which also had a main armament of six 6in and seven 5.9in (150mm) guns, so the US Navy proposed that its new class should have a speed of 35 knots and an armament of eight 6in guns on a displacement of 7,100 tons. The guns were in casemated installations fore and aft, and included four guns that could bear on either beam: it was therefore decided to add four more 6in guns in two twin turrets located fore and aft, although this meant an increase of 400 tons in displacement, a 9in (0.23m) increase in draught, a 1 knot decrease in speed, and the trimming of the belt to a length on each beam alongside the machinery spaces. It was then decided that the originally planned torpedo armament of two submerged tubes should be replaced by 10 tubes above the waterline and that two catapults and aircraft should be added, so the further increase in weight resulted in the omission of the after 6in casemated guns in half of the class, for improved stability. The ships were launched between 1920 and 1924, and during World War II were generally used in the South Atlantic and in a few secondary actions in the Pacific as well as for the gunfire support role in a number of secondary amphibious landings. As completed, the ships had a full-load displacement of 9,150 tons, an armament of twelve or ten 6in guns including four in twin turrets, eight 3in anti-aircraft guns in single mountings and ten 21in (533mm) torpedo tubes, protection in the form of a 3in (76mm) belt and 1.5in (38mm) deck, and a speed of 33.5 knots on the 90,000hp (67,105kW) delivered to four shafts by steam turbines.

With their four tall funnels in two pairs, the 'Omaha' class light cruisers were not visually attractive, but the same cannot be said of the 'Brooklyn' class that followed the last 'Omaha' class ships after an interval of more than 10 years. The spur for the development of this classic class was the Japanese 'Mogami' class of large light cruisers that began to appear in 1935 after Japan's completion of its quota of 12 heavy cruisers permitted under the restrictions of the Washington Naval Treaty. The 'Mogami' class was planned as a light cruiser type able to offer heavy cruiser capabilities through the combination of a large hull with an armament of no fewer than fifteen 6.1in (155mm) guns in five centreline turrets (three forward,

The *Diadem* was completed in 1943 as one of the five-strong second group of the 'Dido' class of British light cruisers optimised for the air defence role with a specification that included a displacement of 5,770 tons, length of 512ft 0in (156.1m), armament of eight 5.25in (133mm) dual-purpose guns in four twin turrets, twelve 2pdr anti-aircraft guns in three quadruple mountings, twelve 20mm cannon in six twin mountings and six 21in (533mm) torpedo tubes in two triple mountings, protection in the form of a 3in (76mm) belt, 2in (51mm) turrets and deck and 1in (25mm) conning tower, propulsion in the form of geared steam turbines delivering 62,000hp (46,225kW) to four shafts for a speed of 33 knots, and complement of 535. The ship survived the war and remained in British service up to 1956, when it was sold to Pakistan for further service as the Babur.

including one superfiring pair, and two aft in a superfiring pair): in the days before radar, when the maximum effective firing range was limited by visibility, the advantage in nocturnal and poor weather operations lay with the ships that could deliver the highest volume of aimed fire, and here the advantage would generally rest with the 'Mogami' class light cruisers even in engagements with heavy cruisers.

The American response to the threat of the 'Mogami' class ships was a type of similar concept but with a greater displacement, thicker armour (to the same basic levels as the 'Astoria' class of heavy cruisers with the exception of a slightly thinner but longer belt) and shorter overall length: the hull was of the flushdecked type, and the main armament of fifteen 6in guns was carried in five triple turrets arranged in the same manner as those of the Japanese ships with the exception that in the American ships it was 'B' rather than 'C' turret that was the superfiring unit of the forward trio.

The nine ships of the 'Brooklyn' class were launched between 1936 and 1938, and their details included a full-load displacement of some 12,700 tons, an armament of fifteen 6in guns in three triple turrets, eight 5in dual-purpose guns in eight single mountings or, in the last two units, four twin turrets, and sixteen 1.1in anti-aircraft guns in four quadruple mountings, protection in the form of a 5in (127mm) belt and 3in (76mm) deck, and a speed of 32.5 knots on the 100,000hp (74,560kW) delivered to four shafts by steam turbines. Wartime alterations included a strengthening of the anti-aircraft armament by sixteen 40mm guns in four quadruple mountings and between twenty and twenty-four 20mm cannon in single mountings. The ships saw very extensive and successful service in World War II, in which only one of the vessels was lost, and in the early 1950s six of the ships were passed in pairs to three US allies in South America, where some of the ships are still operational.

The next class of American light cruisers was completely different from the 'Brooklyn' class and, indeed, from any other type of American light cruiser as it was an anti-aircraft and flotilla leader type inspired by the British 'Dido' class of anti-aircraft cruisers. Although the 'Atlanta' class of four ships, launched in 1941, mirrored the role of the 'Dido' class, it was wholly American in its interpretation of how this role should be achieved to maximum effect. The type had the right armament (including two banks of torpedo tubes) and the high speed required for use with destroyer flotillas operating round the edges of a carrier task force, but was really too large for this role: wartime experience revealed that more success might have been achieved by a reduction in the number of main-calibre guns to allow the incorporation of more than just two high-angle directors, which limited each ship's ability to the engagement of only two aircraft at any one time. As completed, the ships had a full-load displacement of 8,100 tons, an armament of sixteen 5in dual-purpose guns in eight twin turrets, twelve or sixteen 1.1in anti-aircraft guns in three or four quadruple mountings, eight 20mm cannon in single mountings and eight 21in torpedo tubes, protection in the form of a 3.5in (89mm) belt and 2in (51mm) deck, and a speed of 33 knots on the 75,000hp (55,920kW) delivered to four shafts by steam turbines.

The following class comprised the 27 light cruisers of the 'Cleveland' class, which was to have numbered 39 including three ships that were cancelled and nine that were converted into aircraft carriers. This class was an enhanced version of the 'Brooklyn' class with one 6in triple turret sacrificed to make space for a much improved anti-aircraft armament. Launched between 1941 and 1944, the ships had a full-load displacement of 13,755 tons, an armament of twelve 6in guns in four triple turrets, twelve 5in dual-purpose guns in six twin turrets, between eight and twenty-eight 40mm

THE 'Substance' operation was undertaken between 21 and 27 July 194,1 intended for the relief of the beleaguered garrison on the island of Malta. At this time Malta's garrison was in sore need of reinforcements and supplies, but as no convoy could be passed westward through the Mediterranean from Alexandria, it was decided to try an eastward convoy from Gibraltar. The British plan was that the troopship *Leinster* and six storeships should be passed to Malta while the auxiliary *Breconshire* and six empty merchantmen escaped from the island to Gibraltar. The convoy departed the River Clyde on 11 July and reached Gibraltar on 19 July, allowing the operation proper to begin on 21 July. The British plan was for Admiral Sir Andrew Cunningham's Mediterranean Fleet to sortie from Alexandria in order to deal with the Italian fleet if this should sail from Taranto, Palermo or Messina; for a patrol group of eight submarines to lurk on the likely approach routes of any Italian surface forces, and for the convoy to head east under escort of the reinforced Force H (two battleships, one aircraft carrier, five cruisers and 18 destroyers), which would turn back in the Sicilian Narrows, leaving the convoy to proceed to Malta, as the ships from Malta escaped westwards. The operation proceeded without undue incident until 23 July, when the convoy was south of Sardinia and came under heavy air attack. Despite the efforts of the fighters flown off the carrier *Ark Royal*, the first casualties were the *Manchester*, which was so heavily damaged by a torpedo that it had to return to Gibraltar, and the destroyer *Fearless*, which had eventually to be sunk by the British. The vital storeships were undamaged, however, and reached the Skerki Channel for the final dash to Malta. Air attacks on the convoy continued, but the only casualty was a warship, this time the destroyer *Firedrake*, which was detached to Gibraltar. Early on 24 July, one of the storeships was torpedoed and damaged by a Pantellaria-based torpedo craft, but managed to get through to Malta. At daybreak the cruisers headed independently for Malta (as there was now chance of interception by Italian heavy warships), unloaded their troops and stores, and made off to Gibraltar late on 24 July. Later on the same day the storeships and their destroyer escort arrived safely as the empty ships that had broken out from the island headed for Gibraltar, all arriving despite the attentions of the Axis air forces.

anti-aircraft guns in four twin or four quadruple and six twin mountings, and between ten and twenty-one 20mm cannon in single mountings, protection in the form of a 5in (127mm) belt and 2in (51mm) deck, and a speed of 33 knots on the 100,000hp (74,560kW) delivered to four shafts by steam turbines.

Next came seven anti-aircraft light cruisers of the 'Oakland' class that were completed in two groups of four ships launched between 1942 and 1944, and three ships launched between 1945 and 1946. The type was a further development of the 'Atlanta' class with a full-load displacement of 8,200 tons, armour protection in the form of a 3.75in (95mm) belt and 2in (51mm) deck, and a speed of 33 knots on the 75,000hp (55,920kW) delivered to four shafts by steam turbines. The two groups differed principally in their armament: the four ships of the first group had twelve 5in dual-purpose guns in six twin turrets, sixteen 40mm anti-aircraft guns in eight twin mountings, sixteen 20mm cannon in single mountings, and eight 21in torpedo tubes; while the three ships of the second group had twelve 5in dual-purpose guns in six twin mountings, thirty-two 40mm anti-aircraft guns in six quadruple and four twin mountings and twenty 20mm cannon in single mountings.

The 'Fargo' class of only two out of a planned 13 units, was a further development of the 'Cleveland' class with changes to improve the efficiency of their guns' fire: these changes included a more compact superstructure and the two uptakes trunked into a single funnel to give the guns larger arcs of fire. The details of the two ships, which were launched in 1945, included a full-load displacement of 13,755 tons, an armament of twelve 6in guns in four triple turrets, twelve 5in dual-purpose guns in six twin turrets, twenty-eight 40mm anti-aircraft guns in six quadruple and two twin mountings, and twenty-eight 20mm cannon in 14 twin mountings, protection in the form of a 5in (127mm) belt and 3in (76mm) deck, and a speed of 33 knots on the 100,000hp (74,560kW) delivered to four shafts by steam turbines.

The last American light cruiser design created during World War II was the 'Worcester' class of which only two out of a planned 10 units were completed, and then only well after the end of the war. The design was basically a development of the 'Oakland' class design with fully automatic 6in twin turrets replacing the manually operated 5in twin turrets, resulting in a longer hull and a larger displacement. The details of the class included a full-load displacement of 18,000 tons, an armament of twelve 6in dual-purpose guns in six twin turrets and twenty-four 3in dual-purpose guns in 11 twin and two single turrets, protection in the form of a 6in (152mm) belt and 3in (76mm) deck, and a speed of 32.75 knots on the 120,000hp (89,470kW) delivered to four shafts by steam turbines.

The other two naval powers involved in World War II on the Allied side were France and the USSR, neither of which played a major part in naval hostilities. The French cruiser force included the three light cruisers of the 'Duguay Trouin' class launched in 1923 and 1924 with a full-load displacement of 9,350 tons and a main armament of eight 6.1in (155mm) guns in four twin turrets; the two heavy cruisers of the 'Duquesne' class launched in 1925 and 1926 with a full-load displacement of 12,200 tons and a main armament of eight 8in (203m) guns in four twin turrets; the four heavy cruisers of the 'Suffren' class launched between 1927 and 1930 with a full-load displacement of 12,780 tons and a main armament of eight 8in (203mm) guns in four twin turrets; the single but outstanding heavy cruiser of the 'Algérie' class launched in 1932 with a full-load displacement of 13,900 tons and a main armament of eight 8in guns in four twin turrets; the single light cruiser of the 'Emile Bertin' class launched in 1933 with a full-load displacement of 8,480 tons and a main armament of nine 6in (152mm) guns in three triple turrets; and the six excellent light cruisers of the 'La

Galissonnière' class launched between 1933 and 1935 with a full-load displacement of 9,100 tons and a main armament of nine 6in guns in three triple turrets. The USSR operated a number of obsolete and obsolescent cruisers in the 1920s and 1930s, and the only truly modern type available in World War II was the 'Kirov' class, of which six were completed before and during the war with a full-load displacement of 11,500 tons and a main armament of nine 7.1in (180mm) guns in three triple turrets.

On the other side of the naval front line in World War II were Germany, Italy and Japan. Germany planned a class of five 'Admiral Hipper' class heavy cruisers from the early 1930s, and these were orthodox but large ships of their type. Launched in the second half of the 1930s, only three of the ships were completed. The main armament was limited to eight 8in guns in four twin turrets located as superfiring pairs forward and aft, and this allowed a considerable proportion of the displacement to be devoted to a sturdy structure and very good protection. One of the ships was sunk by Norwegian shore batteries in April 1940, but the other two survived the war after playing a distinguished part in its first phases. The basic details of these impressive ships included a full-load displacement of 18,400 tons, an armament of eight 8in guns in four twin turrets, twelve 4.1in (105mm) dual-purpose guns in six twin turrets, twelve 37mm anti-aircraft guns in six twin mountings, twenty-four 20mm cannon and twelve 21in (533mm) torpedo tubes, protection in the form of a 3.1in (80mm) belt and 2in (51mm) deck, and a speed of 33.4 knots on the 132,000hp (98,430kW) delivered to three shafts by steam turbines.

The other major element of Germany's cruiser strength was provided by the six light cruisers of the 'Köln' class, which were relatively modern ships but not particularly notable with their armament of nine 5.9in (150mm) guns and six 3.4in (88mm) anti-aircraft guns.

Italy was a firm believer in the cruiser concept, which it saw as tactically efficient for the support of its battle force in the central Mediterranean and also as a cost-effective means of providing powerful warships suited for the command and support of flotilla operations in more confined waters such as those of the Aegean. In the years after World War I the Italian navy lacked the financial resources to undertake the construction of many new ships, and for this reason retained a number of obsolescent types such as the two 'San Giorgio' class armoured cruisers, the single 'Libia' and 'Campania' class protected cruisers, and the one 'Quarto', two 'Bixio', three 'Poerio', three 'Mirabello', four 'Aquila' and three 'Leone' class scout cruisers. During the 1920s, however, relations between France and Italy began to worsen, and when the French started work on the two 'Duquesne' class heavy cruisers to the limits imposed by the Washington Naval Treaty, Italy responded with the 'Trento' class offering firepower and speed comparable with those of the French class but with somewhat better protection. The 'Trento' class ships were still under construction when France replied with its four 'Suffren' class heavy cruisers in which a measure of speed was sacrificed to greater protection. Italy did not immediately respond to these impressive ships, largely as a result of financial and industrial limitations, and this gave the Italian navy the time to digest the nuances of the 'Suffren' class design before proceeding three years later with the four ships of the 'Zara' class. This class sacrificed some performance, the propulsion arrangement being reduced to 108,000hp (80,535kW) delivered to two shafts by steam turbines for a speed of 32 knots, so that better protection could be worked into the design: this protection took the form of a 5.9in (150mm) belt and 2.75in (70mm) deck, and the firepower of these impressive heavy cruisers was provided by a main battery of eight 8in guns in two pairs of superfiring

An overhead view of the US Navy's nuclear-powered cruiser *Long Beach* reveals some of the salient features of this important ship's layout. From bow to stern, these include the two twin launchers for surface-to-air missiles, the forward pair of SPG-55 fire-control radars, the forward superstructure flanked by two Mk 32 triple mountings for anti-submarine torpedoes and carrying the air and surface search radars as well as two more SPG-55 fire-control radars, the ASROC launcher and 5in (127mm) gun turret, the after superstructure carrying the long-range air search radar as well as the two quadruple launchers for Harpoon anti-ship missiles and the two Phalanx close-in weapon system mountings for last-ditch defence against attack aircraft and anti-ship missiles, and the two quadruple launchers for Tomahawk cruise missiles.

turrets, a secondary battery of sixteen 3.9in (100mm) dual-purpose guns in eight twin mountings, and a tertiary battery of eight 37mm anti-aircraft guns.

So far as light cruisers were concerned, the Italians also responded to French initiatives. Thus the construction of the three 'Duguay Trouin' light cruisers spurred the laying down from 1928 of the first four of an eventual 12 light cruisers of the 'Condotierri' type produced in five subclasses as four 'Bande Nere', two 'Diaz', two 'Montecuccoli', two 'Aosta' and two 'Garibaldi' class ships. Like their French counterparts, the 'Bande Nere' class ships carried a primary armament of eight 6in guns in two pairs of superfiring twin turrets and carried armour protection that can only be described as vestigial, but they were very fast. The four later subclasses of the 'Condotierri' type were a response to the French light cruisers of the 'La Galissonnière' class with improved protection, and successive subclasses introduced greater size and displacement to permit the incorporation of better protection and a more potent propulsion arrangement so that speed did not suffer. The last pair of ships, launched in 1933, were the 'Garibaldi' class with a further enlargement in beam and draught to allow the incorporation of two additional main-calibre guns. The details of these ships included a full-load displacement of 11,260 tons, an armament of ten 6in guns in superfiring pairs of triple and twin turrets, eight 3.9in anti-aircraft guns, eight 37mm anti-aircraft guns, ten 20mm anti-aircraft cannon and six 21in torpedo tubes, protection in the form of a 5.1in (130mm) belt and 1.6in (40mm) deck, and a speed of 32 knots on the 102,000hp (76,060kW) delivered to two shafts by steam turbines.

Although the concept of the small scout cruiser had generally lapsed after the end of World War I except in Japan, where a number of such ships were built in the 1920s, the French reverted to such a type in the mid-1930s with the 'Mogador' class of ships (officially rated as large destroyers but which were in fact scout cruisers), with a full-load displacement of 4,010 tons, a main armament of eight 5.5in (140mm) guns in two superfiring pairs of twin turrets and complemented by four 37mm anti-aircraft guns in two twin mountings and ten 21.7in (550mm) torpedo tubes, and the remarkable speed of 39 knots on the 92,000hp (68,630kW) delivered to two shafts by

The *Yorktown* was completed as the second unit of the 'Ticonderoga' class of guided missile cruisers, numerically the most important type of cruiser for the defence of US Navy major surface forces. The details of this and other early units, before the introduction of the vertical-launch missile system in the sixth ship, include a full-load displacement of 9,410 tons, length of 567ft 0in (172.8m), armament of two 5in (127mm) dual-purpose guns in single turrets, two 20mm Vulcan six-barrel cannon in two Phalanx close-in weapon system mountings, two twin launchers for up to 68 weapons (Standard Missile surface-to-air missiles and up to 20 ASROC anti-submarine rockets), two quadruple launchers for eight Harpoon anti-ship missiles and six 12.75in (324mm) tubes in two triple mountings for lightweight anti-submarine torpedoes, propulsion in the form of gas turbines delivering 80,000hp (59,650kW) to two shafts for a speed of 30 or more knots, and complement of 360.

steam turbines. The capability of these destroyers, of which only two were built to a standard that effectively outgunned the British 'Dido' class light cruisers, was seen by the Italians as a major threat that was countered by the 'Capitani Romani' class of fast light cruisers: 12 ships were laid down, but only four of these were completed. The key to the design was a long and relatively beamy hull able to accommodate a sizeable propulsion arrangement: the machinery of the Italian ships was capable of generating 125,000hp (92,310kW), which was about the same as that of the four times heavier 'Des Moines' class heavy cruisers, and this was delivered to two shafts for the astonishing speed of 43 knots. However, the ships carried virtually no protection, and the armament comprised eight 5.3in (135mm) guns in two superfiring pairs of twin turrets, eight 37mm anti-aircraft guns, eight 20mm anti-aircraft cannon and eight 21in torpedo tubes.

Like the Italians, the Japanese viewed the cruiser as an ideal weapon for a country that lacked a large industrial base and indigenous raw materials, especially iron ore: the cruiser offered the possibility of striking at larger and potentially more threatening warships by using its speed and agility, in combination with daring Japanese tactics, to close to effective torpedo range. The first result of this philosophy, which had seen the laying down of the two 'Tenryu' class light cruisers in the closing stages of World War I, was the five-strong 'Kuma' class of light cruisers with a displacement of 5,100 tons, an armament of seven 5.5in (140mm) guns in a single mounting and eight 21in torpedo tubes, protection in the form of a 2in (51mm) belt and 1.5in (37mm) deck, and a speed of 36 knots on the 90,000hp (67,105kW) delivered to four shafts by steam turbines. Two of the vessels, it is worth noting, were adapted in 1941 into the ultimate torpedo-armed cruisers after the introduction of the 24in (610mm) 'Long Lance' long-range/high-speed torpedo with liquid oxygen propellant: the *Kitakami* and *Oi* were altered by the revision of the gun armament to four 5.5in weapons in two twin mountings and up to thirty-six 25mm anti-aircraft guns in six triple and 18 single mountings: the deck was extended on each beam with sponsons to carry a total of 10 quadruple mountings for the 'Long Lance' torpedo.

After World War I, Japan planned a programme of major military and naval expansion designed to turn the country into the decisive military power in the western half of the Pacific Ocean and in eastern and south-eastern Asia. An early decision was that the Japanese navy was lacking in balance, for construction in the period before and during World War I had been concentrated on capital ships and destroyers. With a major capability in the western half of the Pacific now envisaged, there was clearly demand for larger numbers of more capable cruisers in the scouting and ambush roles. The first result of this was the 'Natori' class of six light cruisers completed in the period between 1922 and 1925. These were unexceptional ships based on the 'Nagara' class with a displacement of 5,170 tons, an armament of seven 5.5in guns in seven single turrets and eight 24in torpedo tubes, protection in the form of a 2in (51mm) belt and 1.5in (37mm) deck, and a speed of 36 knots on the 90,000hp (67,105kW) delivered to four shafts by steam turbines.

The same philosophy was maintained in the following 'Sendai' class of six light cruisers, of which only three were completed. This class had the same basic dimensions, armament and protection as the two preceding classes, although a change was made in the propulsion arrangement that now included 11 oil- and one mixed-burning boilers by comparison with the eight oil- and four coal-burning boilers of the 'Nagara' class and the 10 oil- and two mixed-burning boilers of the 'Kuma' class.

As the 'Sendai' class was being planned and laid down, the final negotiations of the Washington Naval Conference were being undertaken

Cruiser Battles off Guadalcanal

THE land campaign that started the American fight-back after Japan's series of runaway victories between December 1941 and mid-1942 was that for the island of Guadalcanal toward the south-eastern tip of the Solomon Islands. This started with the landing of the US 1st Marine Division in Operation 'Watchtower' on 7 August 1942, and continued with increasing fury until the final Japanese evacuation of the island by 7 February 1943. In the course of this campaign, which was entirely reliant on maritime support for the delivery of men and equipment, seven major naval engagements took place, four of them involving mainly cruisers and destroyers. These were the nocturnal Battle of Savo Island on 8/9 August 1942 in which a Japanese force of seven cruisers under Vice Admiral Mikawa inflicted a severe reverse on the American and Australian force of six cruisers under the command of Rear Admiral Crutchley, who lost four of his major vessels but foiled the Japanese attempt to reinforce Guadalcanal; the nocturnal Battle of Cape Esperance on 11/12 October 1942 in which a Japanese force including four cruisers under the command of Rear Admiral Goto fought a tactically inconclusive action with an American force under Rear Admiral Scott and including five cruisers; and the actions of 12 November and 30/31 November 1942 in 'Ironbottom Sound' between Guadalcanal and Tulagi Islands. The first resulted in a modest American victory when a force under the command of Rear Admiral Callaghan (five cruisers and eight destroyers) saw off a Japanese force under Vice Admiral Abe (two battleships, two cruisers and 14 destroyers), in the process sinking two cruisers and damaging all of the other Japanese ships for the loss of two cruisers and four destroyers. The second was a Japanese victory when Rear Admiral Tanaka's force of eight destroyers encountered Rear Admiral Wright's force of five cruisers and seven destroyers, sinking one cruiser and damaging three others for the loss of only one destroyer.

and the probability of new types of cruiser persuaded the Japanese navy to build the single 'Yubari' class light cruiser as an experimental type offering the same broadside weight as its predecessors on a displacement of only 2,900 tons. This was achieved by limiting the protection to a 2in (50mm) belt, trunking the two uptakes into a single funnel, limiting the torpedo armament to four 24in (610mm) tubes, locating the main armament of six 5.5in (140mm) guns on the centreline in two twin and two single turrets with the twin turrets in superfiring positions, and revising the propulsion arrangement for a speed of 35.5 knots on the 57,900hp (43,170kW) delivered to three shafts by steam turbines. The ship was a considerable success at the technical level, and paved the way for the design and construction of both light and heavy cruisers within the constraints of the Washington Naval Treaty.

The first result of this process was the 'Kako' class of two heavy cruisers completed in 1926. These were impressive ships, well within the treaty limits for the new class of heavy cruisers with 8in (203mm) guns and a maximum displacement of 10,000 tons, as they were armed with six 7.9in (200mm) guns in single turrets (three forward and three aft) and had a displacement of 8,100 tons. Their other primary details included a secondary armament of four 3in (76mm) anti-aircraft guns in single mountings and twelve 24in (610mm) torpedo tubes, protection in the form of a 3in (76mm) belt and 1.5in (37mm) deck, and a speed of 34.5 knots on the 102,000hp (76,050kW) delivered to three shafts by steam turbines. The overall capabilities of the class were improved in the late 1930s, when the original six single gun turrets were replaced by three twin turrets (a superfiring pair forward and a singleton aft) carrying 8in weapons.

The following two ships of the 'Aoba' class were generally similar with the exception of having their six 7.9in guns, later replaced by 8in weapons, in three twin turrets and the strengthened anti-aircraft armament of four 4.7in guns in single mountings. With a displacement of 8,300 tons and protection in the form of a 3in (76mm) belt and 1.5in (37mm) deck, the 'Aoba' class cruiser attained a speed of 34.5 knots on the 102,000hp (76,050kW) delivered to four shafts by steam turbines.

Further development of the concept embodied in these first two classes of Japanese heavy cruiser resulted in the mid-1920s in the considerably improved 'Myoko' class of four ships completed in 1928 and 1929 with a displacement of 10,940 tons, an armament of ten 7.9in guns, later replaced by 8in weapons, in five twin turrets (three forward and two aft), six 4.7in anti-aircraft guns in single mountings, twelve 24in torpedo tubes, protection in the form of a 4in (102mm) belt and 5in (127mm) deck, and a speed of 35.5 knots on the 130,000hp (96,930kW) delivered to four shafts by steam turbines. The most important features of the additional size and displacement introduced with this class were the significantly heavier main armament, carried as a triplet forward with the central unit as the superfiring turret and as a superfiring pair aft, and the considerably thicker armour that made these vessels particularly resistant to terminal battle damage.

The following four ships of the 'Takao' class were to an improved 'Myoko' class design with a more 'piled' superstructure of streamlined design, extensive use of welding rather than riveting and the use of light alloy in place of steel wherever possible to keep weight to a minimum, an increase in the armour protection for the magazines, and a primary armament of 8in guns. The details of the ships therefore included a displacement of 11,350 tons, an armament of ten 8in guns in five twin turrets (three forward and two aft), four 4.7in anti-aircraft guns in single mountings and eight 24in torpedo tubes, protection in the form of a 4in (102mm) belt and 1.5in (37mm) deck, and a speed of 35.5 knots on the 130,000hp (96,930kW) delivered to four shafts by steam turbines.

The Battle of Midway

OPERATION 'MI' was the Japanese operation between 25 May and 5 June 1942 for the capture of Midway Island, and led to the Battle of Midway that was one of the decisive battles of World War II resulting, as it did, in the reversal of Japan's expansion south and east into the Pacific, already checked in the Battle of the Coral Sea, and the removal of the strategic initiative from the Japanese in favour of the Americans. Approval of Admiral Isoroku Yamamoto's plan was given when the navy provided assurances that the occupation of Midway (together with the launching of Operation 'AL' against the Aleutians as a strategic diversion) was only a lure to draw out the Pacific Fleet for the decisive battle. The scheme devised by Yamamoto was essentially simple in concept (though complex in detail) and strategically sound, and used virtually the whole strength of the Imperial Japanese navy's surface fleet. The plan was predicated on the assumption that of the four aircraft carriers available in May to Admiral Chester W. Nimitz, US Commander-in-Chief Pacific Fleet, at least one (*Lexington*) had been sunk in the Battle of the Coral Sea, another (*Yorktown*) had sunk after the battle or was too severely damaged to be operational, and the other two (*Enterprise* and *Hornet*) were absent in the South-West Pacific Area. In fact Nimitz had three carriers available for Rear Admiral Frank J. Fletcher as the *Enterprise* and *Hornet* had reached Pearl Harbor to join the *Yorktown*, which had been repaired with extraordinary rapidity (repairs that had been estimated to need 90 days of work were completed between 27 and 30 May by 1,400 men working 24 hours per day).

Yamamoto attached great importance to the distraction of American attention by the activities associated with 'AL', which was to be undertaken just before 'MI' by Vice Admiral Boshiro Hosogawa's 5th Fleet. The main weight of Yamamoto's plan was in the south, however, and here Vice Admiral Chuichi Nagumo's 1st Mobile Force sortied from Hashirajima in Japan on 27 May with the fleet carriers *Akagi*, *Kaga*, *Soryu* and *Hiryu* (with a total of 72 dive-bombers, 90 attack aircraft and 72 fighters) escorted by the battleships *Haruna* and *Kirishima*, the heavy cruisers *Tone* and *Chikuma*, the light cruiser *Nagara*, 12 destroyers and a fleet train of eight tankers. This was to provide cover and support for Rear Admiral Raizo Tanaka's 2nd Fleet Escort Force, which sailed from Saipan in the Mariana Islands on 28 May with one light cruiser and 10 destroyers as escort for the Midway Occupation Force of 5,000 troops in 15 transports, together with a mine-sweeping group, these being supported by Rear Admiral Takeo Kurita's 2nd Fleet Occupation Support Force (the heavy cruisers *Kumano*, *Mogami*, *Mikuma* and *Suzuya*, two seaplane tenders and three destroyers) from Guam. The basic plan was for these forces to close in Midway from the north-west and west in order to attack Midway at dawn on 4 June unless US Navy forces were detected in the area, in which case Nagumo's carrier aircraft would attack these before neutralising Midway's defences so that the troops could land; to the west lurked a powerful reserve in case US opposition (at sea or on Midway) was stronger than expected. This reserve was Vice Admiral Nobutake Kondo's 2nd Fleet Strike Force (the light carrier *Zuiho* with 24 aircraft, the battleships *Hiei* and *Kongo*, the heavy cruisers *Atago*, *Chokai*, *Myoko* and *Haguro*, the light cruiser *Yura* and eight destroyers supported by four tankers), which was to crush US Navy forces in the region or to shatter the defences of Midway with gunfire. Yamamoto expected that all these operations would finally compel Nimitz to commit all naval forces available at Pearl Harbor, which would then be totally destroyed by the 2nd Fleet in conjunction with his own 1st Fleet Main Body (the light carrier *Hosho* with 19 aircraft, the battleships *Yamato*, *Nagato* and *Mutsu*, the light cruiser *Sendai* and nine destroyers) from Japan.

Intrinsic to the success of this complex operation, involving as it did some 71 major units of the Imperial Japanese navy, were security (already breached by the US Navy breaking of the Japanese JN-25 code), good and timely communications (impossible as everything had to be routed through Yamamoto) and accurate reconnaissance to upgrade the current intelligence picture. This last factor was denied the Japanese by the fact that operation 'K' had been cancelled, so removing Japan's capability for the aerial reconnaissance of Pearl Harbor, and that the screen of 13 submarines on picket duties between Pearl Harbor and Midway arrived only after the US carrier force had passed to the east; the result was that the Japanese forces did not know of the presence of US naval units near Midway, a situation exacerbated by the fact that neither Nagumo nor Kondo had been informed of the cancellation of 'K', and thus did not think to put up significant aerial reconnaissance patrols; thanks to the breaking of JN-25, Nimitz knew what was afoot, and Midway was

Continued on page 77

By 1931, Japan had completed the maximum of 12 heavy cruisers permitted under the terms of the Washington Naval Treaty, so further construction had to be limited to light cruisers carrying guns with a calibre of no more than 6.1in (155mm). The Japanese answer to this dilemma was the creation of the four-strong 'Mogami' class of cruisers with the prodigious armament of fifteen 6.1in guns in five triple turrets, and it was the threat of these ships that persuaded the Americans and British into the design and construction of the 'Brooklyn' and 'Southampton' classes respectively. Displacement was clearly going to be a critical problem with so many turrets, so the use of welding and light alloys, already pioneered in the 'Takao' class, was taken to a greater extreme. This was not without its problems, however, and sea trials with the first two ships were hampered by excessive top weight and structural problems due to poor welding, which resulted in hull deformations that prevented the main turrets from being trained over their full arcs. The two ships were therefore rebuilt with a wider hull carrying external bulges, and this provided greater structural strength as well as improving stability. The latter pair of ships were completed to this revised standard, and in 1939 all four ships were revised to full heavy cruiser standard with their fifteen 6.1in guns in triple turrets replaced by ten 8in guns in twin turrets. As completed to definitive initial standard, the ships had a displacement of 11,200 tons, an armament of fifteen 6.1in guns in five triple turrets, eight 5in anti-aircraft guns in four twin turrets, four 40mm anti-aircraft guns in single mountings and twelve 24in torpedo tubes, protection in the form of a 4in (102mm) belt and 1.5in (37mm) deck, and a speed of 35 knots on the 152,000hp (113,330kW) delivered to four shafts by steam turbines.

The final type of Japanese heavy cruiser was the 'Tone' class of two ships completed in 1938 and 1939. The design was an improved version of that developed in the 'Mogami' class with the main armament reduced to twelve 6.1in guns in four triple turrets all located forward with one unit in a superfiring position. This arrangement was adopted as the ships were intended specifically for the scouting role associated with Combined Fleets operations deep in the Pacific, and allowed the after part of the ship to be dedicated to the floatplane complement of five aircraft (as opposed to the three and two aircraft carried respectively by the preceding two classes) and two beam catapults. The details of the 'Tone' class included a displacement of 11,215 tons, an armament of eight 8in guns in four twin turrets, eight 5in anti-aircraft guns in four twin turrets, twelve 25mm anti-aircraft guns in six twin mounting, and twelve 24in torpedo tubes, protection in the form of a 4in (102mm) belt and 2.5in (63mm) deck, and a speed of 35 knots on the 152,200hp (113,480kW) delivered to four shafts by steam turbines.

In the late 1930s the Japanese navy decided that the time was ripe for the replacement of its older light cruisers built in the early 1920s with a main armament of 5.5in (140mm) guns. The first result of this decision was the completion between 1942 and 1944 of the four ships of the 'Agano' class with a full-load displacement of 8,535 tons, an armament of six 5.9in (150mm) guns in three twin turrets (a superfiring pair forward and a singleton unit aft), four 3in (76mm) anti-aircraft guns in two twin turrets, up to fifty-nine 25mm anti-aircraft guns in ten triple and 29 single mountings and eight 24in torpedo tubes, protection in the form of a 2.25in (57mm) belt and 0.75in (19mm) deck, and a speed of 35 knots on the 110,000hp (82,015kW) delivered to four shafts by steam turbines.

The final cruiser to be completed by the Japanese in World War II was the single light cruiser of the 'Oyodo' class, which was based on the 'Agano' class design but with revisions suiting it to the somewhat different role of commanding a scouting and hunting group of aircraft and submarines. The

primary gun armament of six 6.1in guns was therefore located forward of the superstructure in a superfiring pair of triple turrets, and this left the after part of the ship clear for the floatplane installation, which comprised two aircraft launched from a single centreline catapult but recovered from the sea at the end of their missions by a pair of beam cranes. The other details of this ship, which was completed early in 1943, included a displacement of 8,165 tons, a secondary armament of eight 3.9in anti-aircraft guns in four twin mountings and twelve 25mm anti-aircraft guns in four triple mountings, protection in the form of a 2in (51mm) belt and 2in deck, and a speed of 35 knots on the 110,000hp (82,015kW) delivered to four shafts by steam turbines.

All these Japanese cruisers were extensively used in World War II, and in general proved to be excellent and sturdy warships well able to undertake the tasks asked of them. Wartime modification was extensive as the ships were refitted and repaired, most of the modification efforts being concerned with the improvement of the ships' short-range anti-aircraft defences in an effort to provide them with a counter to the overwhelming air superiority that the Americans were able to bring to bear from a time late in 1942. Virtually every spare part of deck area was used for single or multiple anti-aircraft mountings, and the need for such enhancement often meant the removal of some or all of the aircraft capability, and also some of the torpedo capability.

The end of World War II signalled the end of the gun-armed cruiser as an effective naval weapon at a time when the guided missile soon came to replace the gun as the primary weapon carried by major warships. The more modern ships were maintained in service to provide an interim capability, but the way forward was revealed by the USA in the first half of the 1950s, when two heavy cruisers of the 'Baltimore' class were converted as guided missile cruisers for the fleet escort role: the after end of each ship was remodelled with two twin-arm launchers (for a total of 144 RIM-2 Terrier medium-range surface-to-air missiles) and their associated surveillance, target acquisition and missile guidance radars together with the fire-control systems. The success of the two conversions, which were recommissioned in 1955 and 1956, paved the way for a conversion of six 'Cleveland' class light cruisers, whose after ends were similarly cleared and adapted for the carriage of one twin-arm launcher for 120 Terrier SAMs and their associated radar and fire-control system. These ships were recommissioned between 1958 and 1960, and were followed between 1962 and 1964 by the most elaborate of the conversions. These were three more 'Baltimore' class ships that were stripped of all their main gun armament turrets to permit their modification into two-ended missile ships with two twin-arm launchers for a total of 104 RIM-8 Talos long-range SAMs complemented by two twin-arm launchers abreast of the forward superstructure for 84 Terrier SAMs. These launchers were complemented by the associated radar and fire-control systems, the provision of four target-tracking/missile-guidance radars allowing the simultaneous engagement of four targets rather than the maximum of two that was possible with the earlier conversions.

The success of these ships paved the way for the creation of purpose-designed guided missile cruisers optimised for the defence of the carrier battle groups that had become the most important surface assets operated

Lead ship of a nine-strong class that was delivered between 1964 and 1967 as one of the most potent escort elements for American surface battle groups, the cruiser *Belknap* had a full-load displacement of 8,200 tons, length of 547ft 0in (166.7m), armament of one 5in (127mm) dual-purpose gun, two 20mm Vulcan six-barrel cannon in two Phalanx close-in weapon system mountings, one twin launcher for 40 Standard Missile surface-to-air missiles and 20 ASROC anti-submarine rockets, two quadruple launchers for eight Harpoon anti-ship missiles, six 12.75in (324mm) tubes in two triple mountings for lightweight anti-submarine torpedoes, and one helicopter; propulsion in the form of geared steam turbines delivering 85,000hp (63,375kW) to two shafts for a speed of 32.5 knots, and complement of 480. The ship therefore had a good blend of anti-aircraft, anti-submarine and anti-ship armament, its principal limitation being its inability to undertake the simultaneous engagement of more than two aircraft targets.

by the US Navy. The first of these new missile cruisers carried the same missiles as their predecessors, but these were replaced in due course by the superb RIM-66 and RIM-67 medium- and long-range versions of the Standard Missile. The missile cruisers were built in two basic forms with conventional or nuclear propulsion, the latter being designed for the support of nuclear-powered aircraft carriers on extended-duration deployments, but financial considerations have dictated that production of nuclear-powered missile cruisers has lagged behind the totals required for protection of the nuclear-powered aircraft carriers, which therefore operate with a mix of conventional- and nuclear-powered cruisers.

The current force of such cruisers operated by the US Navy includes the single nuclear-powered ship of the 'Long Beach' class completed in 1961; the nine conventionally powered ships of the 'Leahy' class completed between 1962 and 1964; the single ship of the 'Bainbridge' class completed in 1962 as a nuclear-powered version of the 'Leahy' class design; the one conventionally powered ship of the 'Belknap' class completed between 1963 and 1965; the single ship of the 'Truxtun' class completed in 1964 as a nuclear-powered version of the 'Belknap' class design; the two nuclear-powered ships of the 'California' class completed in 1974 and 1975; the four nuclear-powered ships of the 'Virginia' class completed between 1976 and 1980; and the planned 27 units of the 'Ticonderoga' class completed from 1983 with the extraordinarily complex and capable AEGIS mission system based on the SPY-1A electronically scanned planar-array radar system.

The *Long Beach* is the largest of these ships with a full-load displacement of 16,600 tons, an armament of two twin-arm launchers for 120 Standard Missiles, one octuple launcher for eight RUR-5 ASROC anti-submarine weapons, one octuple launcher for eight BGM-109 Tomahawk cruise missiles, two quadruple launchers for eight RGM-84 Harpoon anti-ship missiles, two 5in (127mm) dual-purpose guns in single turrets, two 20mm Vulcan six-barrel cannon in two Phalanx close-in weapon system mountings, and two triple tubes for 12.75in (324mm) anti-submarine torpedoes; the vessel has a speed of 30 knots on the 80,000hp (59,650kW) delivered to two shafts by steam turbines powered by two Westinghouse C1W pressurised water-cooled reactors. In all, this represents a prodigious capability against targets ranging from aircraft to pinpoint land objectives via submarines, ships and other surface targets on both sea and land.

The later nuclear-powered ships are somewhat smaller and have reduced, although still formidable, capabilities, but the most modern of the cruiser classes currently in service is the large 'Ticonderoga' class. This is based on a development of the hull designed for the 'Spruance' class destroyer, and its details include a full-load displacement of 9,450 tons, an armament of two twin-arm or, in later ships, two vertical-launch systems for a total of 68 or 122 weapons respectively in the form of various mixes of Standard Missile, up to 20 RUR-5 ASROC anti-submarine and 20 BGM-109 Tomahawk cruise missiles, two quadruple launchers for eight BGM-84 Harpoon anti-ship missiles, two 5in dual-purpose guns in single turrets, two 20mm Vulcan six-barrel cannon in Phalanx close-in weapon system mountings and two triple tubes for six 12.75in anti-submarine torpedoes; ships of the class are capable of a speed of 30 or more knots on the 80,000hp (59,650kW) delivered to two shafts by four General Electric LM2500 gas turbines.

Other Western countries that have built cruisers since the end of World War II include France with the single 'de Grasse' class light cruiser with a main armament of sixteen 5in (127mm) dual-purpose guns in eight twin turrets grouped in superfiring quadruplets forward and aft, and the single 'Colbert' class light cruiser with a similar main armament but later rebuilt as

reinforced to some 3,000 men under the command of the 6th Marine Defense Battalion, extra aircraft were flown in (bringing the island's air strength to 109), and reconnaissance patrols were flown in a great fan from the north-west to the south west of the island; the naval support for these measures was the dispatch from Pearl Harbor of Fletcher's forces, consisting of Fletcher's Task Force 17 (the fleet carrier *Yorktown* with 13 torpedo bombers, 37 dive-bombers and 25 fighters, the heavy cruisers *Astoria* and *Portland*, and six destroyers) and Rear Admiral Raymond A. Spruance's Task Force 16 (the fleet carriers *Enterprise* and *Hornet* with a total of 29 torpedo bombers, 75 dive-bombers and 54 fighters, the heavy cruisers *New Orleans*, *Minneapolis*, *Vincennes*, *Northampton* and *Pensacola*, the light cruiser *Atlanta* and 11 destroyers). Other forces involved on the US side were Task Group 7.3 (a patrol of four submarines guarding the approaches to Oahu) and Task Group 7.1 (a patrol of 12 submarines in the western approaches to Midway). As the Japanese forces approached Midway, TFs 16 and 17 were ready to the north-north-east of the island, and the Japanese were first sighted at 09.00 on 3 June.

Operations began at 04.30 on 4 June, when Nagumo launched a first strike against Midway; the second wave of aircraft on board the Japanese carriers were armed with armour-piercing bombs or torpedoes in anticipation of an American naval counterattack. US aircraft took off from Midway to engage the incoming raid and to attack the carriers, but were generally knocked about by the superior Japanese aircraft and pilots; however, the leader of the Japanese strike called for another raid against the Midway defences, and at 07.00, Nagumo ordered his carrier crews to begin the lengthy task of replacing the second wave's anti-ship weapons with conventional bombs. Work had just begun when Nagumo was informed at 07.28 that a Japanese scout aircraft had spotted 10 US ships some 200 miles (320km) to the north-east; the report made no mention of this force's composition, but at 07.58 came another report that the US ships were five cruisers and five destroyers; thus work could proceed with the rearming of the second strike, although at this time the carriers' remaining fighters had to be scrambled to intercept an attack by Midway-based aircraft; then at 08.20 came yet another scout report, this time to the effect that the US naval force included one carrier.

Continued on page 79

a guided missile cruiser with an armament of one twin-arm launcher for Masurca SAMs aft and two 3.9in (100mm) guns in a pair of superfiring single turrets forward; Italy with the two 'Andrea Doria' class helicopter cruisers with an armament of one twin-arm launcher for Terrier (later Standard Missile) SAMs forward, eight 3in (76mm) dual-purpose guns in single turrets, and up to four anti-submarine helicopters aft; and the single 'Vittorio Veneto' class helicopter cruiser with an armament of one twin-arm launcher for Terrier (later Standard Missile) SAMs forward, eight 3in dual-purpose guns in single turrets, and up to nine anti-submarine helicopters aft; the Netherlands with two 'de Ruyter' class light cruisers with an armament of eight 6in (152mm) guns in two pairs of superfiring twin turrets; and the UK with three 'Tiger' class cruisers with an armament of two 6in guns in one twin turret, two launchers for Sea Cat SAMs, and up to four anti-submarine helicopters.

On the other side of the politico-military divide that emerged in the period after World War II, the only country to have built cruisers in the Warsaw Pact bloc was the USSR. This country had a strength of 15 cruisers in 1947, comprising two Russian ships from World War I, one American 'Omaha' class ship, one ex-German 'Nürnberg' class ship, one ex-Italian 'Aosta' class ship, two 'Kirov' class ships, four 'Maksim Gorky' class ships and four 'Chapayev' class ships. The USSR's next cruiser type was the 'Sverdlov' class: 24 of these were ordered, 20 were laid down, 17 were launched and only 14 were completed between 1951 and 1955 to a standard that included a full-load displacement of 17,200 tons, an armament of twelve 6in guns in two pairs of superfiring triple turrets, twelve 3.9in dual-purpose guns in six twin turrets, sixteen 37mm anti-aircraft guns in eight twin mountings and ten 21in (533mm) torpedo tubes, protection in the form of a 4.9in (125mm) belt and 3in (76mm) deck, and a speed of 32.5 knots on the 110,000hp (82,015kW) delivered to two shafts by steam turbines. These

The *Jeanne d'Arc* is the French navy's primary training ship, and in this task had accommodation and facilities for 140 cadets. The vessel is in fact a cruiser-sized helicopter carrier that in time of war would be used for the carriage of a 700-man commando battalion that would be landed by the eight helicopters carried on the large flightdeck abaft the superstructure/funnel assembly. The details of this interesting ship include a full-load displacement of 12,365 tons, length of 597ft 1in (182.0m), armament of four 3.9in (100mm) dual-purpose guns in single turrets, two triple launchers for six MM.38 Exocet anti-ship missiles, and four helicopters, propulsion in the form of geared steam turbines delivering 40,000hp (29,825kW) to two shafts for a speed of 26.5 knots, and complement of 625.

ships were obsolete even as they were being built, but in the later 1950s the USSR started to create considerably more powerful cruisers of two new types within the context of the Soviet ambition to create a navy with genuine blue-water capability. This might not have been able to wrest command of the seas from the US Navy, but was schemed to create the strength that could inflict major casualties on any American force attempting an amphibious invasion of the USSR.

The first of the new types was intended specifically for the engagement and destruction of American aircraft carriers and their supporting warships in operationally vital carrier battle groups, and its first example was the 'Kynda' class of four ships completed between 1962 and 1965 with a full-load displacement of 5,600 tons, an armament of two quadruple launchers for sixteen SS-N-3 'Shaddock' nuclear-tipped anti-ship missiles, one launcher for 24 SA-N-1 SAMs, four 3in dual-purpose guns in two twin turrets, two 12-tube anti-submarine rocket launchers, and six 21in torpedo tubes, and a speed of 34 knots on the 100,000hp (74,560kW) delivered to two shafts by steam turbines.

The 'Kynda' class ships provided a very useful initial capability against the American aircraft carrier force, but were complemented in 1967 and 1968 by the four 'Kresta I' class cruisers that still provided a major offensive punch but were better able to provide their own protection against aircraft and submarine attack. The ships therefore had a full-load displacement of 7,500 tons, an armament of two twin launchers for just four SS-N-3 'Shaddock' anti-ship missiles, two twin-arm launchers for 44 SA-N-1 SAMs, four 57mm anti-aircraft guns in two twin mountings, two 12-tube and two six-tube anti-submarine rocket launchers, ten 21in torpedo tubes, and one anti-submarine and/or missile-guidance helicopter, and a speed of 34 knots on the 100,000hp (74,560kW) delivered to two shafts by steam turbines.

At this time the nuclear-powered ballistic missile submarine was beginning to come to the fore as a decisive strategic weapon, and the threat of the USA's growing force of such boats was reflected in the construction of the 'Kresta II' class of ten cruisers adapted from the 'Kresta I' class design for the specialised task of hunting and killing American nuclear-powered submarines. In this task the primary sensor was an advanced sonar system located in the forefoot of the lengthened bow section, and the primary weapon, the SS-N-14 'Silex' missile, was used to deliver a homing torpedo or nuclear depth charge to the area pinpointed by the sonar (either shipborne or helicopter-carried) as the location of the target submarine.

From 1971 the 'Kresta II' class cruisers were complemented by seven 'Kara' class anti-submarine cruisers, which were the first full-size cruisers to enter service with the Soviet navy after the 'Sverdlov' class ships. With a full-load displacement of 9,900 tons, the ships of this class carry an armament of two quadruple launchers for eight SS-N-14 'Silex' anti-submarine weapons, two twin-arm launchers for 72 SA-N-3 'Goblet' SAMs, two twin-arm launchers for 40 SA-N-4 'Gecko' SAMs, four 3in dual-purpose guns in two twin turrets, four 30mm six-barrel anti-aircraft cannon in single mountings, up to ten 21in torpedo tubes, and two 12- and two six-tube anti-submarine rocket launchers. Propulsion is based on the delivery of 134,000hp (91,710kW) to two shafts by a combined gas turbine or gas turbine (COGOG) arrangement of four large and two small gas turbines for a speed of 34 knots.

The 'Kara' class ships seem to have persuaded the Soviets of the advantage of a full-size cruiser hull for good ocean-going and weapon-carrying capability, and the most recent Soviet class comprises the four ships of the 'Slava' class optimised for the dual-role anti-ship and anti-submarine task with a full-load displacement of 11,200 tons for the carriage of a weapons fit that includes eight twin launchers for SS-N-12 anti-ship

Nagumo's position was now impossible, for the scrambled fighters needed refuelling, the first Midway attack wave was due back, and the second wave was in no position to attempt either sort of attack; while still dithering, Nagumo turned north-east at 09.18 to attack the US forces.

Now it was Fletcher's turn, and he launched a first strike at 07.52 from the *Enterprise* and *Hornet*, following with a strike from the *Yorktown* at 09.00 as she was farther to the north. At 09.30 the US torpedo bombers found the Japanese carriers and attacked. The aircraft were obsolete Douglas Devastators and were destroyed, in the process convincing Nagumo that the Americans' first strike had been beaten, giving the Japanese time to complete the arming of his aircraft for an anti-ship strike. Thus the decks of the Japanese carriers were packed with aircraft as the Douglas Dauntless dive-bombers of Fletcher's first strike arrived overhead and screamed down at 10.25, within five minutes devastating the *Akagi*, *Kaga* and *Soryu*. Between 19.00 and 19.30 the *Soryu* and *Kaga* sank, and the *Akagi* was finished off with torpedoes on the following day. It was a devastating blow from which only the *Hiryu*, cruising separately, escaped. Thus the sole Japanese carrier launched two strikes, and these found and struck the *Yorktown* between 12.05 and 12.15, and at 14.30. The US carrier was abandoned at 15.00 and later sunk by submarine attack while under tow. Now it was the turn of the *Hiryu*, which was devastated by aircraft from the *Enterprise* at 17.00 and scuttled at 05.10 on the following day, being finished off later by Japanese torpedoes. This was a disaster from which the Japanese could not really recover, though Yamamoto tried desperately to entice the US forces into combat with his battleship forces. Fletcher made the right tactical and strategic decision, and thus withdrew.

The Americans had lost 307 dead and 147 aircraft, as well as one carrier and one destroyer; on the other side the Japanese had lost some 3,500 dead (including highly trained and irreplaceable aircrews) and 332 aircraft, as well as four carriers. The Japanese heavy cruisers *Mogami* and *Mikuma* were also damaged in a collision, both ships then being damaged further by air attacks and the *Mikuma* later sinking. The Japanese had suffered a blow of mortal proportions, and Yamamoto had no option but to call off the rest of 'MI', which can justly claim to have cost the Japanese the war; the Battle of Midway was thus one of history's truly decisive battles.

The key to the genuine anti-aircraft capability of most US Navy modern surface warships and those of the USA's allies is the General Dynamics Standard Missile. This was an evolutionary development of the RIM-2 Terrier and RIM-24 Tartar weapons, and is currently operated in four forms as the single-stage RIM-66A/B Standard Missile I MR in the medium-range role, the two-stage RIM-67A Standard Missile I ER in the long-range role, the single-stage RIM-66C Standard Missile 2 MR in the medium-range role and the two-stage RIM-67B Standard Missile 2 ER in the long-range role. The Standard Missile 2 series had an improved guidance package by comparison with the Standard Missile I, allowing a considerable increase in range through optimisation of the missiles' trajectories. Seen here is a RIM-66A/B being fired from the type of single-arm launcher typical of American frigates. The missile weighs either 1,276lb (579kg) for the RIM-66A or 1,342lb (609kg) for the RIM-66B, is either 14ft 8in (4.47m) or 15ft 6in (4.724m) long for the RIM-66A and RIM-66B respectively with a diameter of 1ft 1.5in (0.343m) and a span of 3ft 0in (0.914m), and its data include a speed of more than Mach 2, a range of 28.75 or 41.6 miles (46.25 or 67km) and an upper altitude limit of 50,000 or 62,500ft (15,240 or 19,050m) for the RIM-66A and RIM-66B respectively.

missiles, eight octuple launchers for 64 SA-N-6 'Grumble' SAMs, two twin-arm launchers for 40 SA-N-4 'Gecko' SAMs, two 5.1in (130mm) dual-purpose guns in a twin turret, six 30mm six-barrel anti-aircraft guns in single mountings, ten 21in torpedo tubes, two 12-tube anti-submarine rocket launchers, and one anti-submarine/missile update helicopter. Propulsion is based on the delivery of 120,000hp (89,470kW) to two shafts by four gas turbines for a speed of 34 knots.

The Soviet cruiser force was completed by the two hybrid helicopter cruisers of the 'Moskva' class that were commissioned in 1967 and 1968 with a full-load displacement of 19,300 tons, an armament of two twin-arm launchers for 48 SA-N-3 'Goblet' SAMs, one SUW-N-1 twin launcher for 18 FRAS-1 anti-submarine weapons, two 12-tube anti-submarine rocket launchers, four 57mm anti-aircraft guns in two twin turrets, and 14 anti-submarine helicopters.

Further development of the cruiser is in abeyance as the CIS lacks the need and financial resources for further such ships, and in these circumstances the USA is well equipped with its current types.

Destroyers and Escorts

The *Manchester* is the lead ship of the four-strong 'Type 42 Batch 3' subclass of the 'Type 42' class of guided missile destroyers operated by the Royal Navy since the commissioning of all 12 of the ships between 1976 and 1985. The 'Type 42 Batch 3' subclass has greater length and beam than the other two subclasses for improved seaworthiness and an enlarged missile capacity, and the details of these four ships include a full-load displacement of 5,350 tons, length of 462ft 10in (141.1m), armament of one 4.5in (114mm) dual-purpose gun, two 20mm Vulcan six-barrel cannon in two Phalanx close-in weapon system mountings, four 20mm cannon in single mountings, one twin launcher for 40 Sea Dart surface-to-air missiles, six 12.75in (324mm) tubes in two triple mountings for lightweight anti-submarine torpedoes and one helicopter, propulsion in the form of a COGOG arrangement with two gas turbines delivering 50,000hp (37,280kW) or two gas turbines delivering 9,700hp (7,230kW) to two shafts for a speed of 30 or 18 knots respectively, and complement of 300.

With the advent of the locomotive torpedo as a viable weapon from 1868, most navies began to expend considerable effort on flotillas of fast torpedo-armed vessels intended mainly for the coast defence role by threatening the battle fleets of any potential invader. So great was the threat of the torpedo boat in the minds of most admirals, who feared for the survival of their fleets of battleships that were several nations' most important military assets, that considerable effort was soon put into the creation of ships to catch and destroy torpedo boats. This demanded a speed comparable with that of the torpedo boat as well as a primary armament of quick-firing guns and a small complement of torpedo tubes, which could be replaced by additional quick-firing guns, so that the type could also be used as a torpedo boat. The first of these torpedo boat catchers, soon to be known

The six large destroyers of the 'L'Audacieux' class were launched in 1933 and 1934 for service with the French navy, and the last units were not scrapped until the early 1980s. In their heyday these were superb destroyers offering considerable firepower and very high speed that could be maintained under all conditions. The ship illustrated here is *Le Fantasque* that was scrapped in 1957, and the details of this important class include a full-load displacement of 3,400 tons, length of 434ft 6in (132.4m), armament of five 5.5in (140mm) guns in single turrets, four 37mm anti-aircraft guns in single mountings and nine 21.7in (550mm) torpedo tubes in three triple mountings, propulsion in the form of geared steam turbines delivering 74,000hp (55,365kW) to two shafts for a speed of 37 knots, and complement of 210.

as torpedo boat destroyers, were launched in the UK in 1886. These lacked the speed to catch their prey, however, and it was only in 1892 that the Admiralty took the plunge in a decisive way, ordering no fewer than 42 'turtleback' torpedo boat destroyers from a number of yards that were given considerable discretion about the manner in which they fulfilled the Admiralty's basic requirement for a given armament, triple-expansion steam engines and a speed of 27 knots. The first of these generally successful 'A' class torpedo boat destroyers were ordered from Yarrow as the *Havock* and *Hornet* with triple-expansion steam engines powering two shafts for a speed of 26 knots with an armament that comprised one 12pdr and three 6pdr guns as well as three 18in (457mm) torpedo tubes that could be replaced by two more 6pdr guns.

The two vessels and their successors quickly displayed so marked an ascendancy over the torpedo boat that the earlier type was soon discontinued in favour of rapid development and construction of the torpedo boat destroyer (soon to be called the destroyer) as a dual-purpose type for torpedo attacks on the enemy's fleet and protection of its own fleet against enemy torpedo attack. These early destroyers were capable of speeds in the order of 26 or 27 knots, although a lengthening of the hull and the installation of more powerful engines soon allowed the creation of improved destroyers with a speed of 30 knots, and 60 of these improved torpedo boat destroyers were ordered for later allocation to the 'B', 'C' and 'D' classes depending on their use of four, three and two funnels respectively. The decisive moment in the development of the early destroyer came in 1897, however, when the Hon.

The Indian navy's three 'Blackwood' class frigates, here exemplified by the *Kuthar*, were built in the UK during the mid-1950s to a standard that included a full-load displacement of 1,535 tons, length of 310ft 0in (94.5m), armament of three 40mm anti-aircraft guns in single mountings, two three-barrel Limbo Mk 10 anti-submarine mortars and four 21in (533mm) torpedo tubes in two twin mountings, propulsion in the form of geared steam turbines delivering 15,000hp (11,185kW) to one shaft for a speed of 27 knots, and complement of 140. The class, which included 12 British ships, was intended as a cheaper successor to the 'Whitby' class frigates with the same anti-submarine capability but with only half the power.

The Brazilian navy's destroyer *Para* was originally the US Navy's Guest of the 'Fletcher' class. Brazil acquired the ship in December 1959, and discarded the vessel as wholly obsolete in 1978, when the cost of refurbishment would have been prohibitive. The armament of the ship in its latter days was five 5in (127mm) dual-purpose guns in single turrets, ten 40mm anti-aircraft guns in two twin and two single mountings, one 'Hedgehog' anti-submarine projector, and depth charge racks.

Charles Parsons produced his *Turbinia* to prove the capabilities of his steam turbine propulsion arrangement. So impressive was the performance of this privately funded experimental type that the Royal Navy switched to the steam turbine for its latest destroyers, starting with the *Viper* that was completed in 1900 with a speed of 33.75 knots on a light displacement of 344 tons with a four-shaft steam turbine propulsion arrangement.

These and other early destroyers, powered by triple-expansion or later by turbine engines, were capable of reaching their legend speed only under ideal conditions, however, and anything but a smooth sea made the vessels very wet and rendered the forward guns all but unworkable. By the early 1900s, therefore, the British and other navies had decided that greater size was not just inevitable but also desirable: this would allow the introduction of more powerful engines so that a high speed could be maintained under adverse conditions, and also make possible the introduction of the raised forecastle that would reduce wetness and allow the forward guns to be fought under most operational conditions. The way was paved by the German 'S90' class in which a raised forecastle replaced the turtledeck for improved seaworthiness, and the British responded with the 34 units of the 'River' or 'E' class with considerably greater displacement and a far more seaworthy basic design matched by a more powerful propulsion arrangement and greater bunkerage for improved seaworthiness and greater range. The ships were built in a large number of subvariants by different yards and to a standard that included a full-load displacement of some 620 tons, a propulsion arrangement of triple-expansion steam engines delivering 7,000hp (5,220kW) for a sustained speed of 25.5 knots, and with the same armament as the smaller 30-knot vessels, although from 1906 this was increased to four 12pdr guns and two 18in (457mm) torpedo tubes.

It is with these 'River' class vessels that the era of the true destroyer may be said to have started in a meaningful way, for all that was now needed to create the 'modern destroyer' was the combination of the improved size and seaworthiness of the 'River' class with turbine propulsion and oil- rather than coal-fired boilers.

The first move in this direction came in the period between 1907 and 1909, when the twelve units of the 'Tribal' or 'F' class were completed in two major subclasses as five and seven ships as what may be regarded as the destroyer equivalents of the 'dreadnought' battleship with a virtual doubling of the displacement, a primary armament of 4in (102mm) guns, and a propulsion arrangement that combined oil-fired boilers and steam turbines. The ships were the first genuinely ocean-going rather than sea-going destroyers, and while the earlier vessels had a displacement of between 865 and 890 tons, a length of between 250 and 270ft (76.2 and 82.3m) and a speed of between 33 and 36 knots with a propulsion arrangement in which steam turbines delivered 14,500hp (10,815kW) to three shafts, the later vessels had a displacement of between 970 and 1,090 tons, a length of 280ft (85.3m) and a speed of between 33 and 36 knots with a propulsion arrangement in which steam turbines delivered 15,500hp (11,555kW) to three shafts.

A portent of things to come was the *Swift*, which was completed in 1907 as a flotilla leader with a displacement of 1,850 tons, an armament of four 4in guns and one 2pdr gun as well as two 18in torpedo tubes, and a speed of 39 knots on the 50,000hp (37,280kW) delivered to four shafts by steam turbines.

All these early destroyers had provided both builders and the Royal Navy with considerable experience in the design and operation of destroyers, and the sensible decision was now taken to concentrate on the introduction of homogeneous classes of ships at the rate of between 16 and 24 units per year. The first of these groups was the 16-strong 'Basilisk' or 'G' class completed in 1909 and 1910 with a displacement of between 885 and 965 tons, an armament of one 4in and three 12pdr guns as well as two 18in torpedo tubes, and a speed of some 28 knots on the 12,500hp (9,320kW) delivered to three shafts by steam turbines supplied from coal-fired boilers, which were adopted as there were fears that oil might be in short supply in the event of war. The speed of this class was on the low side, but the ships were very seaworthy. The following 'Acorn' or 'H' class, of which 20 were completed in 1910 and 1911, was somewhat smaller with a displacement of 780 tons, but was capable of a speed between 27 and 30 knots on the 13,500hp (10,065kW) delivered to three shafts by steam turbines supplied from oil-fired boilers, which now became a standard feature of British destroyers. The armament comprised two 4in guns and, for the first time in British destroyers, two 21in (533mm) torpedo tubes. The ships were each built in an average time of 18 months, a rate considerably faster than earlier types as a result of claims by the Germans that they were building large numbers of destroyers in a time of between twelve and 15 months.

The 'Acheron' or 'I' class that followed in 1911 and 1912 totalled 20 ships

The US Navy's force of destroyers built in the 1930s, many of them to a design with the uptakes from two boiler rooms trunked into a single funnel, provided invaluable fleet capability in the early years of the US involvement in World War II, after which they were phased into less taxing service as they were supplemented and then replaced by more modern destroyers of the 'Fletcher', 'Gearing' and 'Allen M. Sumner' classes.

that comprised 14 to a standard pattern and six slightly different ships with a more powerful propulsion arrangement and a number of innovatory features. The standard type had a displacement of between 750 and 780 tons, an armament of two 4in and two 12pdr guns as well as two 21in torpedo tubes, and a speed of between 27 and 30 knots on the 13,500hp (10,065kW) delivered to three shafts by steam turbines, while the more powerfully engined type had a speed of between 29 and 31 knots on the 15,000–16,500hp (11,185–12,300kW) delivered to three shafts by steam turbines. Another six ships were delivered to the Royal Australian Navy, three of them from original British contracts which were replaced by another three ships built by Yarrow to an improved standard with a displacement of 790 tons and a speed of between 32 and 35 knots on the 20,000hp (14,910kW) delivered to three shafts by steam turbines. The last three ships were in effect the prototypes for the later Yarrow variants of the Admiralty standard destroyer design.

The final two destroyer classes introduced before World War I were the 'Acasta' or 'K' class and the 'L' class, which introduced a new British system of nomenclature in which all the ships of a given class had names beginning with the same letter. The 'Acasta' class completed in 1912 and 1913 comprised 12 standard ships, six ships with a different armament disposition and with two rather than three shafts, and two prototypes for the two- and three-funnel versions of the following 'L' class. The standard version had a displacement of 780 tons, an armament of two 4in guns and two 21in torpedo tubes, and a speed of between 27 and 30 knots on the 13,500hp (10,065kW) delivered to three shafts by steam turbines.

The 'L' class was the definitive version of the British destroyer in the period leading up to World War I, and totalled six two-funnel and sixteen three-funnel ships that introduced a raked rather than vertical stem, twin torpedo tube mountings and a 'bandstand' mounting for the amidships gun. The ships each possessed a displacement of between 965 and 1,070 tons, an armament of three 4in guns and one 2pdr gun as well as four 21in torpedo tubes, and a speed of between 29 and 31 knots on the 22,500–24,500hp (16,775–18,265kW) delivered to two shafts by steam turbines.

Not surprisingly, Japanese destroyers of the World War II period revealed a number of conceptual similarities to the same navy's light cruisers. The ships were generally notable for their armament of 5in (127mm) guns in twin turrets, and multiple banks of 24in (610mm) tubes for the exceptionally potent 'Long Lance' anti-ship torpedo, a weapon in which the Japanese navy placed great reliance and which proved very successful up to the middle of 1943, when the US Navy had perfected the radar-directed tactics that negated the favourite Japanese tactic of night destroyer attacks.

As the war broke out in August 1914, the first of the new 'M' class destroyers were coming into service as improved versions of the 'L' class ships, with a displacement in the order of 994 – 1,042 tons, an armament of three 4in guns and one 2pdr gun as well as four 21in torpedo tubes, and a speed of 34 knots (often exceeded by a considerable margin) on the 25,000hp (18,640kW) delivered to three shafts by steam turbines. The 'M' class was built to a total of 112 ships, which was so great that the Admiralty ran out of suitable names and therefore gave many of the ships 'N', 'O', 'P' and even 'R' and 'T' names.

The 'M' class ships were followed by 49 'R' class ships with 'R', 'S', 'T' and 'U' names to a standard that differed from that of the 'M' class mostly in their 'bandstand' mounting for the after 4in gun and their propulsion arrangement of 27,000hp (20,130kW) delivered to three shafts by geared steam turbines for a speed of 36 knots. The final class of 1,000-ton British destroyers comprised the 67 units of the 'S' class with 'S' and 'T' names, a displacement of 1,075 tons, an armament of three 4in guns and one 2pdr gun as well as four 21in and two 14in (356mm) torpedo tubes (which were later removed), and a speed of 36 knots on the 27,000hp (20,130kW) delivered to two shafts by geared steam turbines.

By the middle of World War I, it was clear that further improvement of the destroyer called for a larger hull with a greater displacement, and this led to the development of the 'VW' class with 'V' and 'W' names, a longer and beamier hull, a displacement of between 1,272 and 1,339 tons, and a speed of 34 knots on the 27,000hp (20,130kW) delivered to two shafts by geared steam turbines. The ships fell into two subclasses: the 'V' subclass had an armament of four 4in guns and one 3in anti-aircraft gun as well as four 21in torpedo tubes, while the 'W' subclass had an armament of three 4in guns and one 3in anti-aircraft gun as well as six 21in torpedo tubes in two triple mountings.

The Royal Navy appreciated that effective control of destroyer flotillas demanded leaders with the additional size to carry a flotilla commander and his staff, but had only the *Swift* at the beginning of the war. The service was fortunate, however, that four strong flotilla leader class were under construction in British yards for Chile and Turkey, and these were taken over as the 'Botha' and 'Talisman' classes for completion in 1914-15 and 1916 respectively. The first new leaders built specifically to British specification appeared in 1916, and these were the seven and six units of the 'Marksman' and 'Later Marksman' classes supplemented in 1917 and 1918 respectively by the three ships of the 'Shakespeare' class and the eight ships of the 'Scott' class that were alternatively known as the 'Thornycroft' and 'Admiralty' types.

The British generally led the world in the design and construction of destroyers in this period. Germany's most advanced destroyer class at the beginning of World War I was the 'S30' class of six ships completed in 1914 and 1915 with a

Opposite top: Although they often lack the technical skills and the financial resources to operate and maintain the advanced ships they sometimes feel compelled to buy for reasons of national prestige, many Third-World countries make effective use of less advanced vessels. Into this latter category falls the *Otobo*, the Vosper Thornycroft Mk 3 corvette of the Nigerian navy. Commissioned in 1972, this vessel has a full-load displacement of 660 tons, length of 202ft 0in (61.6m), armament of one 3in (76mm) dual-purpose gun in a single turret and two 40mm anti-aircraft guns in a twin turret, propulsion in the form of diesel engines delivering 8,000hp (5,965kW) to two shafts for a speed of 22 knots, and complement of 70. Such ships allow the development of greater naval skills in the tactical and technical senses, and in the shorter term provide a useful capability for the patrol of the country's coastal waters.

Opposite centre: The *Herstal* of the Belgian navy, which originally had 16 of the class, is a good example of the type of inshore minesweeper required to keep clear the approaches to a port such as Antwerp.

Opposite bottom: Among the many lesser known but still important types of ships are mine warfare vessels, here epitomised by the French navy's *Circé*, lead ship of a class of five minehunters commissioned in the early 1970s. The ships have only the lightest of conventional armament, namely one 20mm cannon, but carry sophisticated sonar for the detection and localisation of sea-bed mines that are then investigated and, if required, destroyed with the aid of the PAP electrically powered and remotely controlled underwater vehicle that carries a TV camera and a 220lb (100kg) explosive charge that can be laid close to the mine and then detonated by remote control.

displacement of 970 tons, an armament of three 3.4in (88mm) guns and six 19.7in (500mm) torpedo tubes, and a speed of between 33 and 36 knots on the 23,500 – 25,000hp (17,520 – 18,650kW) delivered to two shafts by steam turbines. After 1916, Germany's priority was submarines rather than surface warships, and this meant that only 22 more destroyers were completed in the period up to the end of the war. The last of these were the three ships of the 'H145' class of which two were commissioned in 1918 and the third only in 1920 for the French navy as part of Germany's war reparations. These ships had a displacement of 1,147 tons, an armament of three 4.1in (105mm) guns and six 19.7in (500mm) torpedo tubes, and a speed of between 34 and 37 knots on the 23,500 – 25,500hp (17,520 – 19,010kW) delivered to two shafts by steam turbines.

Advanced destroyers were also built in this period by France, Italy, Japan and the USA, and less advanced ships were constructed by countries such as Austria-Hungary and Russia.

After World War I, all the British destroyers up to and including the 'M' class were soon discarded, and further development was based on the 'VW' and 'Marksman' classes. Throughout the 1920s and 1930s, the older destroyers were gradually replaced by newer vessels and, on the outbreak of World War II, the only earlier destroyers still in service were one 'R' class ship, 11 'S' class ships used mainly in the minelaying role, most of the 'VW' class ships used mostly in the escort role, and eight leaders.

With large numbers of comparatively new ships on strength, the Royal Navy ordered no new destroyers in the period between 1918 and 1924, and then made the sensible decision to give Thornycroft and Yarrow, the two

The Royal Navy's frigate *Seymour* of the 'Captain' class was a destroyer escort built in the USA during World War II with a displacement of 1,300 tons, length of 306ft 0in (93.3m), armament of three 3in (76mm) anti-aircraft guns in three single mountings, two 30mm anti-aircraft guns in single mountings and eight or ten 20mm cannon in single mountings, propulsion in the form of a turbo-electric drive delivering 12,000hp (8,945kW) to two shafts for a speed of 26 knots, and complement of 200.

premier builders of British destroyers, a relatively free hand in the creation of two prototypes (*Amazon* and *Ambuscade*) to provide the basis of a new standard type offering improvements over the 'VW' class in terms of greater speed, improved habitability and greater range. Both ships were launched in 1926, and from them were evolved for the Royal Navy and Royal Canadian Navy the 11 ships of the 'A' class with an armament of four or five 4.7in (120mm) guns and quadruple mountings for their eight 21in (533mm) torpedo tubes, nine generally improved ships of the 'B' class, 14 ships of the 'C/D' class with a single 3in (76mm) anti-aircraft gun in place of the earlier ships' two 2pdr anti-aircraft guns, 18 ships of the 'E/F' class with provision for rapid conversion to the minelaying task, 18 generally improved ships of the 'G/H' class, and nine ships of the 'I' class with a tripod rather than pole main mast and quintuple rather than quadruple torpedo tube mountings.

The 'I' class destroyers were launched in 1936 and 1937, and at this stage the British halted further development along this course to produce the 'Tribal' class of an eventual 27 destroyers for the Royal Navy, Royal Australian Navy and Royal Canadian Navy. These ships reflected British concerns that their destroyers were being outstripped technically and operationally by the large destroyers being built in a number of other countries. The result was a highly capable although expensive destroyer with a doubled gun armament, a halved torpedo armament, and much enhanced anti-aircraft and anti-submarine armaments. The 'Tribal' class destroyers possessed a displacement between 1,870 and 1,925 tons, an armament in their baseline British form of eight 4.7in guns in four twin turrets, four 2pdr anti-aircraft guns in a quadruple mounting and four 21in torpedo tubes, and a speed of 36 knots on the 44,000hp (32,805kW) delivered to two shafts by geared steam turbines.

The expense of the 'Tribal' class was too high for its capabilities to be repeated in later classes, which therefore dropped one 4.7in twin turret, reintroduced two quintuple mountings for 21in torpedoes, and reduced the number of boilers to just two so that a single funnel could be used. This scheme resulted in the nine and eight ships of the generally similar 'J' and 'K' classes launched in 1938 and 1939. The sixteen ships of the equally sized 'L' and 'M' classes differed mainly in having dual-purpose guns in fully enclosed twin turrets, but the additional expense of this arrangement resulted in the eight ships of the 'N' class reverting to the earlier and simpler arrangement.

By the time that the 'N' class destroyers were under construction, the UK had accepted the inevitability of war with Germany and, reminded by its merchant shipping losses to submarine attack in World War I, had decided to waste no time in the introduction of a convoy system as soon as war did finally break out. This raised the need for a large number of specialised escort vessels if the Royal Navy's force of fleet destroyers was not to be stripped to the point that it could not support major surface forces. The result was a series of dual-role and escort destroyer classes optimised for the escort role with the same basic hull construction and boiler arrangement as the latest fleet destroyers but with an armament of main guns in single mountings, improved anti-submarine weapons, and enhanced anti-aircraft weapons in which the standard arrangement of four 2pdr guns in a quadruple mounting was supplemented by four single (later twin) mountings for 20mm cannon, replaced later in the war by 40mm weapons in single mountings.

The dual-role destroyer classes comprised the eight ships of the 'O' class fitted for minelaying and with 4in (102mm) rather than 4.7in guns in four of the vessels; the eight ships of the generally similar 'P' class with 4in rather than 4.7in guns and in four of the vessels one 4in anti-aircraft gun in place of one of the two quintuple mountings for 21in (533mm) torpedoes; the eight ships of the 'Q' class with the light anti-aircraft armament increased from four to six 20mm cannon; the eight ships of the 'R' class with eight 20mm cannon and surface warning radar; the eight ships of the 'S' class that introduced the 4.5in (114mm) dual-purpose gun in one ship, had eight 20mm cannon in all ships, and in some ships replaced the 2pdr quadruple mounting with two 40mm guns or four 20mm cannon, the eight ships of the 'T' class with ten and later twelve 20mm cannon; the eight ships of the 'U' class with lattice masts and a diverse arrangement of anti-aircraft guns; the eight ships of the 'V' class with a light anti-aircraft armament of two 40mm guns in a twin mounting or four 2pdr guns in a quadruple mounting and eight 20mm cannon in four twin mountings; the eight ships of the 'W' class with a light anti-aircraft armament of two 40mm guns in a twin mounting and eight 20mm cannon in four twin mountings or, in some ships, four or five 40mm guns in single mountings; and the eight ships of the 'Z' class with the 4.5in dual-purpose gun and a light anti-aircraft armament of two 40mm guns in a twin mounting and six 20mm cannon in two twin and two single mountings.

Finally in the first series of this family of dual-role ships came the 32 destroyers of the 'C' class in four equal 'CA', 'CH', 'CO' and 'CR' subclasses with a displacement of some 1,720 tons, an armament of four 4.5in dual-purpose guns in single mountings, four 40mm anti-aircraft guns in one twin and two single mountings, four 20mm anti-aircraft cannon in two twin mountings and four 21in torpedo tubes in a quadruple mounting, and a speed of 36.75 knots on the 40,000hp (29,825kW) delivered to two shafts by geared steam turbines.

Late in the war, with the defeat of Germany certain and greater emphasis now placed on longer-range operations in the Pacific against the Japanese, the British designed a new destroyer type as the 'Battle' class on the basis of a larger hull to provide greater seaworthiness, a longer range, enhanced self-sufficiency in the course of protracted operations away from a major base, and a much heavier anti-aircraft armament for the protection not only of itself but of the larger warships (especially the aircraft carriers) it was supporting. Some 44 of the class, including two

The *Centauro* was completed in 1957 as one of the Italian navy's four 'Canopo' class frigates designed for the destroyer escort rather than conventional frigate role, and was based on a scaled-down version of the hull of the 'Impetuoso' class destroyer. The details of this small but nicely planned type included a full-load displacement of 2,250 tons, length of 338ft 4in (103.1m), armament of four 3in (76mm) dual-purpose guns in two twin turrets, four 40mm anti-aircraft guns in two twin mountings, one three-barrel Menon anti-submarine mortar in a turreted installation and two 21in (533mm) torpedo tubes (later altered to three 3in/76mm dual-purpose guns in single turrets, one Menon mortar and six 12.75in/324mm tubes in two triple mountings for lightweight anti-submarine torpedoes), propulsion in the form of geared steam turbines delivering 22,000hp (16,405kW) to two shafts for a speed of 26 knots, and complement of 210.

for the Royal Australian Navy, were ordered but only 28 were completed as sixteen units of the second group were cancelled. The ships had a displacement of some 2,325 tons and a speed of 35.75 knots on the 50,000hp (37,280kW) delivered to two shafts by geared steam turbines, and two types of armament: in the first group this comprised four 4.5in dual-purpose guns in two twin turrets, one 4in anti-aircraft gun, fourteen 40mm anti-aircraft guns in four twin and six single mountings or alternatively twelve 40mm anti-aircraft guns in three twin and six single mountings, and eight or ten 21in torpedo tubes; the second group had five 4.5in dual-purpose guns in two twin and one single turrets, eight 40mm anti-aircraft guns in three twin and two single mountings, and ten 21in torpedo tubes.

Another type ordered only slightly later and completed to the extent of only two ships was the 'Weapon' class, optimised for the anti-aircraft and anti-submarine roles with anti-ship capability offered only by the low-angle fire of its six 4in dual-purpose guns, which were installed in three twin turrets, and its ten 21in torpedo tubes.

The standard type of escort destroyer built by the British was the 'Hunt' class of which 86 units were completed in four subclasses including the 'Hunt Type IV' class of only two ships. These ships were essentially small and simple, and the three main subclasses were the 'Hunt Type I' class of 20 ships (generally used in home waters) with a displacement of 907 tons, an armament of four 4in anti-aircraft guns in two twin turrets, four or five 2pdr anti-aircraft guns in one quadruple and one single mounting and two 20mm cannon, and a speed of 26 knots on the 19,000hp (14,165kW) delivered to two shafts by geared steam turbines; the 'Hunt Type II' class of 36 ships (common in home and Mediterranean waters) with a displacement of 1,050 tons, an armament of six or four 4in anti-aircraft guns in three or two twin turrets, four or five 2pdr anti-aircraft guns in one quadruple and one single mounting, and two or three 20mm cannon in single mountings, and a speed of 25 knots on the 19,000hp (14,165kW) delivered to two shafts by geared steam turbines; and the 'Hunt Type III' class of 28 ships (also used in home and Mediterranean waters) with a displacement of 1,085 tons, an armament of four 4in anti-aircraft guns in two twin turrets, four or five 2pdr anti-aircraft guns in one quadruple and one single mounting, two or three 20mm cannon in single mountings and two 21in torpedo tubes, and a speed of 25 knots on the 19,000hp (14,165kW) delivered to two shafts by geared steam turbines.

In World War I the Royal Navy ordered the construction of an eventual 72 ships of the 'Flower' class, generally known as the 'herbaceous borders' and officially designated as fleet minesweeping sloops. These were built in three

Name ship of an 18-strong class of destroyers built in the late 1930s and operated with great success by the Imperial Japanese navy in the early part of World War II, the *Kagero* was built to an improved 'Asashio' class design and proved so good that all later Japanese destroyer classes in World War II were merely developments of the 'Kagero' class. The details of this excellent destroyer included a displacement of 2,033 tons, length of 388ft 6in (118.4m), armament of six 5in (127mm) dual-purpose guns in three twin turrets, four 25mm anti-aircraft guns in two twin mountings and eight 24in (610mm) torpedo tubes in two quadruple mountings, propulsion in the form of geared steam turbines delivering 52,000hp (38,770kW) to two shafts for a speed of 35 knots, and complement of 240. The Kagero was badly damaged by a mine in May 1943 and then finished off by US Navy aircraft off Rendova Island in the Solomons chain, but sister ships that survived to 1943 and 1944 generally had the 5in gun turret in the X position replaced by six 25mm anti-aircraft guns in two triple mountings, thereby raising the number of such weapons to fourteen as four 25mm guns had already been added to the original fit, and from 1944 seven of the ships were further improved in anti-aircraft capability by an increase to between 18 and twenty-eight 25mm guns.

subclasses as the 'Acacia', 'Azalea' and 'Arabis' types, and although intended mainly for the fleet minesweeping role soon proved themselves very versatile and were therefore adapted for other roles such as escort or, in the case of 39 more ships, completed as Q-ships with hidden armament that was designed for the destruction of submarines lured to the surface by the apparently innocuous appearance of these 'merchant' ships. A further 24 ships were built in the '24' class of general-purpose sloops with a central funnel, a dummy bridge aft, and a straight stem and stern to present a double-ended appearance that made it difficult to detect the way the ships were moving at slow speed, especially as effective dazzle painting was employed. These two classes of sloop provided most of the Royal Navy's coastal escort strength in the second half of World War I, and remained in service through the 1920s and 1930s.

In the later 1930s, the apparent inevitability of war with Germany, and with it the renewed threat of submarine attack on the UK merchant navy fleet, persuaded the Admiralty to reconsider its escort capabilities, a process that resulted in the ordering of 20 fast escorts, the ordering of 56 whale-catcher type vessels for the coastal escort role, the conversion of old destroyers to the escort task, and the construction of a new class of oceanic escort as the 'Black Swan' class of sloops. This last class appeared from mid-1939, and eventually totalled 37 ships including four for the Royal Indian Navy, with the final five (including another two Indian ships) cancelled in the closing stages of the war. The ships were built in two forms: as the 'Black Swan' class with a displacement of 1,250 tons, an armament of six 4in anti-aircraft guns in three twin turrets, four 2pdr guns in a quadruple mounting, and four 0.5in (12.7mm) machine guns in a quadruple mounting or twelve 20mm cannon in six twin mountings, and a speed of 19.25 knots on the 3,600hp (2,685kW) delivered to two shafts by geared steam turbines; and as the 'Modified Black Swan' class with a displacement of 1,350 tons, an armament of six 4in anti-aircraft guns in three twin turrets and twelve 20mm cannon in six twin mountings, and a speed of 20 knots on the 4,300hp (3,205kW) delivered to two shafts by geared steam turbines.

The 'Black Swan' and 'Modified Black Swan' classes offered very useful escort capabilities, but they were fairly large vessels built to full warship standards with a geared steam turbine propulsion arrangement, and this made for considerable cost and slow production. The Admiralty had already appreciated this fact and in 1939 ordered the 'Flower' class of escort corvette, of which an eventual 270 were completed in the UK and Canada for service with the navies of the British empire as well as a number of Allied navies. The type, based on a whale-catcher design, was designed for construction to mercantile (and therefore cheaper and quicker) standards with a triple-expansion steam propulsion arrangement, and was produced in two forms. The basic 'Flower' class had a displacement of 950 tons, an armament of one 4in gun, one 2pdr anti-aircraft gun or four 0.5in machine guns in a quadruple mounting and four 0.303in (7.7mm) machine guns in two twin mountings, and a speed of 16 knots on the 2,750hp (2,050kW) delivered to one shaft by a triple-expansion steam engine; the 'Modified Flower' class had a displacement of 980 tons, an armament of one 4in gun, one 2pdr anti-aircraft gun, six 20mm cannon in single mountings, and one 'Hedgehog' anti-submarine projector, and a speed of sixteen knots on the 2,880hp (2,145kW) delivered to one shaft by a triple-expansion steam engine.

The importance of the two 'Flower' classes to the eventual Allied victory over Germany cannot be overestimated, but from an early date the Admiralty realised that the hull was slightly too small for the oceanic escort role and therefore complemented the 'Flower' classes with the larger and faster 'River' class of frigates, which were built to mercantile standards and had a two-shaft propulsion arrangement powered by triple-expansion steam engines. Some 139 of this class were completed in the UK, Australia and Canada for service with the navies of the British empire as well as several Allied navies. The type had a displacement of 1,370 tons, a varied armament of anti-ship and anti-aircraft weapons as well as a Hedgehog anti-submarine projector, and a speed of 20 knots on the 5,500hp (4,100kW) delivered to two shafts by triple-expansion steam engines.

Economical to build and capable in operational terms, the 'River' class was a highly effective type, but its length precluded its construction in many of the yards that had been able to build the 'Flower' classes of corvette. The Admiralty therefore tapped this production source with the 'Castle' class of corvettes, which was built from 1943 and totalled 44 units with a large number of others cancelled at the end of the war. The details of this excellent class included a displacement of 1,010 tons, an armament of one 4in gun, ten 20mm cannon in two twin and six single mountings and one 'Squid' anti-submarine projector, and a speed of 16.5 knots on the 2,880hp (2,145kW) delivered to one shaft by a triple-expansion steam engine.

The 'River' class was followed into production by the 'Loch' and 'Bay' classes of general escort and anti-aircraft frigates, which were built from prefabricated elements to speed production. Some 56 of the two classes were completed, with another 54 cancelled late in the war, and the details of the 'Loch' class included a displacement of 1,435 tons, an armament of one 4in gun, four 2pdr anti-aircraft guns in a single mounting, six 20mm cannon in two twin and two single mountings, and two Squid anti-submarine projectors, and a speed of 20 knots on the 6,500hp (4,845kW) delivered to two shafts by geared steam turbines or 5,500hp (4,100kW) delivered to two shafts by triple-expansion steam engines; the details of the 'Bay' class included a displacement of 1,580 tons,

The *Parramatta* was the second of four (originally to have been six) 'River' class frigates commissioned into the Royal Australian Navy in the early 1960s after construction in Australia to a slightly modified British 'Whitby' class design with a full-load displacement of 1,560 tons, length of 370ft 0in (112.7m), armament of two 4.5in (114m) dual-purpose guns in a twin turret, two 40mm anti-aircraft guns in a twin mounting, twelve 21in (533mm) torpedo tubes in two twin and eight single mountings and two Limbo Mk 10 three-barrel anti-submarine mortars, propulsion in the form of geared steam turbines delivering 30,000hp (22,370kW) to two shafts for a speed of 29 knots, and complement of 230.

Lead ship of a three-strong class of Australian guided missile destroyers modelled closely on the American 'Charles F. Adams' class and delivered from an American yard in the mid-1960s, the *Perth* has a full-load displacement of 4,525 tons, length of 437ft 0in (133.2m), armament of two 5in (127mm) dual-purpose guns in single turrets, one twin launcher for Standard Missile surface-to-air missiles, two Ikara launchers for anti-submarine rockets and six 12.75in (324mm) tubes in two triple mountings for lightweight anti-submarine torpedoes, propulsion in the form of geared steam turbines delivering 70,000hp (52,190kW) to two shafts for a speed of 33 knots, and complement of 350.

Built as a light cruiser in World War II, the *Oklahoma City* was recommissioned into the US Navy in 1960 as one of six such cruisers converted to the fleet escort role with a completely revised armament and associated electronic fit. The ships remained in service into the period 1970-79, and their revised standard included a full-load displacement of 15,150 tons, length of 610ft 0in (186.0m), armament of three 6in (152mm) guns in a triple turret, two 5in (127mm) dual-purpose guns in a twin turret and one twin launcher for 46 RIM-8 Talos surface-to-air missiles, propulsion in the form of geared steam turbines delivering 100,000hp (74,560kW) to four shafts for a speed of 32 knots, and complement of 1,380.

an armament of four 4in anti-aircraft guns in two twin turrets, four 40mm anti-aircraft guns in two twin mountings, four 20mm cannon in two twin mountings and one Hedgehog anti-submarine projector, and a speed of 20 knots on the 6,500hp (4,845kW) delivered to two shafts by geared steam turbines or 5,500hp (4,100kW) delivered to two shafts by triple-expansion steam engines.

At the time of its involvement in World War II in December 1941, the US Navy had 171 operational destroyers, including 71 of the two related 'flushdeck' types that had been built to the extent of 272 destroyers in World War I. Some 31 of these were of the 'Wickes' class with a displacement of 1,090 tons, an armament of four 4in guns in single mountings, one 3in anti-aircraft gun and twelve 21in torpedo tubes, and a speed of 35 knots on the 26,000hp (19,410kW) delivered to two shafts by geared steam turbines. The other 40 of the 'flushdeck' destroyers were units of the 'Clemson' class with a displacement of 1,190 tons, with similar armament, speed and propulsion arrangement.

Construction of destroyers was halted in the USA until the early 1930s, when destroyer developments in other parts of the world finally persuaded the Americans to undertake the construction of a more advanced type in the form of the 'Farragut' class of seven ships with a displacement of 1,395 tons, an armament of five 5in guns in single mountings and eight 21in torpedo tubes in two quadruple mountings, and a speed of 36.5 knots on the 42,800hp (31,910kW) delivered to two shafts by geared steam turbines. In the period leading up to World War II, the US Navy developed the conceptual design of the 'Farragut' class via the 'Mahan' class of 18 ships with twelve 21in torpedo tubes in three quadruple mountings to the 'Craven' class of 22 ships with an armament of four 5in guns in single mountings, four 1.1in anti-aircraft guns in single mountings and sixteen 21in torpedo tubes in four quadruple mountings.

A parallel course of evolution produced the eight and five ships of the 'Porter' and 'Somers' classes respectively for the squadron leader task. The basic design of the 'Porter' class included a displacement of 1,850 tons, an armament of eight 5in guns in four twin mountings and eight 21in torpedo tubes in two quadruple mountings, and a speed of 37 knots on the 50,000hp (37,280kW) delivered to two shafts by geared steam turbines, and the 'Somers' class differed mainly in its uprated propulsion arrangement with 52,500hp (39,145kW) for a speed of 37.5 knots.

Further development of the basic fleet destroyer concept in the late 1930s led to the 'Sims' class of twelve ships that proved to be top-heavy, so one of their five 5in guns and one of their three quadruple 21in torpedo tube mountings were soon removed. The same fate befell the early units of the 'Benson' class, which was an improved version of the 'Sims' class, and itself later upgraded as the 'Livermore' class: construction of the 'Benson' and 'Livermore' classes totalled 32 and 64 ships respectively.

Experience with these classes paved the way for the 'Fletcher' class destroyer that was the US Navy's most important ship of its type in the first part of the war. Built to the extent of 178 ships that were delivered from 1942 with a beamier, flushdecked hull, an increased displacement of 2,050 tons, an armament of five 5in guns in single mountings, between six and ten 40mm and 20mm anti-aircraft guns and ten 21in torpedo tubes in two quintuple mountings, and a speed of 37 knots on the 60,000hp (44,870kW) delivered to two shafts by geared steam turbines.

The 'Fletcher' class destroyers were complemented from 1944 by the 'Allen M. Sumner' and 'Gearing' class destroyers, which were bigger and more heavily armed vessels well suited to the demands of long-range operations in the western Pacific, where they were often exposed to intensive Japanese air attack by *kamikaze* as well as conventional aircraft. The 58 'Allen M. Sumner' class ships were completed to a standard that included a displacement of 2,200 tons, an armament of six 5in dual-purpose guns in three twin turrets, twelve 40mm anti-aircraft guns and ten 21in torpedo tubes in two quintuple mountings, and a speed of 36.5 knots on the 60,000hp (44,870kW) delivered to two shafts by geared steam turbines, and the 99 ships of the 'Gearing' class, completed during and after the closing stages of the war as a development of the 'Allen M. Sumner' class with a lengthened hull, had a displacement of 2,425 tons, an armament of six 5in dual-purpose guns in three twin turrets, twelve or sixteen 40mm anti-aircraft guns and ten 21in torpedo tubes in two quintuple mountings (except in ships with 40mm guns), and a speed of 35 knots on the 60,000hp delivered to two shafts by geared steam turbines.

The US Navy had not initially appreciated the need for dedicated destroyer escorts, and the type was originally ordered in 1941 by the UK, which contracted with American yards for an initial 50 destroyer escorts, or escort destroyers as they were called by the British, before increasing this total to 250 in the following year. After entering the war, the USA soon appreciated the unglamorous but nonetheless vital important of the destroyer escort for the protection of troop and equipment convoys in the Pacific, where their faster and more heavily armed destroyer half-brothers were better employed for the protection of carrier and amphibious task forces. Thus only 55 of these American ships were finally transferred to the British, and of the orders placed by 1943 for 1,005 destroyer escorts, 508 were completed – 452 as destroyer escorts (29 of them for transfer to Allies other than the UK) and the other 56 as high-speed transports.

The ships were completed with two types of hull. The original group of 61 ships comprised the 'Evarts' class with an overall length of 283ft 4in (86.36m), while the others had a hull with an overall length of 306ft 0in (93.27m) and were the 'Buckley', 'Rudderow', 'Cannon', 'Edsall' and 'John C. Butler' classes. The 'Evarts' class had a displacement of 1,140 tons, an armament of three 3in guns in single mountings, four 40mm anti-aircraft guns and five 20mm cannon, and a speed of 21 knots on the 6,000hp

The *Zaal* is one of four 'Saam' or 'Vosper Thornycroft Mk 5' class frigates launched in the UK for the Iranian navy in the late 1960s with a full-load displacement of 1,400 tons, length of 310ft 0in (94.5m), armament of one 4.5in (114mm) dual-purpose gun in a single turret, two 35mm anti-aircraft guns in a single turret, one quintuple launcher for five Sea Killer Mk 2 anti-ship missiles, one triple launcher for nine Seacat surface-to-air missiles and one Limbo Mk 10 three-barrel anti-submarine mortar; propulsion in the form of a CODOG arrangement with gas turbines delivering 46,000hp (34,300kW) and diesels delivering 3,800hp (2,835kW) to two shafts for a speed of 40 or 17.5 knots respectively, and complement of 135.

(4,475kW) delivered to two shafts by a diesel-electric propulsion arrangement. The ships of the 'Buckley' class had a displacement of 1,400 tons, an armament of three 3in guns in single mountings, six 40mm anti-aircraft guns and three 21in torpedo tubes, and a speed of 23.5 knots on the 12,000hp (8,950kW) delivered to two shafts by a turbo-electric propulsion arrangement. The following 'Rudderow' class had a displacement of 1,450 tons, an armament of two 5in guns in single mountings, ten 40mm anti-aircraft guns and three 21in torpedo tubes, and a speed of 24 knots on the 12,000hp (8,950kW) delivered to two shafts by a turbo-electric propulsion arrangement. However, in the 'Cannon' class a diesel-electric propulsion arrangement had to be adopted, as in the 'Buckley' class, because of shortages of turbo-electric equipment, and this resulted in a displacement of 1,240 tons, an armament of three 3in guns in single mountings, six 40mm anti-aircraft guns and three 21in torpedo tubes, and a speed of 21 knots on the 6,000hp (4,475kW) delivered to two shafts by a diesel-electric propulsion arrangement. The 'Edsall' class was similar, and its details included a displacement of 1,200 tons, an armament of three 3in guns in single mountings, eight 40mm anti-aircraft guns and three 21in torpedo tubes, and a speed of 21 knots on the 6,000hp (4,475kW) delivered to two shafts by a diesel-electric propulsion arrangement. The final 'John C. Butler' class was somewhat different, and its details included a displacement of 1,350 tons, an armament of two 5in guns in single mountings, ten 40mm anti-aircraft guns and three 21in torpedo tubes, and a speed of 24 knots on the 12,000hp (8,950kW) delivered to two shafts by geared steam turbines.

Of the other Allied powers in World War II, only France operated a large navy to any effect, and then only to June 1940 in any strategically meaningful manner. The French destroyer force, in order of design, included the six large destroyers of the 'Jaguar' class launched in 1923 and 1924 before completion with a full-load displacement of 3,050 tons and a primary armament of five 5.1in (130mm) guns in single mountings; the 24 medium destroyers of the 'Simoun' class launched in two groups between 1924 and 1929 before completion with a full-load displacement of 2,000 tons and a main armament of four 5.1in guns in single mountings; the 18 large destroyers of the 'Guépard' class launched in four groups between 1928 and 1932 before completion with a full-load displacement of 3,400 tons and a primary armament of five 5.5in (140mm) guns in single mountings; the six large destroyers of the 'Le Fantasque' class launched in 1933 and 1934 with a full-load displacement of 3,400 tons and a primary armament of five 5.5in guns in single mountings; the 12 small destroyers of the 'La Melpomène' class launched between 1935 and 1937 before completion with a full-load displacement of 900 tons and a primary armament of two 3.9in guns in single mountings; the two ships of the 'Mogador' class that were the epitome of large destroyer design and capability after launch in 1936 and 1937 before completion with a full-load displacement of 4,020 tons, a primary armament of eight 5.5in guns in four twin mountings, and a speed of 39 knots on the 92,000hp (75,265kW) delivered to two shafts by geared steam turbines; and the eight large destroyers of the 'Le Hardi' class launched between 1938 and 1939 before completion with a full-load displacement of 2,575 tons and a primary armament of six 5.1in guns in three twin mountings.

On the other side of the military divide were Germany, Italy and Japan. The first destroyers to be built in Germany were the 22 ships of the 'Type 34' or 'Maass' class, which were laid down from 1934 for launch in 1937 and 1938. Despite their attempts to keep abreast of current design trends during the time they had been denied the right to build such ships, the Germans found themselves with a number of problems, most notably in the

The *D'Estienne d'Orves*, lead ship of the French navy's large 'A69' class of frigates, fires one of its MM.38 Exocet anti-ship missiles. Completed between 1976 and 1984, these seventeen ships (with another three delivered to Argentina) have a full-load displacement of 1,250 tons, length of 262ft 6in (80.0m), armament of one 3.9in (100mm) dual-purpose gun in a single turret, two 20mm cannon in single mountings, two or four launchers for two or four MM.38 or MM.40 Exocet anti-ship missiles, one 14.75in (375mm) six-barrel anti-submarine rocket launcher and four 21.7in (550mm) tubes for anti-submarine and anti-ship torpedoes.

The *Glasgow* is the third unit of the 'Type 42 Batch 1' subclass of the 'Type 42' class of guided missile destroyers operated by the Royal Navy since the commissioning of all twelve of the ships between 1976 and 1985. The 'Type 42 Batch 1' subclass has less length and beam than the definitive 'Type 42 Batch 3' subclass and thus suffers in terms of seaworthiness and missile capacity, and the details of these four ships include a full-load displacement of 4,350 tons, length of 412ft 0in (125.6m), armament of one 4.5in (114mm) dual-purpose gun, two 20mm Vulcan six-barrel cannon in two Phalanx close-in weapon system mountings, four 20mm cannon in single mountings, one twin launcher for twenty-six Sea Dart surface-to-air missiles, six 12.75in (324mm) tubes in two triple mountings for lightweight anti-submarine torpedoes, and one helicopter.

The *Southampton* is one of the four ships of the 'Type 42 Batch 2' subclass within the 12-strong 'Type 42 class of guided missile destroyers operated by the Royal Navy.

Below: The *Erinomi* is a simple corvette of the 'Vosper Thornycroft Mk 9' class, of which the Nigerian navy operates two with a specification that includes a full-load displacement of 780 tons, length of 226ft 0in (69.0m), armament of one 3in (76mm) dual-purpose gun in a single turret, one 40mm anti-aircraft gun in a single mounting, two 20mm cannon in single mountings, one triple launcher for Seacat surface-to-air missiles and one 14.75in (375mm) three-barrel anti-submarine mortar.

propulsion arrangement, and the ships acquired an unfortunate but justified reputation for unreliability. Considerable size was chosen for advantages in weapon installation and seaworthiness, but the use of a short bow section with insufficient flare and freeboard meant that they were very wet ships in any sort of sea. In an attempt to match the projectile weight of the latest French destroyers, a new 5in (127mm) weapon was designed to supersede the well-proved 4.1in (105mm) gun, but although this was in itself a successful weapon it was installed in an obsolescent mounting that precluded its use as a dual-purpose weapon. The details of the ships included a full-load displacement of 3,160 tons, an armament of five 5in guns in single mountings, four 37mm anti-aircraft guns in two twin mountings, six 20mm cannon in single mountings and eight 21in torpedo tubes in two quadruple mountings, and a speed of 38 knots on the 70,000hp (52,200kW) provided to two shafts by geared steam turbines.

The survivors of these ships were complemented from the mid-war years by the 15 ships of the 'Type 36A' or 'Narvik' class, which was a development of the 'Type 34' design with greater weight of fire provided by a change to a main-armament calibre of 5.9in (150mm) in a gun that was difficult and slow to work. The details of this class included a full-load displacement of 3,600 tons, an armament of five 5.9in guns in one twin and three single turrets, four 37mm anti-aircraft guns in two twin mountings, five 20mm cannon in single mountings and eight 21in torpedo tubes in two quadruple mountings, and a speed of 36 knots on the 70,000hp (52,200kW) delivered to two shafts by geared steam turbines.

The problems with the main armament of the 'Type 36A' class persuaded the German naval high command that the switch to a 5.9in gun had been wrong, and the next type laid down was the 'Type 36B' class that reverted to the 5in gun. Only three of the ships were completed, with a full-load displacement of 3,505 tons, an armament of five 5in guns in single mountings, four 37mm anti-aircraft guns in twin mountings, fifteen 20mm cannon in three quadruple and three single mountings, eight 21in torpedo tubes in two quadruple mountings, and a speed of 36 knots on the 70,000hp (52,200kW) delivered to two shafts by geared steam turbines.

At the smaller end of the destroyer spectrum, Germany operated a number of ships including the twelve ships of the 'Albatros' and 'Iltis' classes laid down in the 1920s with an armament of three 4.1in guns in single mountings as well as a useful torpedo armament, 21 ships of the 'Type 35' and 'Type 37' classes that were too small for real utility, and then the 15 ships of the 'Type 39' or 'Elbing' class that were launched between 1942 and 1944. These were still comparatively small ships, but had an appearance sufficiently imposing that they were often mistaken for larger fleet destroyers. Their details included a full-load displacement of 1,755 tons, an armament of four 4.1in guns in single mountings, four 37mm anti-aircraft guns in two twin mountings, six 20mm cannon in single mountings and six 21in torpedo tubes in two triple mountings, and a speed of 33.5 knots on the 32,000hp (23,860kW) delivered to two shafts by geared steam turbines.

Italy also operated a mix of small and large (fleet) destroyers, some of them fairly old. The small type of destroyer was epitomised by a basic design originating in World War I with a 239ft 6in (73m) hull. The first of these were the eight 'Pilo' class ships of 1914-15 with an armament of five 4.1in guns in single mountings and four 17.3in (440mm) torpedo tubes in two twin mountings, and there followed the four 'Sirtori' class ships of 1916-17 with an extra gun, the eight 'La Masa' class ships of 1917-19 with the main armament restored to four guns, and the six 'Generale' class ships of 1921-22 with a full-load displacement of 890 tons, an armament of three 4in

(102mm) guns in single mountings, two 3in anti-aircraft guns in single mountings and four 17.3in torpedo tubes in two twin mountings, and a speed of 30 knots on the 15,000hp (11,185kW) delivered to two shafts by geared steam turbines.

A 269ft (82m) hull was used in the four 'Palestro' class ships of 1919-20 for almost a 50 per cent increase in power offering a higher speed with the same basic armament as the 'La Masa' class, and the same hull was retained for the improved 'Curtatone' class of 1922-23.

There followed a long gap in Italian small destroyer design and construction until the advent of the 32 'Spica' class ships from 1936. These had their boiler uptakes trunked into one funnel to maximise usable deck area, and their armament was based on a trio of 3.9in (100mm) guns in single mountings complemented by four 17.7in (450mm) torpedo tubes located initially as four single tubes but later as two twin mountings. Further development of the same concept resulted in the 'Ariete' class. Planned in 1941, the class was to have numbered more than 40 ships, but only 16 were laid down: only one of these was delivered to the Italian navy before Italy's September 1943 armistice with the Allies, but another 13 were later completed in northern Italy for German use. The type had a full-load displacement of 1,125 tons, an armament of two 3.9in guns in single mountings, two 37mm anti-aircraft guns in single mountings and six 17.7in torpedo tubes in two triple mountings, and a speed of 31 knots on the 22,000hp (16,405kW) delivered to two shafts by geared steam turbines.

Further development in Italian destroyer thinking resulted in the very similar 'Sauro' and 'Turbine' class destroyers of which four and eight respectively were built in the mid- and late 1920s with details that included, for the 'Turbine' class, a full-load displacement of 1,700 tons, an armament of four 4.7in (120mm) guns in two twin mountings, two 40mm anti-aircraft guns in single mountings and six 21in torpedo tubes in two triple mountings, and a speed of 36 knots on the 40,000hp (29,825kW) delivered to two shafts by geared steam turbines.

Between 1928 and 1930, and as successors to the four 'Sauro' class destroyers, the Italians produced, the 12 units of the 'Navigatore' class in which a heavy armament and considerable power were squeezed into a comparatively small hull for a full-load displacement of 2,580 tons, an armament of six 4.7in guns in three twin mountings, three 37mm anti-aircraft guns in single mountings and four or six 21in torpedo tubes in two twin or triple mountings, and a speed of 38 knots on the 50,000hp (37,280kW) delivered to two shafts by geared steam turbines.

During 1930-32, the Italian navy introduced the four ships of the 'Dardo' class in which maximum possible use of the deck area was facilitated by the trunking of the boiler uptakes into a single funnel. This permitted a main armament of four 4.7in guns in two twin mountings. Further development of the same concept led to the four destroyers of the improved 'Folgore' class with each gun mounting provided with its own director to make possible the simultaneous engagement of two targets. The main limitation of the 'Dardo' and 'Folgore' classes was their lack of seaworthiness, and in the following 1934 'Maestrale' class of four ships the hull was lengthened by some 32ft 9in (10m) and also increased in beam. Basically the same hull was used in the 1936 'Oriani' class of four ships. With the threat of war increasing at this time, the Italian navy in 1937 and 1938 placed orders for another twelve destroyers modelled on the 'Oriani' class design. These were the 'Soldato' class destroyers with a full-load displacement of 1,460 tons, and armament of four or five 4.7in guns in two twin and one single mounting, one 37mm anti-aircraft gun and six 21in torpedo tubes in two triple mountings, and a

The *Forbin* was one of the French navy's five 'Duperré' or 'T53' class destroyers completed in the mid-1950s as a development of the 'T47' class, with improved capability for the tracking and controlling of aircraft through the introduction of improved radar and specialised control equipment.

The *Athabaskan* is one of four 'Iroquois' or 'Tribal' class destroyers in service with the Canadian navy. The ships were commissioned in the first half of the 1970s as ocean escorts optimised for the anti-submarine role, but in the later 1980s were taken in hand for modernisation in the tribal update and modernization project (TRUMP) to re-emerge with a full-load displacement of 4,700 tons, length of 426ft 0in (129.8m), armament of one 3in (76mm) dual-purpose gun in a single turret and one 20mm Vulcan six-barrel cannon in a Phalanx close-in weapon system mounting, one vertical-launch system for 32 Standard Missile surface-to-air missiles, six 12.75in (324mm) tubes in two triple mountings for lightweight anti-submarine torpedoes and two large helicopters.

The *Scylla* is a 'Leander Batch 3A' frigate of the Royal Navy. One of the most successful warship types developed in the UK since World War II and built in large numbers for the export as well as domestic markets, the 'Leander' class was built in three basic forms in the 1960s, and the 'Leander Batch 3' or 'Broad-Beam Leander' class ships introduced greater beam for improved sea-keeping qualities. The specification for the 'Leander Batch 3' ships includes a full-load displacement of 2,960 tons, length of 372ft 0in (113.4m), armament of two 4.5in (114mm) dual-purpose guns in a twin turret, two or three 20mm cannon in single mountings, one quadruple launcher for Seacat surface-to-air missiles, one Limbo Mk 10 three-barrel anti-submarine mortar and one light helicopter. Some of the ships were later upgraded to 'Leander Batch 3A' standard, losing the 4.5in gun turret and Limbo mortar but gaining two twin launchers for four MM.38 Exocet anti-ship missiles, one sextuple launcher for 32 Sea Wolf surface-to-air missiles, and six 12.75in (324mm) tubes in two triple mountings for lightweight anti-submarine torpedoes.

speed of 39 knots on the 48,000hp (35,790kW) delivered to two shafts by geared steam turbines.

Up to the end of World War I, the Japanese had adhered closely to British destroyer concepts, either buying directly from the UK or building ships based directly on British thinking, and worked within the overall scheme of large first- and smaller second-class destroyers. In the closing stages of World War I, however, the Japanese decided that there was something to be learned from German destroyer thinking especially in the matter of a well between the forecastle and the forward part of the superstructure to break the force of water streaming over the bows in any kind of weather. This resulted in the 13 'Minekaze' and 21 'Momi' class first- and second-class destroyers launched in the years immediately following World War I as what were basically large- and small-scale versions of the same basic design. The 'Minekaze' class ships had a full-load displacement of 1,650 tons, an armament of four 4.7in guns in single mountings and six 21in torpedo tubes in two triple mountings, and a speed of 39 knots on the 38,500hp (28,685kW) delivered to two shafts by geared steam turbines. The nine 'Kamikaze' class destroyers that followed were basically similar to the 'Minekaze' class ships, and further improvement of the same concept came with the twelve 'Mutsuki' class destroyers that introduced the 24in (610mm) torpedo as an exceptionally potent anti-ship weapon.

The Japanese launched the first of an eventual 20 'Fubuki' class first-class destroyers in 1927, and in the process created a type that was a trend-setter in destroyer design as it eschewed British and German design influences for a Japanese concept with a higher forecastle, no well between the forecastle and the forward part of the superstructure, and a strengthened superstructure

The Royal Navy's eight 'County' class destroyers were commissioned between 1962 and 1980, and are here epitomised by the *Antrim*. The basic specification for these useful ships, which offered little short of cruiser capabilities, included a full-load displacement of 6,800 tons, length of 521ft 6in (158.9m), armament of four 4.5in (114mm) dual-purpose guns in two twin turrets, two 20mm cannon in single mountings, one twin launcher for Seaslug long-range surface-to-air missiles, two quadruple launchers for Seacat short-range surface-to-air missiles, and one helicopter; propulsion in the form of a combined steam and gas turbine (COSAG) arrangement with geared steam turbines delivering 30,000hp (22,370kW) and gas turbines delivering 30,000hp (22,370kW) to two shafts for a speed of 30 knots, and complement of 470. None of the ships remains in British service, four and one having been sold to Chile and Pakistan respectively in the 1980s.

The *Tromp* is the lead ship of the Dutch navy's two-ship class optimised for the air defence role and possessing the accommodation to support the commander of an anti-submarine escort squadron. The ships were commissioned in the mid-1970s and in their current form have a full-load displacement of 4,310 tons, length of 454ft 0in (138.4m), armament of two 4.7in (120mm) dual-purpose guns in a twin turret, one single launcher for 40 Standard Missile long-range surface-to-air missiles, one octuple launcher for 16 Sea Sparrow short-range surface-to-air missiles, two quadruple launchers for eight Harpoon anti-ship missiles, six 12.75in (324mm) tubes in two triple mountings for lightweight anti-submarine torpedoes, and one light helicopter.

that was thus considerably less prone to damage in heavy seas. These impressive ships had a standard displacement of 2,090 tons, an armament of six 5in (127mm) guns in three triple turrets and nine 24in torpedo tubes in three triple mountings with no fewer than 18 torpedoes, and a speed of 38 knots on the 50,000hp (37,280kW) delivered to two shafts by geared steam turbines.

In 1931 the Japanese introduced a small destroyer type as the 'Tomodzura' class, whose four units were planned to complete the destroyer tonnage allocated to the Japanese in the Washington Naval Treaty. These ships were designed for coastal operations off Japan and along the shore of eastern Asia, and were ambitious attempts to pack maximum capability into minimum hull, for with a standard displacement of only 650 tons, the ships carried an armament of three 5in guns in one twin and one single mounting as well as four 21in torpedo tubes in two twin mountings, and were capable of a speed of 30 knots on the 11,000hp (8,200kW) delivered to two shafts by geared steam turbines. That too much had been attempted on this hull was revealed by the top-heaviness of the class in general and the capsize of the lead ship in particular, and this problem was addressed in the following 'Ootori' class of eight ships launched between 1935 and 1937 with a longer but still very narrow hull and a reduced armament. The details of the 'Ootori' class included a full-load displacement of 1,050 tons, an armament of three 4.7in guns in single mountings, one 40mm anti-aircraft gun and three 21in torpedo tubes in a triple mounting, and a speed of 30 knots on the 19,000hp (14,165kW) delivered to two shafts by geared steam turbines.

Although the 'Fubuki' class destroyers had offered considerable capabilities at the time of their introduction – a

decade before the capable British 'J' class destroyers with a slightly inferior specification but a very high reputation – the trend-setting nature of the class had resulted in a number of operational problems that were addressed in succeeding classes. The first of these was the 'Akatsuki' class of four ships launched between 1931 and 1933 with a lightened topside structure on a shorter hull, and there followed the 'Hatsuhara' class of six destroyers with a hull that was shortened still further, resulting in the loss of one 5in gun mounting and one torpedo tube triple mounting, and a propulsion arrangement of reduced power as Japanese designers sought to comply with the limitations imposed by the first of the London Naval Agreements. Further development of the 'Hatsuhara' class design led to the 'Shiratsuyu' class of ten ships with a further shortening of the hull but an improvement in torpedo armament to eight 24in tubes in two quadruple mountings with reloads.

In 1937 there appeared the first of ten 'Asashio' class ships that ignored the London Naval Agreement limitations and were therefore very similar to

The *Boxer* is the lead ship of the six-strong 'Broadsword Batch 2' subclass of the Royal Navy's 'Broadsword' class of 10 guided missile frigates. The ships of the 'Broadsword Batch 1' subclass proved too short to carry the planned towed-array sonar and two medium helicopters, so the 'Broadsword Batch 2' subclass was lengthened by an appreciable degree and fitted with an uprated propulsion arrangement to create a highly effective type with excellent anti-ship, anti-aircraft and anti-submarine capabilities.

The *Duchess* was the last of the eight-strong 'Daring' class of standard gun-armed destroyers commissioned into the Royal Navy in the first half of the 1950s. The details of the class included a full-load displacement of 3,580 tons, length of 390ft 0in (118.8m), armament of six 4.5in (114mm) dual-purpose guns in three twin turrets, two 40mm anti-aircraft guns in single mountings and one 'Squid' anti-submarine projector, propulsion in the form of geared steam turbines delivering 54,000hp (40,260kW) to two shafts for a speed of 34.75 knots, and complement of 330.

The modular outfitting scheme devised in Germany by Blohm und Voss allows easy installation, repair, replacement and updating of equipment, weapons, sensors and other units installed in one of several types of standard module, and has resulted in the 'Meko' series of warships built in destroyer and frigate sizes. This is the *Aradu*, a 'Meko 360' class destroyer of the Nigerian navy.

the original 'Fubuki' class ships. The excellence of this basic design was further attested by the completion of 18 'Kagero' class destroyers that introduced a slightly beamier hull and were launched between 1938 and 1941 before completion to a standard that included a full-load displacement of 2,490 tons, an armament of six 5in guns in three twin mountings, four 25mm anti-aircraft guns in two twin mountings and eight 24in torpedo tubes in two quadruple mountings, and a speed of 35 knots on the 52,000hp (38,770kW) delivered to two shafts by geared steam turbines. So successful was the type considered, moreover, that the following 20 'Yugumo' class destroyers were basically similar.

The final type of large destroyer to be built by the Japanese in World War II was the 'Akitsuki' class, of which twelve units were launched between 1941 and 1944. These were planned as anti-aircraft escorts for major surface forces, and were designed to offer the same capabilities as the American 'Atlanta' and British 'Dido' class cruisers on a smaller hull that would therefore be cheaper and quicker to build. One of the keys to this capability was the adoption of a main gun of somewhat smaller calibre than those used in the Western ships, the loss of projectile weight in the Japanese gun being more than balanced by its considerably higher rate of fire. The details of the class included a full-load displacement of 3,700 tons, an armament of eight 3.9in (100mm) dual-purpose guns in two pairs of superfiring turrets, four 25mm anti-aircraft guns in two twin mountings and four 24in torpedo tubes in a quadruple mounting, and a speed of 33 knots on the 52,000hp (38,770kW) delivered to two shafts by geared steam turbines. During the course of the Pacific campaign, the Japanese came to appreciate that all their warships lacked adequate firepower to cope with saturation attacks by American warplanes, and in the surviving 'Akitsuki' class destroyers, the defensive anti-aircraft armament was steadily increased to fifty 25mm guns.

So far as convoy escorts were concerned, the Japanese were sadly let down by their high command, which had persistently based its plans on the winning of a quick victory and therefore had ignored the possibility of a protracted war and a long defensive effort in which Japan would be strangled by American submarine and air power unless vital convoys could be protected. The belated realisation that such ships were desperately needed resulted in the 'Matsu' class of escorts, of which only 17 of a planned 28 were completed in 1944 and 1945 with a full-load displacement of 1,530 tons, an armament of three 5in guns in one twin and one single mounting, twenty-four 25mm anti-aircraft guns in four triple and twelve single mountings, four 24in torpedo tubes in a quadruple mounting, and a speed of 27.5 knots on the 19,000hp (14,165kW) delivered to two shafts by geared steam turbines. Another and somewhat more austere escort was the 'Tachibana' class type of which more than 90 were planned, 27 laid down and only a few completed.

Since World War II, it has been the US Navy that has dominated the Western approach to destroyer design. Soon after the end of the war, relations between the USA and the USSR began to deteriorate rapidly, especially after the Soviet development of nuclear weapons, and as it became

The *Brave* is one of the six 'Broadsword Batch 2' class guided missile frigates currently operated by the Royal Navy.

clear that the Soviet navy was planning to develop a major submarine capability based on the design of the German 'Type XXI' class boat, the US Navy decided that a major upgrade of its escort forces was required to protect the carrier battle groups that were now the core of the service's operational thinking. Consequently, many of the surviving 'Fletcher', 'Gearing' and 'Allen M. Sumner' class fleet destroyers were revised to oceanic escort standard with a reduced gun armament but much improved anti-submarine capability. This made economic sense as the Americans had large numbers of these ships, which were still almost new, and the Soviet threat was slow to materialise in numbers and also in basic capability. Thus the conversions of World War II fleet destroyers into anti-submarine escorts provided the US Navy's main surface strength with a more than adequate defensive element, and the service could thus use its relatively limited funding to provide more modern escorts for the protection of convoys, which were seen to fall into two basic categories – as merchant ships providing fuel, food and raw materials for the USA's allies in Europe, and as amphibious warfare vessels transporting formations of the US Marine Corps and US Army for offensive operations in any part of the world.

These smaller ocean escorts, which were the equivalent of the destroyer escorts of World War II, were the 13 ships of the 'Dealey' class, four units of the 'Claud Jones' class, and two units of the 'Bronstein' class used as prototypes of more advanced types, the first two created in the 1950s and the last in the early 1960s with basically conventional weapons, although the 'Bronstein' class introduced the RUR-5 ASROC weapon which was a rocket used to deliver a homing torpedo or nuclear depth charge to the position of a target submarine detected and localised by sonar.

Further development of this ocean escort type, now generally reckoned to be a frigate rather than a destroyer, resulted in the ten ships of the 'Garcia' class, and the seven units of the 'Brooke' class that suffered in the replacement of one of the two 5in dual-purpose gun mountings by a launcher for sixteen RIM-24 Tartar surface-to-air missiles in recognition of the growing threat posed from the early 1960s by Soviet warplanes. This tendency was continued in the 46 ships of the 'Knox' class optimised for the anti-submarine role but offering a useful anti-aircraft capability with its octuple launcher for RIM-7 Sea Sparrow short-range SAMs.

The current mainstay of the US Navy's frigate force is the 'Oliver Hazard Perry' class of 51 ships commissioned from 1977. Although small, the type has a fair measure of electronic sophistication, and its primary details include a full-load displacement of 4,100 tons, an armament of one 3in dual-purpose gun, one 20mm Vulcan six-barrel cannon in a close-in weapon system mounting, one single-arm launcher for 40 missiles (generally four RGM-84 Harpoon anti-ship and 36 RIM-66 Standard Missile surface-to-air missiles), six 12.75in (324mm) torpedo tubes in two triple anti-submarine

Built for Iran but eventually taken into US Navy service, the *Chandler* is one of four 'Kidd' class guided missile destroyers developed from the 'Spruance' class and currently constituting one of the world's most potent destroyer classes with capabilities that verge on those of the cruiser. The details of the class include a full-load displacement of 9,750 tons, length of 563ft 4in (171.8m), armament of two 5in (127mm) dual-purpose guns in single mountings, two 20mm Vulcan six-barrel cannon in Phalanx close-in weapon system mountings, two twin launchers for 52 Standard Missile surface-to-air missiles and 16 ASROC anti-submarine rockets, two quadruple launchers for eight Harpoon anti-ship missiles, six 12.75in (324mm) tubes in two triple mountings for lightweight anti-submarine torpedoes, and two light helicopters, propulsion in the form of gas turbines delivering 80,000hp (59,655kW) to two shafts for a speed of 33 knots, and complement of 340.

mountings and, in some ships, provision for one anti-submarine helicopter, and a speed of 29 knots on the 41,000hp (30,570kW) delivered to one shaft by two General Electric LM2500 gas turbines.

In a slow process that started in the early 1950s, the mantle of fleet escort destroyer was gradually assumed from World War II conversions by new ships. The first of these were the four highly capable but also highly expensive destroyers of the 'Mitscher' class optimised for the anti-submarine role, then the ten destroyers of the 'Farragut' class optimised for the dual-role anti-submarine and anti-aircraft roles with ASROC missiles, homing torpedoes and one twin-arm launcher for 40 RIM-2 Terrier SAMs, and finally the 18 destroyers of the 'Forrest Sherman' class optimised for the general-purpose role with neither ASROC nor SAM weapons.

By the 1960s the Soviet threat was of a far higher order, and this led to the introduction of the 23 'Charles F. Adams' class destroyers with ASROC anti-submarine and RIM-24 anti-aircraft weapons, and then in the 1970s to the 31 'Spruance' and four 'Kidd' class destroyers with significant anti-submarine, anti-aircraft and anti-ship capabilities in the form of missiles, torpedoes and a multi-role helicopter. The final expression of this tendency,

This view of the stern section of the French destroyer *De Grasse* of the 'Tourville' or 'F67' class highlights the helicopter installation that lies at the heart of modern anti-submarine capability. Located just forward of the gear for the variable-depth sonar, that is one of the ship's key systems for the detection and localisation of submarines, is the helicopter platform and the fully enclosed hangar for two light anti-submarine helicopters that can also be outfitted for anti-ship operations. The hangar is topped by the Crotale Naval octuple launcher for short-range surface-to-air missiles.

which continued throughout the 1980s, is the 'Arleigh Burke' class, of which 26 are planned primarily for the anti-aircraft role with a slightly downgraded version of the AEGIS weapon system (SPY-1 radar and Standard Missile weapons) designed for the 'Ticonderoga' class cruisers.

These American leads have generally been followed in Western Europe, particularly in the UK, France, Italy, Germany and the Netherlands, and in the Far East, where Japan has built up an impressive destroyer and frigate force since the early 1960s.

The USSR also developed a major destroyer and frigate force from the late 1950s, and although the earlier of these classes were intended at the time of their introduction mainly for the destruction of American surface battle groups with large anti-ship missiles, later classes were completed to a more balanced standard with anti-submarine, anti-aircraft and anti-ship capabilities. The more modern of these classes, in order of introduction, were the 14 destroyers of the two 'Kashin' subclasses, the 22 destroyers of the 'Sovremenny' class and the twelve destroyers of the 'Udaloy' class; the 40 frigates of the three 'Krivak' subclasses and the three frigates of the 'Neustrashimy' class.

The most impressive of these are the 'Sovremenny' and 'Udaloy' class destroyers delivered from 1980. The 'Sovremenny' class design is optimised for the anti-ship and anti-aircraft roles with a full-load displacement of 7,300 tons, an armament of four 5.1in dual-purpose guns in two twin turrets, four 30mm six-barrel cannon in single mountings, two quadruple launchers for eight SS-N-22 'Sunburn' anti-ship missiles, two launchers for 44 SA-N-7 'Gadfly' SAMs, two 12-tube anti-submarine rocket launchers, four 21in torpedo tubes in two twin mountings, and one helicopter, and a speed of 32 knots on the 110,000hp (82,015kW) delivered to two shafts by geared steam turbines. The 'Udaloy' class design is optimised for the anti-submarine and anti-aircraft roles with a full-load displacement of 8,700 tons, an armament of two 5.1in dual-purpose guns in single turrets, four 30mm six-barrel cannon in single mountings, two quadruple launchers for eight SS-N-14 'Silex' anti-submarine missiles, eight octuple vertical launchers for 64 SA-N-9 SAMs, eight 21in torpedo tubes in two quadruple mountings, two 12-tube anti-submarine rocket launchers and two multi-role helicopters, and a speed of 30 knots on the 110,000hp (82,015kW) delivered to two shafts by a COGOG arrangement with four gas turbine engines.

This artist's impression conveys elements of the trends that may be incorporated in future frigates with a crew possibly as low as 50 through the incorporation of increased automation and highly sophisticated computer systems. Key features are the small size, with the helicopter located as near to the centre of movement as possible to minimise the ship's pitching on helicopter operations, the clean and uncluttered deck, and the inward slope of the small superstructure elements to minimise radar reflectivity.

Fast Attack Craft

Many of the world's navies, including a large number without any claim to a long-standing naval or even maritime tradition, now operate forces of small but comparatively heavily armed fast combat craft. These can be defined as vessels possessing a displacement of up to 600 tons and a top speed of 25 knots or more, and fall into two basic categories: the fast patrol boat (FPB) and fast attack craft (FAC). The FPB is generally fitted with only light armament (usually machine guns and cannon of up to 40mm calibre) together with minimal sensor and fire-control suites. The FAC is very formidable type usually capable of higher speeds and carrying a heavier, longer-ranged armament that can include anti-ship guided missiles, guns of up to 3in (76mm) calibre, heavyweight anti-ship torpedoes of up to 21in (533mm) calibre, and anti-submarine weapons such as lightweight homing torpedoes, rocket-propelled grenades and depth charges, all controlled with the aid of very sophisticated sensor and fire-control suites. The nature of the primary armament is generally indicated by a suffixed letter: thus the FAC(G) carries a medium-calibre gun, the FAC(M) carries anti-ship missiles, and the FAC(T) carries anti-ship torpedoes.

Recent developments have tended to obscure the fact that the FAC is a type with more than a century of pedigree behind it. The first small warship may be regarded as John I. Thornycroft's torpedo boat *Lightning* built for the Royal Navy in 1876-77. About ten years earlier Robert Whitehead had demonstrated the capabilities of his new invention, the locomotive torpedo, and since that time Thornycroft had urged the Admiralty for permission to develop a torpedo-armed launch based on his successful series of fast steam launches. Displacing 32.5 tons and possessing an overall length of 87ft (26.52m), the *Lightning* was powered by a compound steam engine delivering 460hp (343kW) to one shaft for a speed of 19 knots. By the beginning of the twentieth century, the Royal Navy alone had operated more than 100 such steam-powered boats. The later units displaced some 200 tons each and could reach 25 knots.

After the end of World War II, the Soviets undertook an intensive programme of missile development with the intention of creating a range of weapons across the tactical and strategic spectrum. In the late 1950s, this programme began to yield useful results in the field of surface-to-surface anti-ship missiles. The first Soviet experiments had been made in the immediate aftermath of the war with captured Fieseler Fi 103 (otherwise V-1) missiles, and led to spectacular success in the development of Soviet cruise missiles, which were placed in service some four years before the first Western equivalents. The first such type to reach operational status was the SS-N-1 'Scrubber', which entered service in 1958 as a large ship-launched weapon carrying a conventional or nuclear warhead to a maximum range of 115 miles (185km) with radar or infra-red homing. Although the 'Scrubber' was a considerable technical achievement and boded well for future Soviet developments, the missile was too large for truly practical use, and its deployment was limited to 'Kildin' and 'Krupny' class destroyers.

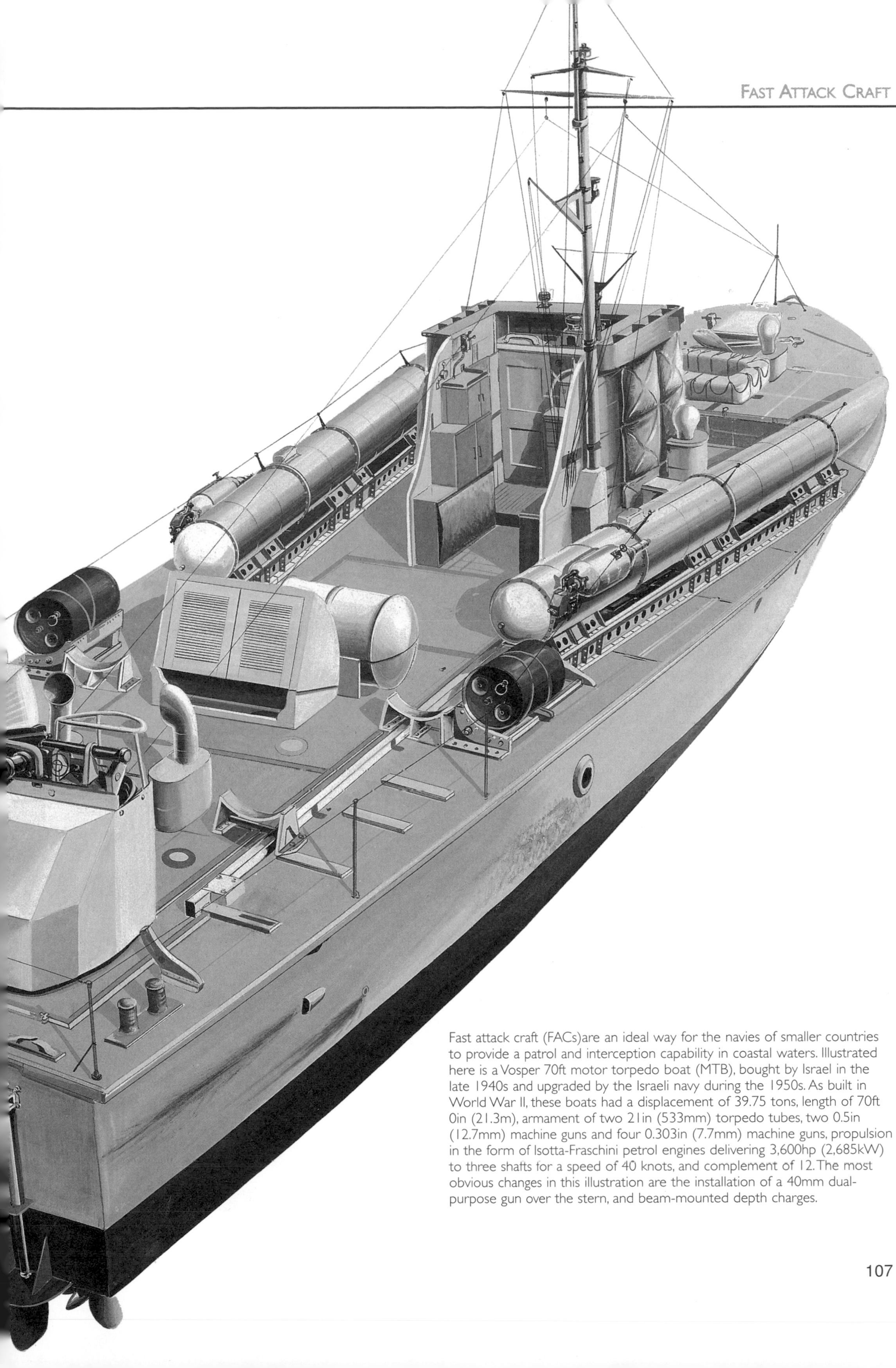

Fast attack craft (FACs) are an ideal way for the navies of smaller countries to provide a patrol and interception capability in coastal waters. Illustrated here is a Vosper 70ft motor torpedo boat (MTB), bought by Israel in the late 1940s and upgraded by the Israeli navy during the 1950s. As built in World War II, these boats had a displacement of 39.75 tons, length of 70ft 0in (21.3m), armament of two 21in (533mm) torpedo tubes, two 0.5in (12.7mm) machine guns and four 0.303in (7.7mm) machine guns, propulsion in the form of Isotta-Fraschini petrol engines delivering 3,600hp (2,685kW) to three shafts for a speed of 40 knots, and complement of 12. The most obvious changes in this illustration are the installation of a 40mm dual-purpose gun over the stern, and beam-mounted depth charges.

Yet the 'Scrubber' did pave the way for more practical weapons of the same aeroplane-type layout, and the first of these more effective weapons was the considerably smaller SS-N-2 'Styx', a missile that can truly be regarded as a weapon that revolutionised naval warfare. The 'Styx' weighed 6,614lb (3,000kg) with a 1,102lb (500kg) high explosive warhead, and its combination of a jettisonable solid-propellant rocket booster and a storable liquid-propellant sustainer rocket provided a theoretical maximum range of 53 miles (85km). The full range could only be usefully employed if mid-course updating of the guidance package was provided by a supporting helicopter (an extremely unlikely contingency in this period), so the effective range of the missile was 23 miles (37km) under the control of an autopilot with an active radar taking over for the terminal phase of the attack. The missile entered production in the late 1950s and reached initial operational capability in late 1958 or early 1959.

By this time the process of designing a specialist fast combat craft for the type was well advanced, but as an interim measure it was decided to convert a number of 'P 6' class torpedo craft into simple launch platforms. This resulted in a total of about 100 'Komar' class craft that entered service probably in late 1958, although the Western powers became aware of the type only in 1960. The Soviets classified this type of craft as the RK, standing for *Raketnyy Kater* (rocket cutter), and this designation has been retained for all later Soviet FAC(M)s. Of the 100 or so 'Komar' class craft completed in the USSR by 1961, some 78 were later transferred to the navies of satellite and client countries, and about 40 of the modified steel-hulled 'Hegu' class were built in China. The 'Komar' class was intended only as a stopgap, and the last craft had been retired from Soviet service by the early 1980s.

The naval operations of the Yom Kippur War saw the fast combat craft come of age in coastal warfare, but even before the war the manifest capabilities of the Israeli 'Saar' class craft had attracted an order for similar 'FPB/TNC-45' type craft from Argentina, which in 1970 ordered two West German-built craft, and these were

PT109 was an American pursuit torpedo (PT) boat of the Elco type built in World War II with a displacement of 38 tons, length of 80ft 0in (24.4m), armament of four 21in (533mm) torpedo tubes, two 20mm cannon in single mountings (or one 40mm gun and one 20mm cannon in single mountings) and four 0.5in (12.7mm) machine guns in two twin mountings, propulsion in the form of petrol engines delivering 4,050hp (3,020kW) to three shafts for a speed of 40 knots, and complement of 14.

commissioned during 1974 in the FAC(G/T) role. Although there was no open warfare in the region, Argentina's possession of these two craft gave it a decided superiority that was only counterbalanced, and indeed reversed, in 1988 when Chile bought from Israel two of its 'Saar 3' class FAC(M)s. The next order came from South-East Asia, where the small nation of Singapore attests its strategic importance and wealth by maintaining moderately large and well-equipped armed forces for the preservation of peace in this potentially volatile region. Also in 1970, Singapore ordered six 'FPB/TNC-45' class FAC(M/G)s as two initial craft from West Germany to be followed by four indigenously built craft. The armament of these craft is a powerful and interesting combination of Swedish and Israeli weapons. The gun armament is Swedish, and comprises one 57mm Bofors SAK 57 weapon on the forecastle and one Bofors 40mm weapon aft. The missile armament initially comprised the first export installation of the Israeli Gabriel weapon, and consisted of five Gabriels in two fixed single container-launchers and one trainable triple container-launcher, though the latter can now be replaced by two twin container-launchers for an American weapon, the RGM-84 Harpoon. The Singapore order was followed by two other contracts from the same region. The first was placed by Malaysia for six licence-built craft completed to a less formidable FAC(G) standard with the same gun armament as the Singapore craft but less capable electronics and reduced performance based on a three- rather than four-shaft propulsion arrangement, and the second came from Thailand in the form of a contract for three licence-built units essentially similar to the Singapore craft. Other orders were received from Ecuador for three FAC(M/G)s with a notably useful armament that includes the 3in (76mm) OTO Melara Compact gun as well as the MM.38 early version of the French Exocet anti-ship missile, from three Persian Gulf states for a total of 17 FAC(M/G)s all carrying the OTO Melara Compact gun and the later MM.40 version of the Exocet missile, and from Ghana for two FAC(G)s with the OTO Melara Compact gun but only a modest two-shaft propulsion arrangement. The 'FPB/TNC-45' is still available, and further orders may yet be placed for this enduring design whose versatility means continued viability through the installation of modern weapons and sensors.

Despite the proved seaworthiness and endurance of the original 'Saar' class craft, Israel decided in the late 1960s that a new type of FAC(M) was required for longer-range operations in the Mediterranean and, to a lesser extent, the Red Sea. A major factor in this decision was the emergence as a major power in the Mediterranean theatre of Libya, a fervently Moslem state. A strong believer in pan-Arab power, Libya was using a very large percentage of its significant oil revenues for the creation of large and offensively oriented armed forces. These included a navy with a considerable missile capability in vessels ranging in size up to corvettes. The result of these Israeli concerns was the 'Saar 4' class of FAC(M)s derived by the Israelis from 1968 on the basis of their experience with the earlier 'Saars'. At a length of 190ft 3in (58.0m) and a full-load displacement of 450 tons, the type is somewhat larger than the 'Saar 2' and 'Saar 3' class units, but as range rather than speed was the prime performance requisite, the four-shaft propulsion arrangement remained essentially unaltered to yield a speed of 32 knots but a range of 4,600 miles (7,400km) instead of a speed of 40 knots or more and a range of 2,890 miles (4,650km). The 'Saar 4' proved its exceptional seaworthiness and range when four of the class made the passage from Israel's Mediterranean coast to the port of Eilat on the Red Sea coast, travelling around Africa via the Strait of Gibraltar and the Cape of Good Hope, and relying exclusively on refuelling at sea.

The American PT boats of World War II were operated with a number of armament fits, this boat having two 21in (533mm) torpedo tubes, eight depth charges, one 20mm cannon and four 0.5in (12.7mm) machine guns in two twin mountings.

Apart from additional fuel bunkerage, the greater volume and deck area of the 'Saar 4' class units are used for greater habitability, improved electronics, a superior weapons layout, and significantly upgraded sensor and countermeasures capabilities. In their original form, the 'Saar 4' class craft each carried two 3in OTO Melara Compact guns, two 20mm Oerlikon cannon in single mountings and/or a maximum of six 0.5in machine guns in twin mountings, and six container-launchers for Gabriel missiles. The after gun mounting was later replaced by a 20mm six-barrel cannon in an American-supplied Phalanx close-in weapon system mounting for improved last-ditch defence against sea-skimming anti-ship missiles, and from 1978 the missile armament was revised after Israel began to receive the RGM-84 Harpoon anti-ship missile, which can be installed in one or two twin or quadruple container-launchers replacing a similar number of Gabriel container-launchers for further enhancement of the 'cocktail' attack concept.

Israel built 10 'Saar 4' class craft for its own use, but subsequently sold two of them to Chile. Another three units of the original configuration were built in the same Israeli yard for South Africa, where another nine were built under licence.

The commissioning of 'Saar 4' class units gave the Israeli navy an impressive force of modern and sophisticated fast combat craft. Early experience in the 1967 war, confirmed by operations in the 1973 war, indicated that these forces could be deployed more effectively in flotillas led by a more sophisticated flotilla leader with specialised equipment and accommodation for the flotilla commander and his staff. This resulted in the 'Saar 4.5' class which was based on the hull, propulsion arrangement, armament (in upgraded form) and electronics of the 'Saar 4' class. The hull was lengthened to allow the incorporation in two units, at the expense of part of the missile armament, of a hangar and deck pad for a single light helicopter used in the surveillance and missile targeting update roles. The Israelis later decided that despite its longer hull, the 'Saar 4.5' class design was not ideally suited to helicopter operations, and this was one of the primary reasons for the design of the 'Saar 5' class of guided-missile corvettes.

The proven success of the 'Saar 2' and 'Saar 3' classes in Israeli service was a very useful advertisement for the quality of Lürssen fast combat craft designs, and resulted in a steady stream of orders for craft based on the 'FPB/TNC-45' design. Lürssen also took a further step up the size ladder, for the company recognised that the type of weapon and electronic fit demanded by its customers was on the verge of swamping the capabilities of the 'FPB/TNC-45' design. Lürssen thus appreciated that greater size would not only facilitate the installation of current weapons and sensors as

In the period before and during World War II, the Italians were some of the most skilled exponents of light craft, which in their MTB forms were designated as MAS craft.

well as a new generation of these items, but would also fit in with the procurement plans of many of the world's smaller navies. Many of these navies belonged to Third-World countries only recently emerged from colonial rule into independence, and for financial and technical reasons thought that their expansion should not encompass major warships optimised for a single role. Instead, they favoured a type one step up from the medium-sized FAC, namely a large fast combat craft type offering multi-role capability through the adoption of a combination of hull and propulsion arrangement that would support later upgrading with more and/or better weapons and sensors.

The two main British designers of fast combat craft are Brooke Marine and Vosper Thornycroft. In general terms, Brooke Marine specialises in robust craft well suited to the demands of Third-World navies with difficulties in finding adequate numbers of trained personnel, while Vosper Thornycroft specialises in the more sophisticated end of the market where an advanced hull and propulsion arrangement are combined with an integrated suite of modern weapons and capable electronics.

Within the spectrum of fast craft, the smallest of Brooke Marine's standard hull types are the 80 and 95ft (24.5 and 29m) designs, and these have proved successful in securing considerable export orders. These are mostly patrol craft of limited performance and light armament, however, and thus fall outside the fast combat craft category. Next up in size, however, is the 107ft (32.6m) design that has formed the basis for two types of fast combat craft, both delivered to African nations and featuring a two-shaft propulsion arrangement for low purchase cost but also low performance. For example, the three units for Kenya were delivered as patrol craft, but as the Kenyan navy became better trained and more experienced it recognised the latent capabilities of the design, and contracted for the craft to be upgraded to limited FAC(M) standard. The original gun armament of two 40mm Bofors guns in single mountings was replaced by the more modern fit of two 30mm Oerlikon cannon in a twin mounting under control of an optronic director, and this core armament was supplemented by four container-launchers for Gabriel II anti-ship missiles.

Amongst Brooke Marine's core designs is the larger 123ft (37.5m) type. This retains a low-powered two-shaft propulsion arrangement similar in concept to that of the 'Brooke Marine 32.6m' design, although with more highly powered engines for better performance. The greater size of the hull provides better seakeeping qualities, and also offers the right combination of larger area and greater volume for a more effective armament layout. Placed by Oman, the first order covered three examples of the 'Al Bushra'

Faced with the possibility of sustained coastal operations in its own waters as well as those along the eastern coast of Asia, the Japanese navy has long been an exponent of the FAC in its torpedo-armed form.

class of FAC(G)s, armed with two 40mm Bofors guns in single mountings forward and aft. These were commissioned in 1973, and were revised between 1977 and 1978 as FAC(M/G)s with two container-launchers for MM.38 Exocet missiles. Another four units were delivered in 1977 as FAC(G)s with a 3in OTO Melara Compact gun on the forecastle under control of an optical director, this useful main gun being supplemented by one 20mm cannon and two medium machine guns. The other main operator of the 'Brooke Marine 37.5m' design is Algeria, which has two British- and seven Algerian-built craft of the 'Kebir' class. This is an FAC(G) type of modest performance, and the armament comprises one 3in OTO Melara Compact gun on the forecastle as well as two 23mm Soviet cannon in a twin mounting aft, where they replace a single 20mm Oerlikon cannon.

The largest of Brooke Marine's designs currently in service is the 137ft (41.8m) type, which is used by Australia in the form of the 'Fremantle' class. This comprises 15 simple FAC(G)s with limited armament, and the craft are used mainly for patrol duties.

The UK had done little with the concept of fast combat craft since the end of World War II. In the second half of the 1960s, however, the Royal Navy became sufficiently concerned with the threat posed by fast combat craft to order a class of three FACs to train the crews of its major warships in the tactics to counter their attacks. The 'Scimitar' class was designed and built by Vosper Thornycroft, and the three craft were delivered in 1969 and 1970. With a full-load displacement of 102 tons on a laminated wooden hull measuring 100ft 0in (30.5m), the craft were each fitted with a CODOG propulsion arrangement whose two shafts were powered by two 90hp (67kW) Foden diesels for cruising or two 4,500hp (3,355kW) Rolls-Royce Proteus gas turbines for a maximum speed of 40 knots. At much the same time, Vosper Thornycroft evolved its 'Tenacity' class design and built a single craft as a private venture. This had a full-load displacement of 220 tons on a hull that measured 144ft 8in (44.1m) in length. The propulsion arrangement was of the CODOG type with the three shafts powered by two 600hp (445kW) Paxman diesels for cruising or three 4,250hp (3,170kW) Rolls-Royce Proteus gas turbines for a maximum speed of 39 knots. This design experience is reflected in a number of types which Vosper Thornycroft evolved for the export market during the 1960s and early 1970s. Typical of these are the 'Vosper Thornycroft 103ft', 'Vosper Thornycroft

Typical features of the British MTBt in World War II were the primary armament of two 21in (533mm) torpedo tubes and a secondary armament of two 0.5in (12.7mm) machine guns in a 'pulpit' twin mounting abaft the bridge and complemented by two or four 0.303in (7.7mm) machine guns in single or twin mountings.

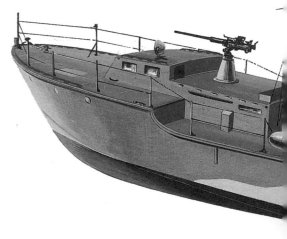

With its *Schnellboote* developed in the period after 1920, Germany opted for a larger type of attack craft that offered greater weapon capability and better sea-keeping qualities at the expense of outright speed. The S10, for example, had a displacement of 78 tons, length of 106ft 4in (32.4m), armament of two 21in (533mm) torpedo tubes and one 20mm cannon, propulsion in the form of three Daimler-Benz MB 502 diesel engines delivering 3,960hp (2,955kW) to three shafts for a speed of 35 knots, and complement of 20.

Built in moderately large numbers during World War II, the Japanese 'Type T14' class of MTBs was characterised by a displacement of 15 tons, length of 49ft 0in (14.9m), armament of two 18in (457mm) torpedoes and one 25mm cannon or 0.51in (13mm) machine gun, and a propulsion arrangement in the form of one Type 91 petrol engine delivering 920hp (685kW) for a speed of 28 knots.

110ft' and 'Vosper Thornycroft 121ft' classes. The first was built as the 24-strong 'Kris' FAC(G) class for Malaysia, the second was produced in three related FAC(G) forms for Abu Dhabi and Singapore, and the third appeared in three forms including a dedicated FAC(M) type for Brunei and related FAC(G) and FAC(M) variants for Venezuela.

The different conceptual approaches of Vosper Thornycroft and Brooke Marine to the design of fast combat craft is highlighted by the superior combat potential of the 'Tenacity' design to Brooke Marine's less powerful types. This superiority received concrete expression in 1977, when Egypt ordered six FAC(M)s to a design which Vosper Thornycroft extrapolated from that of the 'Tenacity' type. The design of the 'Ramadan' class is a good example of the way in which careful design thinking can pack maximum offensive capability into a comparatively small hull, in this instance possessing a full-load displacement of 310 tons on a length of 170ft 7in (52.0m). The armament is impressive and of Italian origins, and comprises two twin container-launchers for Otomat Mk 1 missiles between the superstructure and the deck house, one 3in OTO Melara Compact gun on the forecastle, and two 40mm Bofors guns in a Breda Compact twin mounting over the stern. The propulsion arrangement is based on West German diesels powering four shafts for a maximum speed of 40 knots.

From the design of the 'Ramadan' class, Vosper Thornycroft developed the 'Province' FAC(M/G) design for Oman, which ordered three craft in the early 1980s and followed with a contract for the fourth in 1986. The design of the 'Province' class provides slightly greater dimensions for a hull of proportionately finer line and, despite the greater displacement, this ensures high performance with a four-shaft propulsion arrangement with basically the same power as that in the 'Ramadan' class. The craft were delivered in two differing standards, for while all have the same barrelled armament of one 3in OTO Melara Compact gun and two 40mm Bofors guns in a Breda Compact twin mounting, the first and last three units have respectively two triple and quadruple container-launchers for the MM.40 variant of the Exocet. The same basic type was ordered by Kenya, which thus received two craft with a well-balanced weapon fit with lighter missile armament than the Omani units.

In the 15 years after World War II, the USA had produced or funded for overseas construction a considerable number of motor gun boats (MGBs) (PGM 33-83, PGM 91 and PGM 102-124), but these were for allied rather than American use. In the early 1960s, however, the Cuban missile crisis highlighted the US Navy's lack of fast combat craft for use in confined waters such as the Gulf of Mexico. It was therefore decided to built a 22-strong class of MGBs, though the classification was altered to 'patrol combatant' during 1967. The resulting 'Asheville' class was developed for coastal patrol and blockade, but in the event only 17 of the class were completed between 1966 and 1971 by Tacoma Boatbuilding and Peterson Builders. The type has a CODOG propulsion arrangement for long range at a modest cruising speed and high speed for combat, and the armament is based on a 3in gun in an enclosed mounting forward of the bridge and a 40mm Bofors gun in an open mounting over the stern. Most of these craft saw extensive patrol service in the Vietnam War, and in the mid-1970s four of them were adapted as FAC(M)s with an armament of four Standard Missiles (in its anti-radar form) for service in the Mediterranean as counters to Soviet 'tattletale' vessels. The craft had a very good reputation for seaworthiness, but were decidedly uncomfortable in any sort of sea and suffered propeller cavitation problems that prevented them from attaining their theoretical maximum speed of 40 knots or more.

Below: As well as being heavier, larger and better armed than their earlier brethren, the German *Schnellboote* built in the later part of World War II were fitted with an armoured bridge. This was originally a cast unit of curved shape, but production difficulties meant that most of these bridge units were of the polygonal type illustrated here. The boats had a normal displacement in the order of 105 tons, length of 114ft 6in (34.9m), armament of two 21in (533mm) torpedo tubes and varying numbers of 37mm and 20mm cannon, propulsion in the form of Daimler-Benz diesel engines delivering 7,500hp (5,590kW) to three shafts for a speed of 39 knots, and complement of 15-20.

In the late 1950s, the US Navy also began to acquire an interest in hydrofoil craft for very high speeds, but the sole class to emerge has been the 'Pegasus' class of six high-speed hydrofoils each armed with a single 3in Mk 75 gun forward of the bridge structure and two quadruple container-launchers for eight RGM-84 Harpoon missiles above the stern. As such, the craft are the US Navy's most potent combatants on the basis of firepower per displacement ton. The craft can be highly effective in the right conditions, but they lack the range, endurance and versatility of larger warships. The 'Pegasus' class FAH(M/G)s thus fall outside the main tactical organisation of their operating service, which is concerned primarily with deep-water operations.

Even though the 'Asheville' class failed to find any real favour with the US Navy, Tacoma Boatbuilding was confident that the basic type had an export potential, especially amongst East and South-East Asian nations. The company therefore used the 'Asheville' design as the basis of its Patrol Ship Multi-Mission Mk 5 (PSMM Mk 5) type with a two-shaft COGOG propulsion arrangement using no fewer than six gas turbines. The first customer for the type was South Korea, which operates a large force of fast combat craft against the constant threat of North Korean aggression. The parent company built the first four of the eight craft, the initial three of them reflecting the type's ancestry in a missile armament of four Standard Missiles (each carrying a seeker designed to home on the target vessel's radar emissions) and an American 3in gun. The last American-built unit switched to the definitive armament of two twin container-launchers for the RGM-84 Harpoon missile and the 3in OTO Melara Compact gun. Construction of the last four units was undertaken by a South Korean subsidiary, and this has also built four somewhat different 'Dagger' class FAC(M)s for Indonesia, with a CODOG propulsion arrangement and the revised armament of two twin container-launchers for four MM.38 Exocet missiles, one 57mm Bofors SAK 57 Mk 1 gun, one 40mm Bofors gun and two 20mm cannon. Another customer for the 'PSMM Mk 5' class was Taiwan, the island nation that until very recently regarded itself as being at war with the communist regime on the Chinese mainland. Clearly, the main Chinese threat to Taiwan's continued independence was a seaborne invasion, and against this threat Taiwan maintains powerful naval defences including a force of FACs for the destruction of any elements of the invading force that break through the main offshore defences. Tacoma Boatbuilding thus produced the first unit of the Taiwanese 'Lung Chiang' class, a type similar to the South Korean class with a two-shaft CODOG propulsion arrangement and a barrelled armament of one 3in OTO Melara Compact gun backed by two 30mm Oerlikon cannon in an Emerson Electric twin mounting. The missile armament comprises four container-launchers for the Hsiung Feng I (licence-built version of the Israeli Gabriel) missile. The second unit was licence-built in Taiwan, which planned a large class with the RGM-84 Harpoon missile and an American fire-control system. Under Chinese pressure, the Americans refused to export the Harpoon to Taiwan, which then dropped its plan for a major 'Lung Chiang' class. The only other operator of the 'PSMM Mk 5' type is Thailand, which has six 'Sattahip' class craft that are FAC(G)s, useful mainly for patrol and training with their low-powered propulsion arrangement and comparatively light gun armament.

Peterson Builders also have construction capability for a range of ship types and sizes, and this is reflected in the company's main export success in the field of fast combat craft, the nine units of the 'Al Siddiq' class of FAC(M/G)s for Saudi Arabia. These feature toward the upper end of the fast combat craft size scale, but have a two-shaft CODOG propulsion

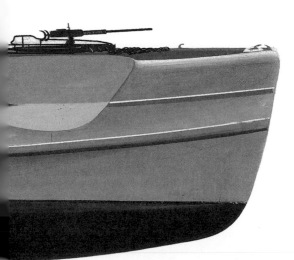

Above: Bahrain is one of 11 countries that operates the 'Lürssen FPB/TNC-45' type of FAC. These four FAC(M)s have a full-load displacement of 259 tons, length of 147ft 4in (44.9m), armament of two twin launchers for four MM.40 Exocet anti-ship missiles, one 3in (76mm) dual-purpose gun in a single turret and two 40mm dual-purpose guns in a twin mounting, propulsion in the form of four MTU diesel engines delivering 15,395hp (11,480kW) to four shafts for a speed of 41.5 knots, and complement of 36.

arrangement for high gas turbine-engined speed and good diesel-engined range. The craft were designed specifically for the anti-ship role, and the armament of each unit is centred on one 3in OTO Melara Compact gun, located on the forecastle forward of the superstructure, and the modest anti-ship missile fit of two twin container-launchers for the RGM-84 Harpoon weapon, located near the stern. Aft of the missile installation is the Phalanx close-in weapon system mounting, whose 20mm six-barrel rotary cannon has excellent fields of fire for its primary task of destroying incoming anti-ship missiles.

By far the world's largest operator of fast combat craft is China, whose navy has been confined almost exclusively to the coast defence role until very recent times, when deeper strategic thinking combined with the possibility of natural resources in the South China Sea to persuade the Chinese to begin development of a technologically more advanced navy possessing offshore capability. China has a long coastline whose many good harbours are supplemented by even larger numbers of well-positioned smaller harbours. With no real naval threat but the posturing and nuisance raids of Taiwan to fear, China rightly decided that the best way to ensure coastal security, and at the same time build the nucleus of a strong navy, lay with the creation of a large force of fast combat craft that could become technologically more sophisticated as Chinese industry and service personnel evolved the necessary skills. The core of this operational philosophy began in the early 1950s, when the Chinese navy used armed examples of local craft. On this basis, and with considerable technical and material assistance from the Soviets, the Chinese began to develop a more advanced fast combat craft capability toward the middle of the decade. Precise details are lacking, but it seems that from 1952, more than 70 'P 4' class motor torpedo boats (MTBs) were transferred from the USSR to China. It is probable that a comparatively small number of improved 'P 6' class MTBs were transferred at a slightly later date, and that these were used as pattern craft for Chinese construction of about 80 boats. This experience allowed the Chinese to begin development of their own types, starting with the 'Huchuan' FAH(T) that entered production in 1966 as the world's first foil-equipped naval vessel. Despite the fact that the type was only of the semi-foil variety, with the forward part of the hull lifted by the foil and the rear part planing, the design was clearly successful in meeting Chinese expectations, and production totalled just under 200 units.

Like the Soviets, however, the Chinese had seen the virtue of combining torpedo- and missile-armed FACs for the type of two-handed punch that could take an enemy force off balance and inflict severe losses. In the early 1960s, the Chinese navy had received from the USSR some seven or eight 'Komar' class FAC(M)s, and from this simple type the Chinese evolved the 'Hegu' design with a steel rather than wooden hull of slightly modified form and the position of the missile container-launchers moved slightly inboard by comparison with the Soviet original. These were limited but effective FAC(M)s, but the Chinese have maintained the type in service long past the time when simple electronic countermeasures have made it easy for any modestly sophisticated navy to defeat the missile carried by the 'Hegu' class craft.

As in the pattern established earlier with the MTBs, the Soviets followed deliveries of the 'Komar' class craft with some four examples of the two improved 'Osa I' class (in this instance with four 30mm rather than 25mm cannon in two twin mountings) as well as the technical information that allowed the Chinese to build this type as the 'Huangfen' class. The Chinese-built craft differ in detail from the Soviet original, and for an unexplained reason the class is credited with a maximum speed of 41 knots to the Soviet

Opposite top: The *Achimota* is one of two 'Lürssen FPB/PB-57' class FAC(G)s operated by Ghana, one of eight countries operating craft of this basic type. The Ghanaian vessels have a full-load displacement of 389 tons, length of 190ft 7in (58.1m), armament of one 3in (76mm) dual-purpose gun in a single turret and one 40mm dual-purpose gun in a single mounting, propulsion in the form of three MTU diesel engines delivering 10,665hp (7,950kW) to three shafts for a speed of 33 knots, and complement of 45.

Opposite centre: The *Roebuck* was one of 23 frigates built in World War II and revised in the mid-1950s as the 'Rapid' class of specialised anti-submarine escorts with a full-load displacement of 2,850 tons, length of 358ft 3in (109.2m), armament of two 4in (102mm) dual-purpose guns in a twin turret, two 40mm anti-aircraft guns in a twin mounting, two 21in (533mm) torpedo tubes, and two 'Squid' or 'Limbo' anti-submarine mortars, propulsion in the form of geared steam turbines delivering 40,000hp (29,815kW) to two shafts for a speed of 36.75 knots, and complement of 195.

The US Navy's current force of FACs is limited to six 'Pegasus' class missile-armed hydrofoils, of which this is the *Aquila*. The details of the class include a full-load displacement of 240 tons, length of 132ft 10in (40.5m) with the hydrofoils extended, armament of one 3in (76mm) dual-purpose gun in a single turret and two quadruple launchers for eight Harpoon anti-ship missiles.

type's 35 knots. The 'Huangfen' class is still the backbone of the Chinese fast combat craft force but, as with the 'Hegu' class operating the same missile, its combat capability has been virtually removed in recent years by the widespread adoption of electronic countermeasures by potentially hostile navies. This fact has been recognised by China, which is now retrofitting a more modern type of anti-ship missile, which has the additional advantages of smaller size and reduced weight so that a greater number of missiles can be installed. In recent years, the Chinese have made considerable but mostly unsuccessful attempts to upgrade their fast combat craft capability, often with the aid of Western companies. Older missiles have been supplemented and largely replaced by more modern weapons, but the Chinese government's suppression of the emergent democracy movement has led to the effective halt on all programmes of Western technical support for types such as the 'H3' class.

Thus in many parts of the world the concept of fast combat craft is alive and flourishing. Many emerging countries find such craft an ideal way to begin development of their navies, with larger and more sophisticated craft bought to match their developing skills and increased operational ambitions. Many less affluent countries have discovered that such craft are a cost-effective method of maintaining a national presence in territorial waters and offshore zones of possible commercial importance. But in general the countries that make the greatest and potentially most effective use of fast combat craft are those with confined coastal waters or chokepoints where major maritime routes are constricted by geographical factors. It is therefore no coincidence that areas where concentrations of fast combat craft are to be found include the Baltic Sea and its exit into the North Sea; the Mediterranean (especially at its western end near the Strait of Gibraltar, its centre near the Sicilian Narrows, its north offshoot in the Adriatic Sea, its north-eastern corner into the Aegean Sea, and its eastern end where Israel and several Arab nations vie with each other); the Persian Gulf; South-East Asia where there are several chokepoints such as the Malacca Strait; the eastern coast of Asia; and various parts of South America where limited finance and confined waters combine with nationalistic and economic rivalries.

The Aircraft Carrier

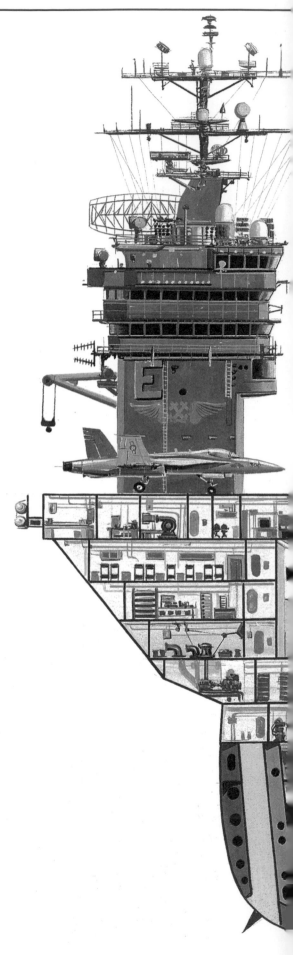

I T was an American who made the first take-off from and first landing on a ship. In November 1909 Eugene Ely flew off the cruiser *Birmingham* and in January 1911 he landed on the cruiser *Pennsylvania*, in both instances using a Curtiss biplane. The mantle then passed to the British, and in 1912 the first British aircraft operations began with a take-off from the moored battleship *Hibernia* during January and continued with a take-off from the moving battleship *Africa* in May. This capability was seen at the time as experimental, and more serious consideration was given to the use of aircraft in their flying boat and floatplane forms as adjuncts of naval operations. The first ship completed for this task was the *Ark Royal*, which was converted during construction from a collier into a seaplane carrier with internal accommodation for seaplanes that were lifted into and out of the water by a crane. Although successful in basic terms, the *Ark Royal* lacked the speed and range to support fleet operations, and the faster English Channel ferries *Empress*, *Engadine*, *Riviera*, *Ben-my-Chree*, *Manxman*, *Vindex*, *Pegasus* and *Nairana* were converted into seaplane carriers and saw valuable service, and these were supplemented by the converted liner *Campania*. Seaplane operations were cumbersome, however, and several of the ships were later fitted with a flying-off platform allowing the operation of wheeled aircraft, which were initially converted floatplanes but later standard 'landplane' types.

As World War I continued, the importance of aircraft for all surface operations, sea as well as land, increased dramatically and thought was given to the creation of larger ships to carry a greater number of aircraft that could be operated from longer platforms at higher weights. The light battle-cruiser *Furious* was converted into an aircraft carrier for service from March 1918, and was supplemented from October 1918 by the *Vindictive* and *Argus*, which had been laid down as a cruiser and a liner respectively. As the war ended in November 1918, the UK was building two more aircraft carriers as the *Eagle*, whose hull had been laid down as that of a sister ship to the battleship *Canada*, and the *Hermes* that was the first ship to be designed as an aircraft carrier.

During the 1920s, *Furious* was rebuilt to full aircraft carrier standard with a flush flightdeck, and her two light battle-cruiser half-sisters *Courageous* and *Glorious* were also converted to this standard, with a starboard-side 'island', in the period between 1924 and 1930. This gave the British a force of four large battleships by the mid-1930s. The two 'Courageous' class ships each had a displacement of 22,500 tons, an armament by the beginning of World War II of sixteen 4.7in (120mm) anti-aircraft guns in single mountings as well as provision for 48 aircraft, protection in the form of a 3in (76mm) belt and deck, and a speed of 30.5 knots on the 90,000hp (67,105kW) delivered to four shafts by geared steam turbines. The *Furious* had a displacement of 22,450 tons, an armament by the beginning of World War II of twelve 4in (102mm) anti-aircraft guns in six twin mountings and twenty-four 2pdr anti-aircraft guns in three octuple mountings as well as provision

118

for 33 aircraft, protection in the form of a 3in (76mm) belt and deck, and a speed of 30.5 knots on the 90,000hp (67,105kW) delivered to four shafts by geared steam turbines. The *Eagle* had a displacement of 22,600 tons, an armament by the beginning of World War II of nine 6in (152mm) guns in single mountings, four 4in anti-aircraft guns in single mountings and eight 2pdr anti-aircraft guns in an octuple mounting as well as provision for 21 aircraft, protection in the form of a 7in (178mm) belt and 4in (102mm) deck, and a speed of 24 knots on the 50,000hp (37,280kW) delivered to four shafts by geared steam turbines.

Experience with these large carriers as well as a few small carriers benefited the British between the world wars, and in the later part of the 1930s they produced a new *Ark Royal* to embody the lessons of this experience in an altogether larger ship with better protection (passive armour as well as active guns) and a large aircraft complement of which most could be accommodated in a large two-storied hangar under the full-length flightdeck. The ship had a displacement of 22,000 tons, an armament of sixteen 4.5in (114mm) anti-aircraft guns in eight twin mountings, forty-eight 2pdr anti-aircraft guns in six octuple mountings and thirty-two 0.5in (12.7mm) machine guns in eight quadruple mountings, as well as 72 aircraft, protection in the form of a 4.5in (114mm) belt and 3in (76mm) deck, and a speed of 30.75 knots on the 102,000hp.

By the period immediately preceding World War II, the British had decided that the threat posed by aircraft to the aircraft carrier had reached such a level that the demands of survivability could only be met by the adoption of an armoured hangar below an armoured flightdeck, and the greater topweight generated by this change dictated that a single-level

This cross-section reveals the great size and complexity of the modern aircraft carrier, in this instance the *Abraham Lincoln* of the US Navy's superb 'Nimitz' class of nuclear-powered ships.

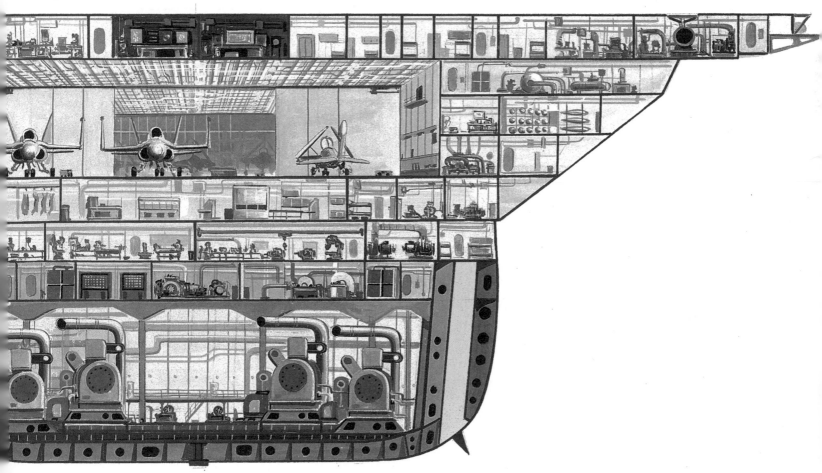

hangar had to be used with a consequent reduction in aircraft capacity to 36 in the 'Illustrious' class carriers, which were the first full series-built carriers to reach British service. The class was planned as six ships, but while the first three were completed to the originally planned standard, the last three were delivered to a modified standard with an additional half-hangar aft even though this meant a reduction in the armouring of the ships' upper sections. The original four 'Illustrious' class carriers were delivered in the first half of World War II and each had a displacement of 23,000 tons, an armament of sixteen 4.5in anti-aircraft guns in eight twin mountings, forty-eight 2pdr anti-aircraft guns in six octuple mountings and eight 20mm cannon in single mountings, as well as 36 aircraft, protection in the form of a 4.5in (114mm) belt and hangar side and 3in (76mm) deck, and a speed of 31 knots on the 110,000hp (82,015kW) delivered to four shafts by geared steam turbines. The last two carriers of the class were delivered later in World War II and each had a displacement of 26,000 tons, an armament of sixteen 4.5in anti-aircraft guns in eight twin mountings, forty-eight 2pdr anti-aircraft guns in six octuple mountings and thirty-eight 20mm cannon in 17 twin and four single mountings, as well as 72 aircraft, protection in the form of a 4.5in (114mm) belt, 1.5in (38mm) hangar side and 3in (76mm) deck, and a speed of 32 knots on the 148,000hp (110,350kW) delivered to four shafts by geared steam turbines.

These were the last fleet carriers to be completed in the UK during World War II, although two of four 'Audacious' class fleet carriers were completed after the end of the war, and further aircraft deliveries were therefore for the light and escort carriers. The light carriers were essentially scaled-down fleet carriers, and the first of them in British service were the 10 units of the 'Colossus' class, of which only six were operational by the end of World War II in the form of four light carriers and two maintenance carriers. The light carriers were completed to a standard that included a displacement of 13,190 tons, an armament of twenty-four 2pdr anti-aircraft guns in six quadruple mountings and nineteen 40mm anti-aircraft guns in single mountings, as well as 48 aircraft, only light protection, and a speed of 25 knots on the 42,000hp (31,315kW) delivered to two shafts by geared steam turbines. The two maintenance carriers had lighter gun armament and no

Seen here in the late 1930s, the *Enterprise* was one of the three aircraft carriers of the US Navy's 'Yorktown' class, and the ship's details included a full-load displacement of 22,900 tons, length of 827ft 4in (252.2m), armament of eight 5in (127mm) guns in single mountings and 81 aircraft launched with the aid of three catapults, propulsion in the form of geared steam turbines delivering 120,000hp (89,470kW) to four shafts for a speed of 33 knots, and complement of 2,920 in war.

aircraft, and were designed for support of the British naval force operating with the US Pacific Fleet. The other four ships were completed after the war, and four of the class were later transferred to friendly nations (Australia, Brazil, Canada, Argentina, France, and the Netherlands).

There followed five of six light carriers of the 'Majestic' class that were launched during the war but completed after it, with a displacement of 14,000 tons, an armament of thirty 40mm anti-aircraft guns in six twin and 18 single mountings, as well as 34 aircraft, only light protection, and a speed of 24.5 knots on the 42,000hp (31,315kW) delivered to two shafts by geared steam turbines. All of these ships were later transferred or sold to friendly nations (two to Australia, two to Canada and one to India).

There should have followed eight units of the larger and more capable 'Hermes' class 'intermediate fleet carrier' type with somewhat higher performance as a result of their considerably more powerful propulsion arrangement, but only four of these were laid down for launch and completion after the end of the war, with a displacement of 18,300 tons, an armament of thirty-two 40mm anti-aircraft guns in two sextuple, eight twin and four single mountings, as well as 50 aircraft, protection in the form of a 1in (25mm) deck, and a speed of 29.5 knots on the 83,000hp (61,885kW) delivered to four shafts by geared steam turbines.

The escort carrier was built to a small and less capable standard as it was designed originally for the convoy escort role and later used additionally for the support of amphibious operations. The ships were initially converted from large merchant ships but later were built specifically for the task although generally to mercantile standards. Most of the ships were of American origin, and the vessels used by the Royal Navy included the five units of the 'Archer' class, 26 units of the 'Ruler' class, and four miscellaneous ships. The 'Ruler' class may be taken as typical of the breed, and its details included a full-length hangar under the flightdeck, a displacement of 11,420 tons, an armament of two 4in anti-aircraft guns in single mountings, sixteen 40mm anti-aircraft guns in eight twin mountings and twenty 20mm cannon in single mountings, as well as 24 aircraft, no protection, and a speed of 17 knots on the 9,350hp (6,970kW) delivered to one shaft by a geared steam turbine.

In the period after World War II, the UK was financially straitened and was already beginning its retreat from empire, so no new aircraft carriers were laid down for some time and the Royal Navy relied on its existing units, albeit in forms that were often upgraded to a

Seen in the background is the British aircraft carrier *Argus*, which was the first ship of its type with a full-length flightdeck. Completed in the last stages of World War I, the ship was used mainly as an aircraft ferry and training carrier in World War II before succumbing to the attentions of the breakers immediately after the end of that war.

The *Amagi* and *Akagi* were Japanese battle-cruisers taken in hand during construction for conversion into aircraft carriers, but the *Amagi* became a constructive total loss while still incomplete during the course of a 1923 earthquake, and was scrapped.

significant degree with features such as the angled flightdeck and the mirror landing system, which were both British inventions. The force available by the middle of the 1950s included the three units of the 'Hermes' class revised as the 'Centaur' class, the lead ship of the 'Audacious' class completed as the sole 'Eagle' class ship with a full-load displacement of 53,390 tons and provision for up to 60 aircraft, the other unit of the 'Audacious' class completed as the sole unit of the 'Ark Royal' class with a full-load displacement of 53,060 tons and provision for up to 36 aircraft, and the *Victorious* of the 'Illustrious' class revised to a more modern standard with a full-load displacement of 35,500 tons and provision for up to 36 aircraft.

The sole later addition in the 1950s was the 'Hermes' class carrier with a full-load displacement of 28,700 tons and provision for up to 28 aircraft. In the late 1960s, the UK decided that large aircraft carriers were no longer appropriate to the country's reduced world status and were also too expensive in maintenance and construction, and they were gradually phased out of service in the 1970s, although two units enjoyed a further lease of life into the early 1980s as commando carriers.

Right: This cross-section of an American aircraft carrier of the World War II period reveals the extensive compartmentalisation and double skinning which, in concert with comparatively lavish and well-disposed armour, made such ships difficult targets for torpedoes and gunfire. The 'aircraft' part of the ship was built as an added superstructure, however, and being considerably less well protected was distinctly vulnerable to bombing attack.

Opposite: This cross-section of the *Illustrious*, a British aircraft carrier of the World War II period, reveals the British system of incorporating the 'aircraft' part of the ship into the main hull, thereby affording it considerably better protection than the comparable section of American aircraft carriers.

The last British aircraft carriers, which are still in useful service after launch between 1977 and 1981, are the three light carriers of the 'Invincible' class, which were designed to carry helicopters and fixed-wing aircraft of the short take-off, vertical landing STOVL type, the latter in the form of the British Aerospace Sea Harrier. These carriers each have a full-load displacement of some 23,000 tons, an armament of one twin-arm launcher for Sea Dart surface-to-air missiles and two 20mm Vulcan six-barrel cannon in Phalanx close-in weapon system mountings, as well as 14 aircraft, and a speed of 28 knots on the 112,000shp (83,505kW) delivered to two shafts by a COGOG propulsion arrangement with four Rolls-Royce Olympus gas turbines.

The American involvement with carrierborne aviation began in 1922 with the conversion of the collier *Jupiter* into the aircraft carrier *Langley*. This ship provided the fledgling naval air arm with initial experience, and this facilitated the entry into service late in the same decade of the two fleet carriers of the 'Saratoga' class which, as a result of the Washington Naval Treaty limitation on capital ship construction, were converted during construction from battle-cruisers into aircraft carriers. When completed, the ships were the largest and probably the most advanced aircraft carriers in the world with a full-load displacement of 39,000 tons, an armament of eight 8in (203mm) guns in four twin turrets and twelve 5in (127mm) anti-aircraft guns in single mountings, as well as 90 aircraft, protection in the form of a 6in (152mm) belt and 3in (76mm) deck, and a speed of 34 knots on the 180,000hp (134,210kW) delivered to four shafts by a turbo-electric propulsion arrangement.

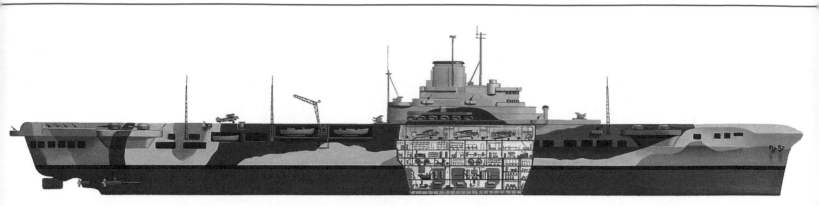

The first American aircraft carrier designed as such was the following *Ranger*, which was launched in 1933 and completed to a standard that included a displacement of 14,500 tons, an armament of eight 5in (127mm) anti-aircraft guns in single mountings, as well as 86 aircraft, protection in the form of a 2in (51mm) belt and 1in (25mm) deck, and a speed of 29.5 knots on the 53,500hp (39,890kW) delivered to two shafts by geared steam turbines.

Experience indicated that the *Ranger*, built to Treaty limitations and therefore lacking in protection and performance to ensure that a large number of aircraft could be embarked, was inadequate as a first-line aircraft carrier. The two following units of the 'Yorktown' class, both launched in 1936, were therefore completed to a larger and more capable standard with a full-load displacement of 25,500 tons, an armament of eight 5in anti-aircraft guns in single mountings, as well as 100 aircraft, protection in the form of a 4in (102mm) belt and 3in (76mm) deck, and a speed of 34 knots on the 120,000hp (82.015kW) delivered to four shafts by geared steam turbines. These two ships were the *Yorktown* and the *Enterprise*, and in 1940 a half-sister was launched as the *Hornet* with a slightly larger flightdeck and a number of other improved features.

The last American aircraft carrier completed before the entry of the USA into World War II was the *Wasp*, which was a small carrier along the lines of the *Ranger* and designed to fill the American quota for aircraft carrier tonnage under the terms of the Washington Naval Treaty. The American philosophy at this time was that all must be subordinated to aircraft-carrying capability, and as the *Wasp* carried very nearly as many aircraft as the ships of the 'Yorktown' class, major sacrifices had to be made in protection and speed. As completed, the ship had details including a full-load displacement

The *Formidable* was a unit of the first subclass of the 'Illustrious' class of British fleet aircraft carriers, and was launched in 1939 for service through World War II before being scrapped in 1953. The details of the ship included a displacement of 23,000 tons, length of 753ft 6in (229.7m), armament of sixteen 4.5in (114mm) dual-purpose guns in eight twin turrets, forty-eight 2pdr anti-aircraft guns in six quadruple mountings, eight 20mm cannon in single mountings, and 36 aircraft, protection in the form of a 4.5in (114mm) belt and hangar sides and 3in (76mm) deck, propulsion in the form of geared steam turbines delivering 110,000hp (82,015kW) to three shafts for a speed of 31 knots, and complement of 1,390.

Seen here in 1950, the *Oriskany* was one of the 15 units of the 'Modified Essex' class of fleet aircraft carriers delivered in the later stages of World War II. The details of the ship included a full-load displacement of 38,000 tons, length of 888ft 0in (270.7m), armament of twelve 5in (127mm) anti-aircraft guns in four twin and four single turrets, seventy-two 40mm anti-aircraft guns in 18 quadruple mountings, 52 20mm cannon in single mountings, and 80 aircraft launched with the aid of two catapults, propulsion in the form of steam turbines delivering 150,000hp (111,840kW) to four shafts for a speed of 33 knots, and complement of 3,450.

of 21,000 tons, an armament of eight 5in (127mm) anti-aircraft guns in single mountings, as well as 84 aircraft, protection in the form of a 4in (102mm) belt and 1.5in (38mm) deck, and a speed of 29.5 knots on the 75,000hp (55,920kW) delivered to two shafts by geared steam turbines.

By the late 1930s, the radical worsening of international relations combined with the US Navy's considerable experience in carrier operations to make feasible the design of a completely new type of aircraft carrier. This was the 'Essex' class, which became the mainstay of the US Navy's carrier force in World War II and was built to the final extent of 26 ships. The design included a size comparable with that of the 'Saratoga' class battle-cruiser conversions with the pure aircraft carrier design features of the 'Ranger', 'Yorktown' and 'Wasp' classes, in a type that was optimised for far-ranging operations through the incorporation of more 'ship' qualities, much improved protection based not so much on thicker armour as on increased compartmentalisation and, for maximum aircraft operating capability (including the possibility of upgrade to larger and heavier warplane types), a large flightdeck with an overhanging port side, two catapults and three large elevators (including one deck-edge rather than inset unit) connecting the hangar and flightdeck. The one weak point of the design, certainly relative to British practice at this time, was the installation of the flightdeck as an essentially unarmoured superstructure element rather than as an intrinsic and armoured part of the hull. Even so, the 'Essex' class carriers were superb warships that possessed the ability to survive considerable combat damage.

The details of the 'Essex' class aircraft carrier included a full-load displacement of 33,000 tons, an armament of twelve 5in anti-aircraft guns in four twin and four single mountings, between forty-four and seventy-two 40mm anti-aircraft guns in 11 to 18 quadruple mountings and fifty-two 20mm cannon in single mountings, as well as 100 aircraft, protection in the form of a 4in (102mm) belt and 3in (76mm) deck, and a speed of 33 knots on the 150,000hp (111,840kW) delivered to four shafts by geared steam turbines.

Experience with the 'Essex' class aircraft carriers showed that while these were excellent ships with considerable offensive and

The Brazilian navy's aircraft carrier *Minas Gerais* was originally constructed as the Vengeance of the British 'Colossus' class in World War II, but after purchase by Brazil in the mid-1950s was rebuilt in the Netherlands to a more advanced standard with an angled flightdeck, mirror landing system and a single steam catapult.

Seen in 1972, the year in which it was deleted, the *Albion* was laid down in World War II as a 'Hermes' class light carrier but completed after the war as one of three 'Centaur' class carriers with a full-load displacement of 27,000 tons, length of 737ft 9in (224.8m), armament of thirty-two 40mm anti-aircraft guns in two sextuple, eight twin and four single mountings, as well as 26 aircraft, propulsion in the form of geared steam turbines delivering 78,000hp (58,155kW) to two shafts for a speed of 28 knots, and complement of 1,100 excluding an air group of 300.

The *Clemenceau*, lead ship of a two-strong class of French aircraft carriers, was completed in 1961 with a full-load displacement of 32,780 tons, length of 869ft 5in (265.0m), provision for 38 aircraft, speed of 32 knots, and complement of 1,340.

Lead ship of a four-strong class that was the first type of aircraft carrier designed after World War II, the US Navy's *Forrestal* was completed in 1955 with details that include a full-load displacement of 80,385 tons, length of 1,086ft 0in (331.0m).

defensive capability, they were hampered by their lack of protection on and below the flightdeck. In the 'Midway' class, of which six were ordered but only three completed in the period after World War II, the opportunity was taken to increase size and displacement by an appreciable degree. This allowed improved horizontal and vertical armour to be worked into the design, and also provided for the carriage of a larger complement of current aircraft or a smaller number of newer and larger types as these entered service. Other features were the two aircraft-launching catapults, three elevators including one deck-edge unit, and the location of virtually all of the defensive armament in long sponsons along the sides of the hull. The details of this class included a full-load displacement of 60,000 tons, an armament of eighteen 5in dual-purpose guns in single turrets, eighty-four 40mm anti-

aircraft guns in 21 quadruple mountings and eighty-two 20mm cannon, as well as 137 aircraft, protection in the form of an 8in (203mm) belt and armoured decks, and a speed of 33 knots on the 212,000hp (158,065kW) delivered to four shafts by geared steam turbines.

Although the US Navy was a firm believer in the overall superiority of the large fleet carrier, the crisis in which it found itself in the days after the Japanese attack on Pearl Harbor persuaded the service to plan for the rapid introduction of a light carrier element based on the hulls of nine incomplete 'Cleveland' class cruisers. Such was the urgency of the programme that all of these very successful ships entered service in 1943, providing the US Navy with an excellent interim carrier capability until the larger 'Essex' class carriers could enter service. The details of this class included a full-load displacement of 15,100 tons, an armament of four 5in dual-purpose guns in single turrets, twenty-six 40mm anti-aircraft guns in two quadruple and nine twin mountings and forty 20mm cannon in single mountings, as well as 45 aircraft launched with the aid of two catapults, protection in the form of a 5in (127mm) belt and 3in (76mm) deck, and a speed of 32 knots on the 100,000hp (74,560kW) delivered to four shafts by geared steam turbines.

The same reasoning that led the British to the concept of the escort carrier was also relevant to the Americans, who saw in this type the possibility of large numbers built in a short time for tasks ranging from

Built basically to mercantile standards and equipped more austerely than fleet carriers, the small escort carriers produced in the USA during World War II were nonetheless vital ships that played a major strategic role in tasks such as convoy escort and the provision of air support for amphibious operations.

The *Ark Royal*, seen here in 1977, was the UK's last large fleet carrier. The ship was completed in 1955 and broken up in 1980, and its details included a full-load displacement of 53,060 tons, length of 811ft 9in (247.4m), provision for 36 aircraft, protection in the form of a 4.5in (114mm) belt, 1.5in (38mm) hangar side and 4in (102mm) deck, propulsion in the form of geared steam turbines delivering 152,000hp (113,330kW) to four shafts for a speed of 31.5 knots, and complement of 2,640 including the air group.

'The Great Marianas Turkey Shoot'

AFTER the US capture of the Gilbert and Marshall Islands between November 1943 and February 1944, the Imperial Japanese navy planned the long-sought 'decisive battle' of the naval war in the Pacific. Admiral Mineichi Koga, commander of the Combined Fleet, and Admiral Soemu Toyoda, succeeding Koga after the latter's death in an air accident on 1 April 1944, appreciated that the next forward move would take the Americans to the Mariana Islands on the Japanese home islands' strategic doorstep. This would enable them to strike at Japan, Iwo Jima in the Volcano Islands, Okinawa in the Ryukyu Islands, and Formosa with the intention of severing Japan's maritime links with the Philippines, South-East Asia and all their raw materials. The resulting Operation 'A' called for the American invasion force off the Marianas (in the event, Vice Admiral Raymond A. Spruance's 5th Fleet with the 5th Amphibious Force and Vice Admiral Marc Mitscher's Task Force 58) to be attacked by powerful surface forces moving in from the south-west, where they were based close to vital oil supplies. The operation was launched on 15 June 1944 under the command of Vice Admiral Jisaburo Ozawa, whose 1st Mobile Fleet from Tawitawi was supported by Vice Admiral Matome Ugaki's Southern Force from Batjan, the two forces rendezvousing east of the Philippines on 16 June, one day after the US forces landed on Saipan in the Marianas. The rendezvous gave Ozawa a fleet of three fleet and six light aircraft carriers (carrying 473 obsolescent warplanes including 222 fighters and about 200 attack aircraft, all manned by indifferent aircrew with a maximum of a mere six months' training), five battleships, 10 heavy and two light cruisers, and 22 destroyers. Task Force 58 comprised seven fleet and eight light aircraft carriers (with 956 modern warplanes manned by skilled aircrew, of whom even the least experienced had two years' training and 300 hours in the air), seven battleships, eight heavy and 13 light cruisers, and 69 destroyers.

The Japanese plan became apparent to Mitscher after the Japanese rendezvous was spotted by US patrol submarines, and the scene was thus set for the climactic Battle of the Philippine Sea (soon to become known as 'The Great Marianas Turkey Shoot') on 19/20 June 1944. Ozawa thought that the land-based warplanes commanded by Vice Admiral Kakuji Kakuta on Guam, Rota and Yap Islands had already struck hard blows at the US ships, and planned that his attack aircraft would rearm and refuel on these island bases. In reality the Japanese land-based aircraft had been virtually wiped out by American carrierborne aircraft, and the island airfields were being kept under constant attack: neither of these facts was reported by Kakuta to Ozawa. The Japanese carriers launched a first air strike early on 19 June, but the radar-warned Americans intercepted this initial wave 50 miles (80km) short of the US force, shooting down more than 200 Japanese aircraft. US submarines had meanwhile attacked Ozawa's force, torpedoeing the carriers *Taiho* and *Shokaku*, both of which sank. The Japanese second strike of 125 aircraft was intercepted on its way to Guam: once more, the Japanese aircraft were decimated, some 100 being lost. Two more Japanese attacks were handled in the same way; thus by the end of the first day, Ozawa had lost two carriers and 346 aircraft, whereas Mitscher had lost some 35 aircraft (29 of them in combat) and suffered damage to one battleship.

It was now the turn of the Americans to go over to the offensive, and Mitscher launched his aircraft from 16.24 on 20 June as TF58 pursued the Japanese fleet that was withdrawing to the north-west to refuel. The American strike sank two tankers and the carrier *Hiyo*, damaged the carriers *Zuikaku*, *Junyo* and *Chiyoda* plus the heavy cruiser *Maya*, and destroyed another 65 Japanese aircraft, for the loss of 20 of their own aircraft. It was night by the time the American aircraft headed for their parent carriers, which Mitscher ordered to turn on their lights as an aid to the pilots. Nevertheless some 80 US aircraft ran out of fuel and ditched, most of their crews being saved. Operation 'A' and the resultant Battle of the Philippine Sea may thus be seen as marking the end of the Imperial Japanese Navy's air arm as an effective weapon.

convoy escort and anti-submarine warfare to support of amphibious operations via the resupply of larger carriers (both fleet and light) and the reinforcement of island bases in the Pacific. The first of these classes was the 'Long Island' type, of which two were retained by the US Navy and the other four passed to the Royal Navy, and further construction yielded the 'Bogue' class of 11 ships excluding 26 transferred to the Royal Navy, the 'Sangamon' class of four ships, the 'Casablanca' class of 50 ships that were the first of the type built from the keel up as escort or 'jeep' carriers, and the 'Commencement Bay' class of 19 ships. The details of the 'Casablanca' class included a full-load displacement of 10,400 tons, an armament of one 5in dual-purpose gun, sixteen 40mm anti-aircraft guns in eight twin mountings and twenty-four 20mm cannon in single mountings, as well as 28 aircraft launched with the aid of one catapult, no protection, and a speed of 19 knots on the 9,000hp (6,710kW) delivered to two shafts by triple-expansion steam engines.

In the aftermath of World War II, the US Navy concentrated on the restoration of its war-weary carrier force to full capability and on the completion of those ships in the final stages of construction. The 1947 fleet strength therefore included 22 'Essex', three 'Midway', three 'Independence', two 'Saipan', four 'Bogue', six 'Casablanca' and 12 'Commencement Bay' class carriers. These ships remained in service or were taken in hand for conversion, either to an improved standard or for other roles, as the US Navy analysed the lessons of World War II. These included the inescapable conclusion that the aircraft carrier had replaced the battleship as the real capital ship, and the development of the US Navy's surface capability was now concentrated even more strongly on the operation of carrier battle groups as the core of American naval strength.

Shipbuilding resumed during the Korean War (1950-53), and included in this first generation of new ships were the four aircraft carriers of the

The *Independence* was the last of the four 'Forrestal' class conventionally powered aircraft carriers to be completed for the US Navy, which commissioned the ship in January 1959. The flightdeck arrangement of this ship includes a fore-and-aft bow section with two steam catapults, an angled section with two steam catapults and four sets of arrester wires, and four large deck-edge elevators located at three on the starboard side (one forward of the island and two abaft it) and one on the port side (near the forward edge of the angled flightdeck section).

Commissioned in the first half of the 1980s, the Royal Navy's three small carriers of the 'Invincible' class, here epitomised by the *Illustrious* photographed in 1983, were designed for the operation only of VTOL and STOVL aircraft, the former represented by helicopters and the latter by BAe Sea Harrier multi-role warplanes that are able to lift off at a moderately high weight as a result of their thrust-vectoring engine configuration and the 'ski jump' forward edge of the flightdeck. The details of the 'Invincible' class include a full-load displacement of 19,500 tons, length of 677ft 0in (206.6m), armament of two 20mm Vulcan six-barrel cannon in two Phalanx close-in weapon system mountings, two 20mm cannon in single mountings, one twin launcher for Sea Wolf surface-to-air missiles, and 21 aircraft (12 rotary-wing and nine fixed-wing machines), propulsion in the form of a COGAG arrangement with gas turbines delivering 94,000hp (70,085kW) to two shafts for a speed of 28 knots, and complement of 785 excluding an air group of 400.

Although larger than the 'Invincible' class ships, the three units of the USSR's 'Kiev' class bear a similarity to the British ships in being designed for the operation only of VTOL and STOVL aircraft. The ships are in effect hybrid missile cruisers and V/STOL aircraft carriers.

'Forrestal' class to a design scaled down from that of the *United States*, a large ship laid down (but then cancelled) as the carrier of the US Navy's new generation of strategic attack warplanes armed with free-fall nuclear weapons. The 'Forrestal' class ships were completed between 1955 and 1959 with all the latest aircraft developments including the angled flightdeck and mirror landing system, and its flightdeck carried four deck-edge elevators as well as four catapults. The details of this epoch-making class included a full-load displacement of 78,510 tons, an armament of eight 5in dual-purpose guns in single turrets, as well as 90 aircraft, unspecified protection, and a speed of 33 knots on the 280,000hp (208,770kW) delivered to four shafts by geared steam turbines.

The next four ships were completed between 1961 and 1968 as the 'Kitty Hawk' class to an improved 'Forrestal' class design, with a full-load displacement of 80,945 tons, an armament of two twin-arm launchers for 80 RIM-2 Terrier surface-to-air missiles, as well as 90 aircraft, unspecified protection, and a speed of 33.6 knots on the 280,000hp (208,770kW) delivered to four shafts by geared steam turbines. The last of the ships to be completed was the *John F. Kennedy*, which differs from the other ships in its improved underwater protection of the type developed for the first American nuclear-powered carrier.

This was the *Enterprise*, which was completed in 1961 with a full-load displacement of 89,085 tons, an armament of 90 aircraft supplemented by three octuple launchers for RIM-7 Sea Sparrow surface-to-air missiles, unspecified protection, and a speed of 32 knots on the 280,000hp (208,770kW) delivered to four shafts by the geared steam turbines supplied from eight Westinghouse A2W pressurised water-cooled reactors. The importance of this ship was enormous, for it opened the possibility of operational cruises of extreme range and endurance. The ship has virtually unlimited range without any need for oil fuel, and this leaves all the bunkerage for aviation fuel with consequent advantages in the amount of flying that can be undertaken before the bunkers need replenishment from supply ships: the real limitations to the length of an operational cruise are crew efficiency and the rate at which consumables (food and other manpower requirements, warplane spares, ammunition and bombs, and warplane fuel) can be replenished.

Opposite below: Although larger than the 'Invincible' class ships, the three units of the USSR's 'Kiev' class bear a similarity to the British ships in being designed for the operation only of VTOL and STOVL aircraft. The ships are in effect hybrid missile cruisers and V/STOL aircraft carriers, and their details include a full-load displacement of 37,100 tons, length of 895ft 9in (273.0m), armament of four 3in (76mm) dual-purpose guns in two twin turrets, eight 30mm six-barrel cannon in eight close-in weapon system mountings, four twin launchers for eight SS-N-12 'Sandbox' anti-ship missiles, two twin launchers for 72 SA-N-3 'Goblet' surface-to-air missiles, two twin launchers for 40 SA-N-4 'Gecko' surface-to-air missiles or, in one ship only, six octuple vertical launchers for 96 SA-N-9 surface-to-air missiles, one twin launcher for 20 FRAS anti-submarine rockets, two 12-tube anti-submarine rocket launchers, 10 21in (533mm) torpedo tubes in two quintuple mountings and 32 aircraft in the form of 19 rotary-wing and 13 fixed-wing machines, propulsion in the form of geared steam turbines delivering 201,180hp (150,000kW) to four shafts for a speed of 32 knots, and complement of 1,200 excluding an air group of unrevealed size.

Aircraft Carrier Attack on Pearl Harbor

OPERATION 'Z' was the Japanese attack on the US Pacific Fleet in Pearl Harbor on 7 December 1941, and this attack marked the entry of Japan into World War II. The operation was designed by Admiral Isoroku Yamamoto, Commander-in-Chief of the Combined Fleet, as a decisive stroke to eliminate Admiral Husband E. Kimmel's US Pacific Fleet at its base on Oahu Island in the Hawaiian group.

The force selected for the attack was Vice Admiral Chuichi Nagumo's 1st Air Fleet, comprising the fleet carriers Akagi, Kaga, Hiryu, Soryu, Shokaku and Zuikaku, the light cruiser Abukuma and nine destroyers, supported by the battleships Hiei and Kirishima, and by the heavy cruisers Tone and Chikuma; there were also three submarines for reconnaissance of the approach route for the 1st Air Fleet, two destroyers for the operation against Midway Island planned on the return journey, and a fleet train of eight tankers and supply ships. The 1st Air Fleet assembled in Tankan Bay in the Kurile Islands from 22 November 1941, and began to sail on 26 November, a circuitous northern route being selected to reduce the chances of detection. At 06.00 Nagumo began to launch his first strike force, consisting of 43 Mitsubishi A6M fighters, 51 Aichi D3A dive-bombers and 89 Nakajima B5N bombers (49 carrying 1,600lb/726kg armour-piercing shells modified as bombs and the other 40 carrying torpedoes specially modified for shallow running).

Shortly before 08.00 the attack began, the fighters peeling off to strafe airfields and the bombers beginning a decisive blow against Pearl Harbor. Only three of the battleships were not hit, and as the Japanese pulled out at 08.35 the West Virginia was sinking, the Arizona had settled on the bottom, the Oklahoma had capsized, the Tennessee was on fire, and the damaged Nevada was making for the harbour mouth. But already a second strike force was approaching the harbour, the pattern was similar to that of the first wave when the attack started at 09.15, and the Nevada was forced to beach herself while the Pennsylvania was severely damaged. The Japanese pulled out at 09.45. American losses were three battleships sunk, one battleship capsized, four battleships severely damaged, three light cruisers and three destroyers damaged, 65 out of 231 US Army aircraft destroyed, 200 out of 250 US Navy and Marine Corps aircraft destroyed, and some 3,225 Americans killed plus another 1,272 wounded.

The Japanese had scored a decisive victory, but this was only of a tactical or perhaps operational nature, the great strategic prizes being missed as the Pacific Fleet's three carriers (Enterprise, Lexington and Saratoga) were absent, and as Nagumo refused his air commanders' pleas for a third strike to eliminate the Pacific Fleet's unprotected oil tank farms and maintenance facilities.

The success of the *Enterprise* paved the way for the US Navy's current generation of carriers, which comprise the eight ships of the 'Nimitz' class delivered from 1975 to an improved 'Forrestal' class design with a smaller nuclear propulsion arrangement. These huge and extremely capable ships each have a full-load displacement of 102,000 tons, an armament of three octuple launchers for RIM-7 Sea Sparrow surface-to-air missiles and four 20mm Vulcan six-barrel cannon in Phalanx close-in weapon system mountings, as well as 90 aircraft, unspecified protection, and a speed of 30 knots or more on the 260,000hp (193,855kW) delivered to four shafts by the geared steam turbines supplied from two Westinghouse A4W or General Electric A1G pressurised water-cooled reactors.

The only other country to have built aircraft carriers in significant numbers is Japan, which completed its first carrier in 1922 as the *Hosho*. This was a small ship of limited operational capability, but provided the Japanese navy with the right type of experience to progress to the design and operation of larger and more capable fleet aircraft carriers. The first of these were two conversions from capital ships whose completion was prevented by the Washington Naval Treaty: the *Kaga* and *Akagi* were conversions from related battleship and battle-cruiser designs respectively. The details of the *Kaga* included a displacement of 26,900 tons, an armament of ten 7.9in (200mm) guns in two twin and six single turrets and twelve 4.7in

guns in six twin mountings, as well as 60 aircraft, protection in the form of an 11in (280mm) belt, and a speed of 27 knots on the 91,000hp (67,850kW) delivered to four shafts by geared steam turbines, while the details of the *Akagi* included a displacement of 26,900 tons, an armament of ten 7.9in guns in two twin and six single turrets and twelve 4.7in guns in six twin mountings, as well as 60 aircraft, protection in the form of a 10in (255mm) belt, and a speed of 31 knots on the 131,200hp (97,825kW) delivered to four shafts by geared steam turbines.

In 1929, Japan laid down its second purpose-designed carrier as the *Ryujo*, which as a result of Washington Naval Treaty limitations had a displacement of less than 10,000 tons as such carriers were not included in Japan's limit of 80,000 tons of carriers. The ship was found to be limited in many operational respects, and after its 1936 refit had details that included a displacement of 10,600 tons, an armament of eight 5in anti-aircraft guns in four twin mountings and twenty-four 25mm anti-aircraft guns in 12 twin mountings, as well as 48 aircraft (36 operational and 12 spare), unspecified but limited protection, and a speed of 29 knots on the 65,000hp (48,465kW) delivered to two shafts by geared steam turbines.

Japan used its experience with these early carriers to plan its first large fleet carriers designed as such from the keel up. These were the two ships of the 'Soryu' class that were completed in 1937 and 1939 with a

Laid down in June 1944 as the Elephant, fifth light carrier of the 'Hermes' class, this ship was completed in November 1959 as the *Hermes* of the 'Centaur' class. This long building period allowed a thorough revision of the ship, which thus emerged with an angled flightdeck and a deck-edge elevator, the latter complementing an inset elevator in the after part of the flightdeck. The deck-edge elevator was adopted as the forward inset elevator originally planned had to be eliminated to allow the incorporation of two steam catapults in the forward end of the fore-and-aft section of the flightdeck. The ship was completed with a full-load displacement of 28,700 tons, length of 744ft 4in (226.9m), armament of ten 40mm anti-aircraft guns in five twin mountings, and 28 aircraft, propulsion in the form of geared steam turbines delivering 76,000hp (56,665kW) to two shafts for a speed of 28 knots, and complement of 1,830 excluding an air group of 270. The ship was later revised with two triple launchers for Seacat surface-to-air missiles in place of the 40mm guns, and in its final form became a carrier of VTOL and STOVL warplanes in the form of up to 10 Westland Sea King anti-submarine helicopters and 20 BAe Sea Harrier multi-role warplanes, the latter launched at high weights with the aid of the 'ski jump' raised section installed at the forward end of the flightdeck. The Hermes was the flagship of the British forces despatched to free the Falkland Islands from Argentine occupation in 1982, and was deleted shortly after this.

Opposite top: The *Coral Sea* was an American fleet carrier of the 'Midway' class built in World War II, but was modernised and survived into the later 1980s, finally as a training carrier based on the American west coast.

Opposite below: Represented here by the lead ship, photographed in 1988, the four fleet aircraft carriers of the 'Kitty Hawk' class were completed in the 1960s to an improved 'Forrestal' class design with a full-load displacement of 80,945 tons, length of 1,947ft 6in (319.4m), armament of two twin launchers for 40 RIM-2 Terrier surface-to-air missiles, and 90 aircraft launched with the aid of four steam catapults, propulsion in the form of geared steam turbines delivering 280,000hp (208,770kW) to four shafts for a speed of 33.6 knots, and complement of 3,305 excluding an air group of 1,380.

Right: The *Ark Royal* was completed in 1978 as the third unit of the Royal Navy's three-strong 'Invincible' class of light aircraft carriers, and differs from the other two ships in details such as its higher-angled 'ski jump', full-load displacement of 20,000 tons, greater length of 685ft 10in (209.1m) and improved defensive armament.

displacement of 15,900 and 17,300 tons respectively, an armament of twelve 5in anti-aircraft guns in six twin mountings and between twenty-eight and thirty-one 25mm anti-aircraft guns in 14 twin mountings or in seven triple and five twin mountings, as well as 69 aircraft (53 operational and 16 spare), moderate but unspecified protection, and a speed of 34.5 knots on the 152,000hp (113,330kW) delivered to four shafts by geared steam turbines.

Further improvement of the concept embodied in the 'Soryu' class and the expiry of Treaty limitations allowed Japan's next pair of carriers to be the somewhat larger ships of the 'Shokaku' class completed in 1941 with a displacement of 25,675 tons, an armament of sixteen 5in anti-aircraft guns in eight twin mountings and thirty-six 25mm anti-aircraft guns in 12 triple mountings, as well as 84 aircraft (72 operational and 12 spare), protection in the form of an 8.5in (215mm) belt and 6.75in (170mm) deck, and a speed of 34.25 knots on the 160,000hp (119,135kW) delivered to four shafts by geared steam turbines.

These were the most important aircraft carriers operated by the Japanese navy up to the time of the Battle of Midway (June 1942), when the service lost no fewer than four of the ships together with most of its experienced naval aviators. The Japanese carrierborne arm then went into a decline from

which it never recovered despite the delivery of new and improved aircraft, fresh aircrews who lacked the experience and the skills of their predecessors, as well as a number of new aircraft carriers to supplement the ships surviving from the early operations of World War II. The other ships included the two 'Soho' class light carriers completed in 1939 and 1940 with a displacement of 11,260 tons and 30 aircraft; the three 'Taiyo' class escort carriers completed in 1940 and 1941 with a displacement of 17,830 tons and between 27 and 30 aircraft; the two 'Hiyo' class fleet carriers completed in 1942 with a displacement of 24,140 tons and an armament of 53 aircraft; the single 'Taiho' class fleet carrier completed in 1944 with a displacement of 29,300 tons and an armament of 74 aircraft; the single 'Ryuho' class light carrier completed in 1942 with a displacement of 13,360 tons and an armament of 31 aircraft; the single 'Shinano' class fleet carrier converted from a 'Yamato' class battleship and completed in 1944 with a displacement of 62,000 tons and an armament of 47 aircraft; the single 'Shinyo' class light

These two views highlight the huge size of the flightdeck of the US Navy's 'Nimitz' class of nuclear-powered aircraft carriers, planned as a total of nine ships. The ship shown is the *Abraham Lincoln*, which was commissioned in November 1989 with a full-load displacement of 102,000 tons, length of 1,092ft 0in (332.9m), armament of four 20mm Vulcan six-barrel cannon in four Phalanx close-in weapon system mountings, three octuple launchers for Sea Sparrow surface-to-air missiles, and 81 fixed-wing and six rotary-wing aircraft, propulsion in the form of nuclear-powered geared steam turbines delivering 260,000hp (193,855kW) to four shafts for a speed of 30 or more knots, and complement of 3,185 excluding an air group of 2,800. The flightdeck, which extends over the full length of the ship, is 252ft 0in (76.8m) wide, served by one starboard- and three port-side deck-edge elevators, carries two steam catapults on the fore-and-aft section of the flightdeck and on the angled section two steam catapults and five sets of arrester wires.

carrier completed in 1943 as a conversion of a German liner with a displacement of 17,500 tons and an armament of 33 aircraft; the single 'Kaiyo' class escort carrier completed in 1943 with a displacement of 13,600 tons and an armament of 24 aircraft; the two 'Chiyoda' class light carriers completed in 1943 and 1944 with a displacement of 11,190 tons and an armament of 30 aircraft; and the three 'Unryu' class light fleet carriers completed in 1944 with a displacement of 17,150 tons and 64 aircraft.

Germany and Italy designed and started work on aircraft carriers for service in World War II, but none of these was completed. The only other countries that have completed true aircraft carriers are France (one before and two after World War II with two others currently building or planned) and the USSR (four 'Kiev' and two 'Kuznetsov' class ships), although Italy and Spain have in recent years each completed one light aircraft carrier suitable for the operation of helicopters and STOVL warplanes.

The *Nimitz* was completed in May 1975 as the lead ship of this important aircraft carrier class, and is seen here with examples of the wide assortment of aircraft that can be carried on these huge machines. The current air group includes 20 Northrop Grumman F-14 Tomcat fleet defence fighters, 20 McDonnell Douglas F/A-18 Hornet dual-role fighter and attack aircraft, 20 Northrop Grumman A-6 Intruder attack aircraft, 10 Lockheed Martin S-3 Viking anti-submarine aircraft, six Northrop Grumman EA-6 Prowler electronic warfare aircraft and five Northrop Grumman E-2 Hawkeye airborne early warning aircraft as well as six Sikorsky SH-3 Sea King or Sikorsky SH-60 Seahawk helicopters.

Although somewhat smaller than the latest 'Nimitz' class nuclear-powered aircraft carriers, the *Forrestal* and its conventionally powered three sister ships are still very substantial warships.

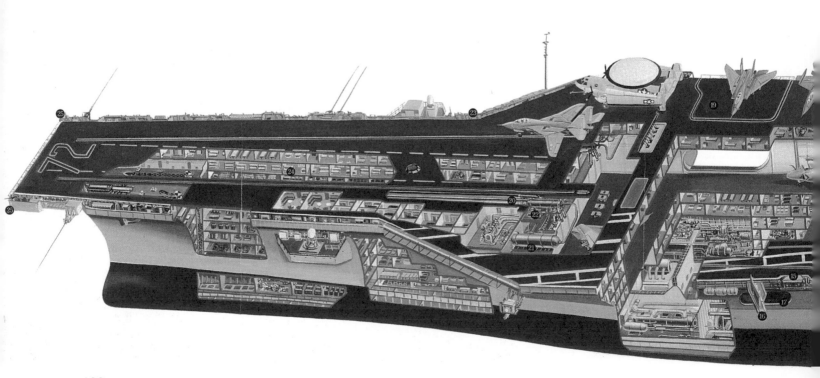

Annotation key

1. Aviation jet engine shop
2. Phalanx 20mm close-in weapons system
3. NATO Sea Sparrow Mk 29 launcher
4. Ship's boats
5. Squadron ready rooms
6. Landing signal officer platform
7. Mk 7 Mod 3 arrester gear engine
8. Aircraft elevator
9. Air search radar
10. Mobile crane
11. Jet blast deflector
12. Missile arming/de-arming platform
13. Island: Primary flight control/air boss, navigation bridge, radar and electronics, chart room, flight deck control, flight deck TV camera
14. Main engine room (arrangemernt notional)
15. Catapult officer launch control station
16. Optical landing system
17. Ship's whaler
18. Main deck (hanger bay)
19. Aircraft elevator
20. Type C-13-2 catapult
21. Catapult steam vessel
22. Catapult piping room
23. Saluting gun
24. Crew living spaces
25. .50-caliber machine gun

One of the two defensive weapons now carried by American aircraft carriers, the RIM-7 Sea Sparrow (seen here being fired from the *John F. Kennedy*) is a development of the AIM-7 Sparrow air-to-air missile intended for the short-range protection of major warships.

This cutaway illustration of the *Abraham Lincoln* reveals the extraordinary complexity of the huge 'Nimitz' class aircraft carriers.

Glossary

BARBETTE   fixed circular mounting carrying a revolving turret

BREECH-LOADING GUN   type of gun in which the projectile and propellant are loaded through an opening breech mechanism

CONNING TOWER   armoured portion of the superstructure carrying the fire-control position and other essential command positions

DUAL-PURPOSE GUN   gun capable of engaging low-angle (surface) and high-angle (aerial) targets

GUN HOUSE   portion of the turret accommodating the gun or guns

GUN MOUNTING   rotating semi-enclosed or open housing for one or more guns

MUZZLE-LOADING GUN   type of gun in which the propellant and projectile are loaded through the muzzle

RAM   waterline forward extension of the bow designed to penetrate the hull of an enemy warship

RIFLED GUN   gun with a rifled barrel and therefore firing a projectile that is spin-stabilised and thus more accurate over long range than a projectile fired from a smooth-bore barrel

SHELL   hollow projectile containing explosive initiated by a fuse mechanism

SHOT   solid projectile containing to explosive

SMOOTH-BORE GUN   gun without a rifled barrel and therefore firing a projectile that is not spun and thus less accurate over long range than a projectile fired from a rifled barrel

TRIPLE-EXPANSION STEAM ENGINE   type of reciprocating steam engine

TURBINE STEAM ENGINE   type of non-reciprocating steam engine with less volume and vibration than a triple-expansion engine

TURRET   rotating enclosed and generally armoured housing for one or more guns

Index

Index of Ships Names